DATE DUE

DEMCO, INC. 38-2931

THE PECKING ORDER

ALSO BY DALTON CONLEY

The Starting Gate

Honky

Being Black, Living in the Red

THE PECKING ORDER

Which Siblings Succeed and Why

DALTON CONLEY

Pantheon Books, New York

Pantheon Books and colophon are registered
trademarks of Random House, Inc.

Library of Congress Cataloging-in-Publication Data

Conley, Dalton [date]
The pecking order : which siblings succeed and why / Dalton Conley.
p.   cm.
Includes bibliographical references and index.
ISBN 0-375-42174-2
1. Family—United States. 2. Brothers and sisters—United States.
3. Successful people—United States. 4. Equality—United States.
5. Income distribution—United States. I. Title.

HQ536.C7455 2004   306.85'0973—dc22   2003058020

www.pantheonbooks.com

Book design by M. Kristen Bearse

Printed in the United States of America
First Edition
2 4 6 8 9 7 5 3

In no particular order,

Yo Xing Heyno Augustus Eisner		*E Harper Nora Jeremijenko-Conley*
Alexander Weiser Knuckles		*&*
Jeremijenko-Conley	*or*	*Yo Xing Heyno Augustus Eisner*
&		*Alexander Weiser Knuckles*
E Harper Nora Jeremijenko-Conley		*Jeremijenko-Conley*

With infinite, equal love

CONTENTS

THE PECKING ORDER

ONE

INEQUALITY STARTS AT HOME

An Introduction to the Pecking Order

Let me start with a story.

Once upon a time a future president was born. William Jefferson Blythe IV entered the world one month premature but at a healthy six pounds and eight ounces. At twenty-three, his mother, Virginia, was young by today's standards, but perhaps a touch old for Arkansas in the 1940s. She was a widow, so times were tight during Bill's early years. In fact, times would be tough during all of Bill's childhood. Nonetheless, he seemed destined for great things. According to family lore, in second grade Bill's teacher "predicted that he would be President someday."[1]

His mother eventually married Roger Clinton, but that didn't make life any easier for Bill. Roger was a bitterly jealous alcoholic who often became physically abusive to his wife. Bill cites the day that he stood up to his stepfather as the most important marker in his transition to adulthood and perhaps in his entire life. In 1962, when Bill was sixteen, Virginia finally divorced Roger, but by then there was another Roger Clinton in the family, Bill's younger half brother.

Though Bill despised his stepfather, he still went to the Garland County courthouse and changed his last name to Clinton after his mother's divorce from the man—not for the old man's sake, but so that he would have the same last name as the younger brother he cherished. Though they were separated by ten years, were only half siblings, and ran in very different circles, the brothers were close. The younger Roger probably hated his father more than Bill did, but he nonetheless started to manifest many of the same traits as he came of age. He was a fabulous salesman: at age thirteen, he sold twice as many magazines as any of his classmates for a school project, winning a Polaroid camera and a turkey for his superior effort. He also had an affinity for substance abuse: by eighteen, he was heavily into marijuana. During Bill's first (unsuccessful) congressional campaign in 1974, Roger spent much of his time stenciling signs while smoking joints in the basement of campaign headquarters.

As Bill's political fortunes rose, Roger's prospects first stagnated and then sank. He tried his hand at a musical career, worked odd jobs, and eventually got into dealing drugs. And it was not just pot; in 1984, then-governor Bill Clinton was informed that his brother was a cocaine dealer under investigation by the Arkansas state police. The governor did not stand in the way of a sting operation, and Roger was caught on tape boasting how untouchable he was as the brother of the state's chief executive. Then the axe fell. After his arrest, Roger was beside himself in tears, threatening suicide for the shame he had brought upon his family—in particular, his famous brother. Upon hearing this threat Bill shook Roger violently. (He, in truth, felt responsible for his brother's slide.)

The next January, Roger was sentenced to a two-year prison term in a federal corrections facility in Fort Worth, Texas. Bill describes the whole ordeal as the most difficult episode of his life. David Maraniss— the author of *First in His Class,* the most comprehensive biography of Clinton to date—summarizes the family situation as follows:

How could two brothers be so different: the governor and the coke dealer, the Rhodes scholar and the college dropout, one who tried to read three hundred books in three months and another who at his most addicted snorted cocaine sixteen times a day, one who could spend hours explaining economic theories and another whose economic interests centered on getting a new Porsche? In the case of the Clinton brothers, the contrasts become more understandable when considered within the context of their family history and environment. They grew up in a town of contrast and hypocrisy, in a family of duality and conflict. Bill and Roger were not so much opposites as two sides of the same coin.[2]

If asked to explain why Bill succeeded where Roger failed, most people will immediately point to genetic differences. After all, they were only half siblings to begin with. Others will pin it on birth order, claiming that firstborns are more driven and successful. But both of these accounts rely on individual explanations—ones particular to the unique biology or psychology of Bill and Roger—and both are incomplete. Was Bill more favored and more driven because he was a firstborn? My research shows that in families with two kids, birth order does not really matter that much. In fact, just under one-fourth of U.S. presidents were firstborns—about what we would expect from chance. The fact is that birth position only comes into play in larger families. But what about genes: was Bill simply luckier in the family gene pool? That may be so, but it still does not explain why sibling disparities are much more common in poor families and broken homes than they are in rich, intact families. In fact, when families have limited resources, the success of one sibling often generates a negative backlash among the others.

Sure, if one kid is born a mathematical genius and the other with no talents whatsoever, their respective dice may be cast at birth. But for most of us, how genes matter depends on the social circumstances around us. A child in one family may be born with innate athletic talent that is never nurtured because the parents in that family value reading ability over all else. Yet in another family, the fit between the individual talents of a particular child—say spatial reasoning—and the values of the parents may be perfect, and those abilities are realized. Finally, what kind of rewards talent brings depends entirely on the socioeconomic structure of the time. Fifty years ago, musical talent might have led to a decent living. Today—in an economy that rewards the most popular musicians handsomely at the expense of everyone else—innate musical ability is more often a route to financial struggle.

In Bill Clinton's case, he obviously had good genes—which contributed to his sharp mind, quick wit, tall stature, and verbal charisma—but there was not much advantage to being the firstborn. What really made a difference in his life was the good fit between his particular talents, the aspirations of those around him, and the political opportunities in a small state like Arkansas. This good fit combined with his family's lack of economic resources to generate an enormous sibling difference in success. However, had Virginia had money, she might not have had to put all her eggs—all her hopes and dreams—in Bill's basket. She might have been able to actively compensate for Bill's success by giving Roger extra financial and nonfinancial support—sending him, for example, to an elite private school when he started to veer off track. Instead, Bill's success seemed to come at the expense of Roger's—particularly when it led Roger to a false sense of invincibility.

On the surface, it may seem that the case of the Clintons is atypical. And, of course, a pair of brothers who are, respectively, the president and an ex-con is a bit extreme. But the basic phenomenon of sibling differences in success that the Clintons represent is not all that unusual. In fact, in explaining economic inequality in America, sibling differences represent about *three-quarters* of all the differences between individuals. Put another way, only one-quarter of all income inequality is between families. The remaining 75 percent is *within* families.[3] Sibling differences in accumulated wealth (i.e., net worth) are even greater, reaching 90-plus percent.[4] What this means is that if we lined everyone in America up in rank order of how much money they have—from the poorest homeless person to Bill Gates himself—and tried to predict where any particular individual might fall on that long line, then knowing about what family they came from would narrow down our uncertainty by about 25 percent (in the case of income). In other words, the dice are weighted by which family you come from, but you and your siblings still have to roll them. For example, if you come from a family that ranks in the bottom 5 percent of the income hierarchy, then you have a 40 percent chance of finding yourself in the lowest 10 percent, a 21 percent chance of making it to somewhere between the 30th and 70th percentile, and only a one in a thousand chance of making it to the top 10 percent. If you come from the richest 5 percent of families in America, then your odds are flipped. And if you start at the dead middle of the American income ladder, then you are about 63 percent likely to end up somewhere in that 30th- to 70th-percentile range, with a 4 percent chance of ending up either in the top or the bottom 10 percent.[5] A similar pattern holds for educational differences. For example, if you attended college there is almost a 50 percent chance that one of your siblings did not (and vice versa).[6]

What do sibling disparities as large as these indicate? They imply an American landscape where class identity is ever changing and not necessarily shared between brothers and sisters. Taken as a whole, the above statistics present a starkly darker portrait of American family life than we are used to. We want to think that the home is a haven in a heartless world. The truth is that inequality starts at home. These statistics also pose problems for those concerned with what seems to be a marked erosion of the idealized nuclear family. In fact, they hint at a trade-off between economic opportunity and stable, cohesive families.

While it may be surprising to realize how common sibling inequality is on the whole, my analysis of national data shows that Americans are quite aware of sibling disparities within their own families. For instance, when given a choice of fourteen categories of kin ranging from parents to grandparents to spouses to uncles, a whopping 34 percent of respondents claimed that a sibling was their most economically successful relative. When the question is flipped, 46 percent of respondents report a sibling being their least successful relative. Both these figures dwarf those for any other category.[7] When respondents were asked to elaborate about why their most successful relative got that way, their most common answer was a good work ethic (24.5 percent); when we add in other, related categories like "responsible, disciplined," "perseverance, motivation," or "set goals, had a plan," the total is well over half of all responses. Contrast that with the 22.6 percent that covers all categories of what might be called socioeconomic influences, such as "inheritance," "coming from a family with money," "marrying money," and so on. When accounting for the success of our kin, individual characterological explanations win out.

The pattern becomes even more striking when we flip the question to ask about the misfortune of the *least* successful relative. Only 9.6 percent of respondents cite social forces like poverty, lack of opportunity, or the pitfalls of a particular field as an explanation. Meanwhile, a whopping 82.4 percent cite individualistic reasons—having a "bad attitude" or "poor emotional or mental health." The single largest category was "lack of determination."[8]

That shows us how harsh we are on our brothers and sisters. Are we fair when we pass this kind of judgment, or terribly biased? I think the latter. In this book I challenge the perceived split between individual personality–based explanations for success and failure, and sociological ones. I argue that in each American family there exists a pecking order between siblings—a status hierarchy, if you will. This hierarchy emerges over the course of childhood and both reflects and determines the siblings' positions in the overall status ordering in society. It is not just the will of the parents or the "natural" abilities of the children themselves that determines who is on top in the family pecking order; the pecking order is conditioned by the swirling winds of society, which envelop the family. Gender expectations, the economic cost of schooling in America, a rising divorce rate, geographic mobility, religious and sexual orientations—all of these societal issues weigh in heavily on the pecking order between siblings. In other words, in order to truly understand the pecking orders within American families, you cannot view them in isolation from the larger economy and social structures in which we live. The family is, in short, no shelter from the cold winds of capitalism; rather it is part and parcel of that system. What I hope you end up with is a nuanced understanding of how social sorting works—in America writ large, and in your family writ small. And just maybe—along the way—we will all have a little more sympathy for our less fortunate brothers and sisters.

Who Gets Ahead?

Books about siblings debate why children raised by the same parents in the same house under the same circumstances turn out differently—sometimes very differently. They offer genetic explanations, or focus on birth order or the quality of parenting. *The Pecking Order* takes all these issues into account, but, based on years of research with three separate studies, it now moves us beyond those factors. Why is there a pecking order in American families, and how does it work? The reasons go way beyond relationships between family members. Americans like to think that their behavior and their destiny are solely in their own hands. But the pecking order, like other aspects of the social fabric, ends up being shaped by how society works.

In fact, siblings serve merely as a tool by which I hope to shed light on why some of us are rich and others poor; on why some are famous and others in America are anonymous. However, in figuring this all out, we do not gain much traction by comparing Bill Clinton with Joe Q. Public, Bill Gates with the average reader of this book, or any pair of randomly associated people. Some books tell you that the best way to understand why one person succeeds and another does not is to examine big amorphous categories like class or economics or race. I say the best way to do it is to examine differences within families, specifically to compare siblings with one another. Only by focusing in on the variety of outcomes that arise within a given family can we gain a real understanding of the underlying forces, of the invisible hands of the marketplace, that push each of us onto our chosen (or assigned) path in life. Siblings provide a natural experiment of sorts. They share much of their genetic endowment.[9] They also share much of the same environment. So it's logical to ask: how and why is it that some siblings end up in radically different positions in life? If we find an answer to that question, I think we will understand something very fundamental to American life.

Of course, no study can hope to explain each individual family. Pluck and luck have a lot to do with where we find ourselves. But there are systematic patterns that emerge when we compare siblings. These relationships are not simple and straightforward. It is just not true that firstborns are richer than secondborns, or that boys do better than girls, full stop.

The family is not a sorting machine. It goes through economic ups and downs; it grows and contracts (with birth, death, divorce, to name a few such transitions); and its many changes are stamped upon the children it rears. You may grow up in the same house—even the same room—as your brother or sister and yet have very different memories of those who raised you. Fifty-three percent of sibling pairs do not remember their father's education similarly; 46 percent remember their mother's education differently. Twenty-one percent of siblings differ on whether their mother worked for a year or more during their childhood. Twenty-five percent even disagree about how old their parents are.[10] Clearly, American siblings remember—and thus experience—their families differently.

Previous accounts of who succeeds in America have focused on either one of two important issues: between-family differences or within-family differences. So-called academic and intellectual discussions of economic opportunity, race, poverty, welfare, education, and almost any other issue of public policy or social concern compare the circumstances of one family with another (such as what parents do for a living); this is what I call *cross-family stratification.* The question of how within-family differences—such as gender or birth order—affect us is left to the realm of pop psychology and self-help books; this dimension I call *intra-family stratification.* But the two axes are not independent—they affect each other dramatically. So in order to gain a complete picture of how social sorting works in America, we need to consider both.

About the Study

A word on how I gathered the information and statistics that fill this book. *The Pecking Order* represents the culmination of several studies that together peel back the veneer of family life in America. They include three national surveys and a series of in-depth interviews. First of all, I rely on the U.S. Census. Previous scholars have generally ignored the census as a means to study how kids turn out, since there is no way to link parents and their adult children. However, I have devised a way to measure how kids are doing while they are still at home, thus avoiding this problem (for details, see the appendix). I examine a measure of parental investment in children—whether or not each sibling goes to private school. Of course, many families cannot afford to send any of their offspring to private school; but when children do attend, it is very instructive to study which siblings tend to go and which do not. Of course, a particular sibling may be sent to private school because she is excelling—and therefore the parents put their eggs in her basket—or because she is lagging, and the parents invest more in her schooling as a compensatory measure. I also examine a measure of academic success for the siblings: whether or not each child has been held back a grade in school. Together these measures help paint a portrait of which siblings receive more parental financial resources and which thrive in the school system—the first step to long-term socioeconomic success, since education has become increasingly important to the economic security of Americans as we have moved from an industrial to an information economy.[11]

Since the census allows me only to examine educational measures, I use other data to examine other outcomes, like occupational prestige and earnings. The second national survey I examine—called the Panel Study of Income Dynamics (PSID), run out of the University of Michigan—has been following the same five thousand families each year since 1968.[12] Every time a child is born, a family breaks up, or someone moves in or out, they are tracked. The result is something like a thirty-five-year family tree that now includes more than sixty thousand individuals. It is considered the preeminent survey of the economic and social status of families in America. The economists' estimates of sibling resemblance in earnings that were mentioned earlier come from this study, as do my own results regarding net worth, income, occupational prestige, and education. The third national survey—run out of the University of Chicago—is called the General Social Survey (GSS) and has been the standard tool for gauging demographic, socioeconomic, and attitudinal trends in America every year since 1972. A special supplement to the 1994 GSS survey—called the Study of American Families (SAF)—surveyed the siblings of the GSS respondents, asking many of the same questions and more. With the GSS-SAF dataset we can compare sibling responses on social attitudes, political positions, and lifestyles. These differences can then be compared with siblings' relative socioeconomic positions.

Finally, these survey studies are complemented by the actual voices of siblings themselves as part of an ongoing, five-year study conducted by myself and a staff of researchers, interviewers, and administrators at New York University's Center for Advanced Social Science Research. If the statistical analyses of national data provide the skeleton for this book, the interview transcripts provide the flesh and blood of the narrative. They give us a glimpse into the black box of the American family so that we can see how the gears of household relations generate disparate outcomes among offspring. In all cases we have interviewed multiple siblings from the same family. In some instances, we have interviewed the parents as well.

I present the interview findings differently than do other, more "academically written" works of sociology. I have tried to foreground the stories and background the commentary. Basically, this strategy represents the opposite approach of what most sociological studies do. I think this manner of presentation makes the material much more engaging to the reader, an important step—I believe—for bringing what sociology has to offer to a wider community. Except where otherwise noted, I present the case studies as a single narrative distilled from the accounts of multiple siblings, rather than as a "he said, she said" back and forth between competing visions. Though siblings often experienced their childhoods differently, there was a remarkable degree of consensus on critical moments in the history of the family, turning points for their respective life paths, and about the particular roles each occupied within the family constellation. Where there is conflict over family history or interpretation, I have tried to draw that disagreement out; otherwise, I have presented a case history as a judge would in rendering his or her opinion: after having reviewed all the testimony and evidence from a variety of sources, and after having brought his or her own legal (or in my case, sociological) expertise to bear on the case. (Likewise, in the interest of a readable and dramatic narrative, a lot of the citations and discussions of the relevant research debates have been presented in the end notes; anyone interested in the intellectual history and development of the ideas presented here should be sure to read the accompanying notes as well as the appendix.)

In addition to fleshing out the quantitative results, these interviews also help us to understand dynamics that cannot be adequately addressed by survey-type studies—for example, how outside influences and special circumstances affect one sibling and not the others, how siblings react differently to family changes like death or divorce, or how sensitive issues like sexual orientation, religious belief, or legal problems set in motion upward or downward mobility. These sorts of issues cannot be gotten at by national surveys since they are often intimate in nature and, more importantly, cannot be adequately anticipated by questionnaires that are meant to take as little time as possible to complete. (Names, places, and other identifying features have been changed to protect the confidentiality of the study subjects and their families.) In combination, these diverse sources of data provide a textured portrait of how American families navigate the economic landscape, how siblings react to their unique positions in the household order, and how sibling differences in success are managed and mediated while the family keeps its bonds intact. More information about how the interviews and quantitative analyses were conducted can be found in the appendix.

Family Background(s)

Every parent with more than one child has heard the question in one form or another: Who do you love most? Among many families there is a scripted answer: Why, I love all of you equally, of course. My interviews show, however, that this spoken norm is by no means universally true. Many families are forced to implicitly—sometimes explicitly— bet on one kid at the expense of another. The novel *Sophie's Choice* dramatizes this in the most terrible terms of all: a mother is made to choose which child will survive and which will die in a Nazi gas chamber. In modern America, the choices parents make are less dramatic, but no less real. When parents have enough "class" resources to go around—time, money, social connections—kids turn out more similarly since parents don't have to choose and can actively compensate for inequities among their kids.[13]

However, when parental resources are stretched thin due to financial hardship, large family size, short spacing between kids, single parenthood, minority racial status, and so on, kids tend to drift apart. This is both because the internal competition between siblings becomes more intense and more critical, and because parents are more likely to have to bet all their resources on one kid to make it against adverse circumstances. For example, children of parents who are poorly educated are much more likely to have unequal outcomes in terms of attending college or not themselves. In other words, they are more likely to have one attend at the expense of the others. Likewise, in families that lack a business to absorb less talented or motivated offspring, or liquid assets that can pay for schooling or finance extended job searches, or even social connections that will ease the transition from school to work by providing the right introduction to a potential employer, kids are left more on their own to make it (or not). When things are really tight in a household, siblings may even be called upon to sacrifice their goals for the sake of the greater good and survival of the family—as was the case for someone like Evan.

Evan always dreamed of becoming a lawyer but, as the eldest, always had to work throughout high school to help his single mother pay the bills for himself and his three younger siblings. When he turned eighteen, he could not even think about college as there were still three kids at home relying on him and his mother. So he joined the Army, sending home the major portion of his checks to help out. He stayed in the military for twenty years, having long given up the dream of college, law school, and being "his own boss." However, his sacrifice is appreciated by his siblings and especially his mother, who wonders how she would have ever gotten the remaining three kids fed, raised, and out of the house if it had not been for Evan's monthly contributions. His siblings, all of whom did go to local commuter colleges, now work at various well-paying office jobs, the youngest having worked his way up to the position of regional manager of a large financial firm. While their mother is well aware of the sacrifices that Evan made, his younger brothers and sisters do not see his life choices as critical to their successes. They're wrong.

My research tells me decisions like Evan's are fairly common when families are not particularly well off. If one child of a mother who herself did not attend college does complete all four years, the chances are about 47 percent that any other given child of that mother also attains a bachelor's degree. Compare that with the 76 percent likelihood that a given child of a college graduate will complete college if his or her sibling did (of course, the chances that any finish college are also higher).[14] Low levels of financial, social, and intellectual capital in a family mean that small differences between siblings get blown up into big ones, whether through the fact that fewer of the children "make it" overall or because of actual sibling sacrifices—as in Evan's case.

His situation stands in stark contrast to that of Carl and Joey. The boys' father owned an electronics company in Massachusetts. He provided his children with everything. When Carl, Joey's older brother, wanted to go to an expensive private college, his dad told him, "Don't even think about the money." When he wanted to go on to get a graduate degree, Carl approached his father for a loan. "Can I work out a payment plan over about five years?" he asked.

"You don't have to pay it back," his dad responded. "This is my pleasure, to see you continue with your schooling." (He himself had never finished college and had made his fortune as an independent entrepreneur.)

Joey, by contrast, did not want to go to college. He had always been the rebel of the family—the black sheep. He started fights with his older brother, got suspended at school, stayed out late. Perhaps all this was because he felt unloved and unwanted by his mother. The rest of the family confirms that this was, sadly, true (though which came first, his behavior or his mother's, is an open question). Joey dropped out of high school for a year but eventually finished. He did try out a local commuter college for a semester but hated it. Time passed, and he continued to languish. Then his father put him to work in his own company as a salesman, and loaned him money to get his own place. After Joey had been on the job a couple of years, his father made him the sales manager. Everyone in the family—including Joey himself—says they think he might have been homeless and on welfare had it not been for the job provided by his father. The family may or may not have made Joey into the black sheep, but it certainly used its resources to bring that black sheep back into the flock.

John Edgar Wideman lives the life of an academic superstar—as an award-winning author, MacArthur Fellow, and distinguished professor at the University of Massachusetts. His brother, meanwhile, is doing hard time: a life sentence for murder.

Jay works for a pharmaceutical company on the West Coast earning a middle-class income while his sister lives back in New York, in their mother's house in the projects. Jay and his sister haven't spoken for several years. He does not approve of her "lifestyle" of illicit activity and welfare dependence.

Both the Widemans and Jay's family are black. Their stories of sibling divergence are not atypical. With respect to college graduation, the similarity of African-American siblings is about half what it is for non-black siblings.[15] For occupational prestige, sibling similarity is also about half as strong for blacks as it is for non-blacks.[16] (Occupational prestige is calculated by survey researchers who get respondents to rank order jobs based on their social status, from "food service preparation and service occupations" on up to medical physicians.[17] There is a remarkable degree of consistency across time and place regarding the status hierarchy of occupations.)[18] As was the case with respect to parental class status, these effects are partially due to the overall lower education and prestige levels of blacks vis-à-vis whites—so if one kid makes it through college or lands a high-status job, he or she is more likely to be alone in that regard. In short, racial or class disadvantage means that inequality rears its head even at home; families that are racially and economically advantaged do not have to face hard choices and divergent outcomes as frequently.

Who Gets Ahead?

Of course, all of these findings lead to the $64,000 question: when there are disparities between siblings, what predicts which siblings will or will not succeed, and why? In *The Nurture Assumption,* psychologist Judith Harris argues that the influence of parents on children has been overstated and that genetics and peer influences are of much greater salience (and thus might explain sibling differences). I am sympathetic to such arguments, but wary. Harris takes the 50 percent sibling similarity and chalks it up to genetics; then she takes the remaining 50 percent and chalks it up to genetics and peer groups. She spins a convincing argument that other than providing their genes, parents have little effect on their kids. For example, she points out that children of the British upper class were at one time raised almost exclusively by working-class nannies. They spent very little time with their parents and were soon sent off to boarding school. Harris points out that with almost no "quality time" to instill parent-child socialization, these kids still came out speaking exactly like their parents and not like their less educated governesses. Why? According to Harris, it did not make much difference who was doing the day-to-day raising of these kids, since they learned how to talk from one another. Strike one against the importance of parents.

Another powerful testament to the noninfluence of parents, Harris claims, is the case of immigrants. If immigrant children arrive before the approximate age of thirteen, then they adopt the syntax and accent of their peers in their adopted country, leaving their parents to speak in broken sentences and thick accents for the rest of their lives. Harris takes this as evidence that peers, not parents, teach us how to speak. Strike two for parents.

However, if I read Harris' examples in another way, they show the enormous power of parents—albeit not through the direct socialization process that she decries. Why do British elites speak like their parents (and often reproduce their parents' class status)? Because of their parents: their parents exercise their class resources to send their children to a select boarding school where they encounter other kids from similar environments, where highly trained teachers instruct their offspring in the "proper" way to speak. In short, while these parents may not have read to their children every night, they do a lot to ensure that they are not disappointed with their offspring. The same is true for immigrant parents. Could there be a more important choice, one that affects the life course of their children more, than their decision to immigrate? They are, indeed, the reason that their children speak differently, though the mechanism is not direct socialization.

In both these cases, parents set up an institutional structure to presumably generate good socioeconomic outcomes for their kids. Clearly, parents do matter.[19]

Siblings also affect one another's level of success and failure. I find that they affect one another's likelihood of success in school, and the further away from the parents the siblings are in birth order, the more strongly they influence each other. For example, the similarity of the likelihood of being held back a grade between the secondborn and thirdborn is three times as strong as the similarity between the firstborn and secondborn—indicating that as the family grows, the influence of siblings on one another grows and the effect of parents probably becomes diluted.[20]

In fact, what all my research shows is that the family is a complex network of affiliations stewing over with the potential for politics and intrigue. Usually the tensions inherent in these interdependent relationships are safely ensconced within the rhetoric of intra-family equality and universal love (*Share; No, it's his turn; Hitting isn't nice*). Other times they spill out into bitter, often lifelong fights: think of sibling battles for large inheritances. The family is a tangled web.

So nothing about it is simple. Therefore, nothing about why one sibling succeeds and another doesn't is reducible to one clear and present factor. Sometimes even simple variables like birth order are difficult to pin down. How do we classify the birth order of Justin, who was born second but never knew his older brother since he died when Justin was an infant? What do we say about Ray, whose older sibling died when he was ten? What about Selena, whose mother's second marriage was to a man with two kids of his own (à la *The Brady Bunch*), thus causing Selena, at age five, to go from being the first of two to the third of four?

Besides, is overall birth order the pivotal factor in success and failure, or is it *gender-specific* birth order that is most important? Naturally, the answer varies depending on the family. There may be such gender-specific specialization that the only real reference group worth talking about is those siblings of the same sex. For instance, being the last-born boy of five is a lot different when the first four children are also boys than when they are girls.

Even defining who is in the family and who is out can be difficult sometimes. Who really has an impact on children? Is it only those who raise them? With one-third of all births to unmarried parents, kids do not always have two parents.[21] Take the case of Malik and Jim. Malik is the product of a relationship his mother had with a Black Panther wanna-be while in high school. His father has, in addition to Malik, four other sons and two daughters with other women. His half brother Jim is the result of a brief marriage their mother had to another man. Jim's father now has three other sons. Jim had some contact with his father growing up—leading a relatively stable life, he would come to important life events like graduations. But, having received enough small doses of his dad over the course of his childhood, Jim's father did not figure so large in his psyche or life history. Jim did his own thing and today is an accountant in San Diego.

By contrast, Malik did not have any contact with his father until he looked him up during his freshman year of college at Stanford. Having won the state championship in debate, he was the shining jewel of his extended family in Bakersfield, California. He was able to go to Stanford due to a combination of loans, work study, and scholarship money. Though the proverbial apple initially fell quite far from the tree in Malik's case, it soon rolled right beside the trunk. In an attempt to establish the relationship he had always craved with his father, he moved in with him for a year in Oakland, which caused quite a bit of trouble for him. By the middle 1980s, his father had developed a heroin habit, and so Malik also began to use the drug. At first he tried to commute to Stanford and take care of his schoolwork while snorting (never shooting) heroin at night as he and his father hit the jazz clubs of San Francisco and the East Bay. Soon, however, the double life proved too difficult and he withdrew from college for a time.

After six years—and tens of thousands of dollars of student debt—Malik eventually finished his degree, but the experience with his father threw him off kilter in a way that—though he no longer uses drugs at all—affects his career path even today. After he finished college he still wanted to emulate his dad and so spent several years trying to found and manage a jazz record label with a couple of friends. After two and a half years of sleeping on couches and mounting arrears on his student loans, the company finally sputtered out. Since then Malik has worked a series of office jobs, interspersed with periods of unemployment. Though he still dreams of politics or big business, he has never fulfilled the promise that he showed back when he aced his SATs and marched triumphantly onto the sun-drenched Stanford campus. Ironically, his father had a much greater impact on his life through his absence than did Jim's dad with his occasional presence.

What constitutes a family? Do we count Malik's or Jim's father as family members even though they didn't raise their children? Malik's absent father turned out to be the seminal influence in his life.

And what about divorce and adoption? They certainly throw family composition into disarray and affect sibling success and failure. Today, slightly more than half of all divorces involve couples with children under age eighteen. In a given year, about 1.7 percent of American children experience a marital disruption—this rate has risen three-fold since 1960.[22] As for adoption, rates have also risen in recent decades. In 1944—the earliest year for which reliable data are available—there were about 50,000 adopted children. That figure peaked in 1970 at about 175,000 and has since stabilized at somewhere between 100,000 and 120,000.[23] The result is that today, about 2 percent of children are adopted. One consequence of the transformation of the American family is that the transmission of class status from one generation to the next is a lot messier thanks to complicated kinship relations.

Take Kara and Kathy. They were both adopted by a couple who had tried for years to have their own biological children. The girls themselves are not biologically related, a fact that probably made it easier for their mother to label them as differently as she did. From the start, Kara was seen as the smart, capable daughter. Kathy was relegated to being the dumb, incompetent one—but she was also treated as prettier and more socially adept. While it may be true that Kara was actually somewhat smarter and Kathy was somewhat prettier, it was their parents' response to that perceived difference that really mattered. For example, they could have chosen to compensate for what they took to be the differences between the two girls, pushing Kathy academically and encouraging Kara's social self-confidence. Instead, they drew out the differences between the two sisters, making them more, rather than less, important. Her mother labeled them as binary opposites not only in her subtle behaviors, but to their faces as well. She tried to convince Kara that she was not interested in boys, while she gave Kathy the green light to date. She would also tell Kara that she was closer to her than she was to Kathy, thus emotionally obligating Kara to spend most of her free time with her mother rather than socializing with her peers.

Of course, labeling of some sort occurs in most families no matter what the intentions of the parents. However, in this case, a particularly manipulative mother combined with the girls' status as adoptees exacerbated the labeling. Neither child was allowed to touch the walls, for fear of dirtying them. They could not sit on the edge of the bed for fear of eroding the support of the mattress edge. Cleaning rituals often took hours, and having been labeled the competent one, Kara bore the brunt of the chores. In the end, however, it was Kara who escaped the household. She is now a professor; meanwhile, Kathy barely graduated high school. Her self-confidence and belief in her own abilities eroded, Kathy continued to live at home until she was twenty-five, at which time she married a man in his fifties who works as a movie usher.

Two adopted daughters of no relation to each other but raised by the same parents. How do we know what made one successful and the other marginal? We can never know for sure how much the labeling is responsible for their divergent outcomes and how much was, say, genes.

But even full siblings only share 50 percent of their genes. And genes can play themselves out in many different ways. However, the rhetoric of genetic difference makes it much easier to recognize, accentuate, and even create differences in adoptees than in children of the same parents.

In other families, the siblings are more "related" than most of us are to our siblings. I am speaking of identical twins. What better way could there be to explore the question of whether genetics determines sibling success and failure? Of course, identical twins are as alike as you can get genetically, but they also occupy a unique social position. This is well illustrated by the twins Pauline and Esther Friedman—better known as (Dear) Abby and Ann Landers. The Friedman twins' mother made them dress alike and do the same things. Ann Landers later wrote, "There was no opportunity for quiet introspection and honest self-appraisal. Granted, the 'togetherness' was great fun, but it denied us the opportunity to develop as individuals. We would never escape the image of the sister act. . . . [All the same,] we traded on our twinship shamelessly. . . ." She went on in her advice column to instruct the mother of twins specifically *not* to dress them alike and to make an active effort to treat them differently.

Twins—long held up by scientists as the lab rats of human genetics—are, however, just as susceptible to social pressures as the rest of us. Genetics cannot be seen in isolation from the social context of family relations. Twinness can just as easily turn the other way, where twins actively work to distinguish themselves from each other. Despite their obvious similarities, Ann Landers and Abby went for many years not speaking to each other after a bitter, public fight. Sometimes being a twin can be too close for comfort.

While in their case their divergence was one of social relations, in other cases twins can separate in more socioeconomic ways as well. For instance, though Laura and Lynne always looked very much alike, Laura was always slightly thinner than Lynne. When they got to high school, this turned out to make a big difference; Laura always garnered much more interest from boys. Always being second choice slowly worked itself under Lynne's skin. Her self-esteem plummeted and her weight rose; her weight rose and her confidence sank further. This critical time in adolescence has affected each of their life trajectories. Today, the unemployed Lynne barely leaves her house while Laura holds down a management position in a large nonprofit organization. They try to remain close socially despite the different paths their lives have taken, but they no longer have as much in common to talk about as they once did. Laura's busy schedule also drives them apart.

So is genetics the key? In the next chapter, I'll explore more twins' stories. That's the best way to put to rest the nature-nurture red herring that plagues most of our assumptions about how and why siblings turn out differently with respect to success.

If not genetics, then is it birth order that explains which brothers and sisters succeed and which do not? Birth position is a subject of intense debate among psychologists. But whether or not birth order matters for personality is largely irrelevant to how it matters for sibling differences in socioeconomic success. For our purposes, family size is what really matters; parental time, attention, and money are somewhat fixed pies and each additional slice means less for everybody. Child-dominated households may also be less intellectually stimulating— think of the chaos of a family with five children as compared with two. But the number of children in a household changes over the life span of a family. Birth order comes into the picture as a stand-in for the number of siblings with whom an individual shares his or her parents over the course of childhood. Firstborns spend at least some of their time as only children. Last borns do as well (if elder siblings leave). However, middle borns experience the crunch of sibling competition for parental resources both coming and going. Chapter 3 fleshes out theories of birth order and family size, offering a unique way to measure the impact of the birth of additional siblings on sibling outcomes.

Not only is coming from a large family a disadvantage overall; it also generates more disparate outcomes among siblings. Bigger families generate wider spreads among any given pair of siblings than do families that are smaller. This is due to the fact that resources are spread more thinly, forcing parents to make choices on child investment. It is also due to the reduced parental influence and control in large, child-dominated families.

Birth order also affects how siblings experience family trauma. Chapter 4 explores trauma in the lives of children—illness, death, parental desertion. When a family disruption occurs, not all siblings are created equally. First of all, kids who have escaped the household by the time family tragedy strikes often fare the best. They may escape largely unscathed from the deleterious economic consequences of negative events. They also see less of the family grieving firsthand. Last, but by no means least, they are less often forced into taking on adult responsibilities in lieu of a missing or incapacitated parent, as are some of the siblings who remain. Among the siblings who do remain, however, it is often the eldest who bears the biggest burden, and suffers for it. This is particularly true for elder girls, who are more likely to be forced into the role of caretaker for younger brothers and sisters when the remaining single parent has to work to support the family.

Chapter 4 also deals with the variable impact of divorce on siblings' success. American families have gone through a revolution in the last four decades. Increasingly, romantic relationships are severed from childrearing arrangements; the old model of lifelong monogamy and clear gender roles is dead in many sectors of U.S. society. This is a result of many factors, ranging from reproductive technologies (such as the pill and in vitro fertilization) to economic changes (like increased female labor force participation) to demographic shifts (like declines in average family size, increases in the age at first birth, and longer life expectancies). There has been much highly charged debate in academia and in the media about what these changes are doing to the fabric of American families in general and the lives of children in particular. In this debate, divorce is seen either as universally bad for offspring or universally harmless. Ignored in divorce research and in the media is the fact that—like trauma—family disruption impacts siblings differently depending on their age and family position. For the most part, divorce follows the same age-related patterns as other family traumas.

Occasionally, however, if the desertion or divorce represents relief from a highly conflictual or otherwise extremely negative situation, it is the siblings still at home who thrive as a result of new and better circumstances, particularly when the remaining parent remarries a higher status partner. Chapter 5 addresses how upward mobility affects siblings differently, whether as a result of remarriage, parental careers taking off, or even a change of location.

Chapter 6 investigates how gender plays out within families. Girls face different challenges than boys do. In some families traditional gender roles are expected (and enforced), generating male advantages over sisters, while in other families girls are expected to achieve as much as boys. Having a mother who worked while the kids were growing up actually attenuates such gender disparities. In other words, female role models matter for girls. In addition to battling different expectations in some families, girls have other gender-specific issues to deal with as well. For example, physical attributes such as attractiveness and weight often predict which sister will attain greater socioeconomic success. This is less true for brothers. Of course, as with all social patterns, there are important exceptions that prove the rules.

While forces like family size, economic class, and gender can explain to a certain extent which siblings succeed and which do not, there is always "luck." Writing thirty years ago, Christopher Jencks found that family background—in other words, the corresponding status of our siblings and parents—explained only about half of ability and success. The other half he chalked up to luck. But even what we call luck has its own logic and patterns. Luck, it turns out, is what the survey designers forgot to ask about (or what is not possible to anticipate and categorize). Chapter 7 examines luck in some detail. The in-depth interviews reveal some interesting patterns with respect to the garbage pail category of "other" influences—which may have remained obscured in large-scale survey research. These unique circumstances that make some siblings radically diverge from their brothers and sisters can be divided into two camps. Some factors bestow "outsider" status upon an individual. Examples of this include being gay or being highly religious. Of course, in one context, being highly religious may make you an outsider vis-à-vis the rest of your family, but in another household, you might be an outsider if you are *not* particularly pious. The same can be said—though to a lesser extent—for sexual orientation (which often makes someone an outsider in *any* heterosexual family). What is even more interesting is the fact that the consequences of outsider status often vary as well. When an individual comes from a high-class family background, being an outsider to that world can be a disadvantage. It often bars that sibling from truly enjoying all the resources and advantages that the family provides other siblings. Shaun is the firstborn, gay son of a wealthy attorney who—by virtue of his sexuality—never really gained acceptance by his dad. Hence it was his straight brother who was groomed to be the heir to the prestigious Atlanta law practice that his father had built with two partners. On the other hand, when a family has lower status, being gay can often trigger upward mobility. Drew's story is typical of so many gay men: he left his homophobic, working-class hometown of one thousand people in order to discover the sexual freedom and satisfaction of the big city (in this case, San Francisco). This sexuality-inspired geographic mobility led to upward socioeconomic mobility for Drew as well. In San Francisco, not only did he encounter the liberation of drag queens and Queer Nation, he also got hooked up with the high-tech industry as a programmer. He has so far survived the dot-com bust and earns several times what his working-class siblings do back in Oklahoma.

Religion, it seems, works in much the same way. If the rest of your family is highly religious, then it does not mark you as distinct in any important way. But if you are much more religious than your family, it can work just like sexual orientation: as a barrier to resources or as a protective shield. Of course, it is not always so easy to distinguish cause and effect. For instance, did Jean's deep religiosity develop to serve as a source of inner strength and identity in the face of her lack of material success vis-à-vis her siblings? Or was it the religiosity that stopped her from pursuing a secular education with as much vigor as her sisters? In other cases it is not so difficult to disentangle: Richard was born deaf, so his outsider status obviously was not caused by his bookish behavior or his upward mobility. Disabilities or special talents can often trump all other considerations. For example, children who are born premature or of low birth weight (less than five and a half pounds) are up to 75 percent less likely than their siblings to graduate from high school in a timely fashion (which, in turn, strongly affects later economic success).[24]

The other type of "luck" comes from the outside—yet is no less problematic with respect to causality. While some individuals enjoy (or suffer from) outsider status, others have their lives shaped differently from those of their siblings, by outside influences. Like outsider status, outside influences can have positive or negative ramifications. Some kids are lucky enough to find a mentor or to get bused to a different school than their siblings. (Again, we do not know for sure what is cause and what is effect here.) More often I heard stories of an unfortunate turn of events that triggered a downward spiral for a particular sibling. Others had legal or health problems. Here, it would appear that causality is more certain, since the random events can be thought of as external and unpredicted. However, it could also be the case that siblings are using these events to "pass blame" for their socioeconomic plight that might have occurred even without the terrible "luck" they experienced. With all these contingencies and caveats it is no wonder that researchers throw up their hands and call it all "luck" or "chance." However, a truly random roll of the dice it is not.

With families experiencing an increasing amount of social and geographic mobility in contemporary U.S. society, how do the varying class positions of adult siblings affect family relations in America? In other words, do large class disparities weaken family structures, making extended kin (i.e., the uncles and aunts that these siblings become to one another's children) less relevant than they once were? Or do reciprocal helping arrangements and other forms of family connection persist over sibling disparities in social status? What kinds of tensions arise between siblings of different class statuses with respect to obligations to, for example, ailing parents? How do social attitudes and social networks differ when sibling socioeconomic status diverges? The conclusion sheds some light on the social consequences of these sibling disparities for family life in America, placing them within a larger historical sweep. It also makes explicit many of the policy choices that have been implicit up till now.

Endnotes: Categorical Confusion,
Nervous Parents, and Only Children

While I will provide many answers here and demonstrate how the family pecking order cannot be viewed in isolation from hierarchies of the wider society, no research study can explain every case. The best we can hope for is to explain overall patterns in society—the average case. There is no simple instruction manual for who succeeds and who does not. Anyone who tells you that they are going to explain your personality, your marriage, your career, or anything else about you with one factor—gender, birth order, income, or astrological sign—might as well be selling you a bottle of snake oil.[25] There are as many explanations for particular family pecking orders as there are families. Furthermore, the patterns surrounding race, gender, family size, and so on that I describe here are in constant flux. About the only thing I can guarantee is that if you read this twenty years after I write, the *particulars*—regarding, for example, the role of mothers working or the particular crunch that secondborns feel—will probably no longer apply. That is because the very rules of the game are always changing. If you take anything away from this book, however, I hope it is a new way of viewing the way family pecking orders emerge. As much as we would like it to be, the family is not a haven in a harsh world. It is part and parcel of that world, rat race and all. Inequality, after all, starts at home.

We have only reached the end of the first chapter, yet parents of more than one child may already be fretting over their family history and parenting decisions—did I favor my son over my daughter in grade school? Did my middle child get short shrift? Is my divorce responsible for the poor grades of my eldest? Those that have one child may suddenly decide that one kid is quite enough lest they face the kind of anxieties that come from the sibling differences in success that invariably emerge. While data do show that only children excel on average, we do not know whether that is because of being the only kid in the family, or because of the types of parents that tend to stop after just one kid. What we can say for sure, however, is that only children do not have to experience the same sort of tensions, perceived inequities, sibling struggles, and intra-family stratification that those with brothers or sisters do. About the only way to guarantee not engendering intra-family stratification is to stop at just one. But for most of us, kids are irresistible like potato chips—we can't stop at one.

BUTTERFLIES IN BIALYSTOK,
METEORS IN MANILA

The Nature-Nurture Red Herring

Polish brothers Jan and Jacek Nodotek grew up in an atmosphere where they happily did "everything" together all the way through school, were treated equally by their parents, and shared the same group of friends. Both attended a special high school for athletes in their hometown of Bialystok, in northeast Poland, but do not report any particular competitiveness; rather, they describe a supportive relationship that even included covering for the other when he hadn't done his homework. Though they always went to the same schools and had the same group of friends, they still demonstrated some important differences. Jan was more socially assertive and thus enjoyed an early string of girlfriends. Jacek was more introspective and sensitive to his own moods and feelings, as well as those of others. The brothers describe this difference as stemming from the different personalities of their parents: they both agree that Jan is more like their father—confident, strong willed, and exacting; Jacek is more like their mother—warm and emotional.

The key moment in their mutual life histories appeared to occur right after high school. Jacek attended school for another year to knock off the prerequisites for an accounting program (seemingly an odd choice, given that Jan believes he is the more detail-oriented of the two). Jan, meanwhile, went to Great Britain to study English intensively. This time apart proved crucial to their future trajectories. After Jan had gained fluency in that oh-so-important lingua franca of world business, he returned to Poland for a short time. Shortly thereafter, he secured the means to live in the United States—he had saved enough money, made a couple of connections in the Polish community in America, and then hit the jackpot in the green card lottery. Jacek came with him; their mother also came, a little later, so that she could "take care of them."[1]

In America, Jan's mastery of English—not to mention his legal status—placed him firmly in charge of the family. After some time spent learning on the job, working as a day laborer with other Polish contractors, Jan is now a licensed, bonded contractor whose business seems to keep growing despite a recent downturn in the economy. Jacek officially works for Jan, and though the money goes into the family pot, Jan is clearly in charge. Even after Jacek became legal and his English had improved enough to deal with clients, the inertia of social roles left Jan as the head of the household. In terms of socioeconomic status, they are the same, especially as long as they live in the same home (though this may change soon, since Jan has finally gotten serious about a woman—another Polish immigrant whom he met in America). However, in terms of power over life choices—say, where to live, what jobs to take, whether to make a break from the contracting business and go back to college (which they have been contemplating)—Jan calls the shots. In fact, ultimately Jan is the capitalist, manager, employer—while Jacek is the employed worker. So while their economic conditions may be more or less the same, their class positions could not be more different.

Who knows whether the year in England was the key moment; or whether winning the green card lottery made the difference; or whether these things are just the signposts on a road that was already well paved. If asked to explain why the pecking order between Jan and Jacek emerged, most people would point to age, assuming that Jan was a bossy older brother who dominated his younger sibling. Others would say that genes are what really matter in predicting Jacek's subordinate position. Innate differences may have led to different personalities (and identification with different parents), which led to the course of events I described above. Both these answers would be wrong, because Jan and Jacek are identical twins. I begin this chapter with their story to show how even in the extreme case of identical twins—where there is no genetic variation whatsoever—seemingly "innate" personality differences can still emerge and, in turn, lead to sibling differences in success.

It does, indeed, appear that their identification with different parents led to some quasi-innate differences that might have preordained their respective roles whether or not England, America, and the contracting business had come into the picture. In other words, had Jan never learned English or won access to the United States, they might have stayed in postcommunist Poland and started a business, yet fallen into a similar fraternal dynamic all the same. The bottom line is that we certainly cannot attribute their respective parental identifications to genetic "leanings." Alternatively, it may be the case that the enormous control that Jan exerts over their life course is merely the result of seemingly random events that have large ripples across time.

If we believe the former—that no matter what, Jan would have been the "leader" due to personality differences—then we can ask, Why did he imprint on his father while their mother had more influence on Jacek? While it may seem inevitable that twins identify differently, we do not know why. Was it something in early childhood (a random accident or other experience that shaped one or the other's personality), in infancy (such as who suckled better), or even in the womb (who had the better placental position and thus was heavier, more robust in health, and probably born first)—or was it more like the flip of a coin? No matter which of these stories is right, the fact remains that small differences at some point after birth (or even before) made ripples deep into the future, which seemed to swell into larger and larger waves, rather than dissipating into sea foam. Like a butterfly flapping in Bialystok creating a hurricane in New York. What is true for twins is no less true for the rest of us.

Identical twins Abby and Amy were born to parents who always declared that they never wanted to have children—and who never let their children forget that fact. Their father was Italian and had met their American mother in Miami; the two fancied themselves bohemians and were not well equipped for the emotional and financial demands of parenthood. Their mother, in particular, nurtured many resentments about raising children (most likely because it fell on her to do most of the raising and because she had wanted to be a writer, without other obligations). The family lived in a very small apartment in the Mission district of San Francisco; their father toiled as a waiter in a small but expensive restaurant.

For most of the sisters' childhood, their parents lived separate lives on completely distinct schedules. Their father could not speak English very well, and their mother could not speak Italian *at all,* so the twins, who are bilingual, were necessary translators for the few family discussions that did occur. But their role in holding together a failing marriage was not limited to linguistics. They constantly managed their mother's black moods, nicknaming her Elvira. On Christmas and their mother's birthday, Abby and Amy would buy and wrap presents for their mother, signing their father's name on the card. Also, from a very young age, the twins had to contribute earnings to the household. They modeled and acted in commercials as children, including a poster for the annual Twins Days Festival in Twinsburg, Ohio.

They ignored their father's attempts to co-opt them into his verbal abuse of their mother. "Don't you think Mom is getting fat?" he would ask them in Italian—or in broken English, if he wanted her to hear. "Aren't her clothes terrible?"

They were silent, letting his anger wash over them and evaporate into the air. Only later did they realize that their mother looked like a movie star during this whole period and that their father's assessments were off the wall. "Elvira" stood at five foot nine, had huge blue eyes, and sharp cheekbones that dipped down to a wide, full mouth; she never did get fat, despite her husband's prognostications.

Her beauty aside, things only got worse; he hardly ever stayed in with the family. "Where were you?" she'd scream on one of his rare appearances at home. "Out sleeping with hookers, I bet."

The girls just accepted the fact that their parents hated each other and took over managing their own lives, earning their own money, shopping for food, cooking their own dinners, cleaning the railroad apartment. Their father was not around much, and their mother simply thought of housework as female slavery and so refused to do it, leaving the burden to her children. Had her marriage been a happier one, had her husband done his share, too, housework might not have felt like insult added to injury. But their mother's bitterness extended well beyond the housework issue: she so resented her husband's absence and the forced responsibilities of single parenting (even as self-limited as they were in her case) that she left nasty notes in her daughters' diaries, leaving them open when Amy would clean the house.

Thanks to behaviors like this, Amy was too afraid to invite friends home. When Abby (who was slightly less self-conscious) did bring friends home, Amy would race around picking up dirty clothes off the floor, used cups and plates from the various surfaces, stuffing them into the sink to be washed by her later—all while Abby relaxed, gabbing to buddies on the couch.

By adolescence, the psychological toll started to mount: Amy developed anorexia. She had control over nothing else about her life, so she would control what went into her body. By the next year she cured herself. The way she changed things was by convincing her mother that she had to get divorced.

"I can't live like this anymore," she and Abby told their mother. The Italian-American union finally dissolved, when, in the face of Amy's divorce request and the increasing flagrance of her husband's affairs, their mother finally took legal action. But nothing really changed; Amy and Abby still fended for themselves with regard to food, clothing, schoolwork, and so on. It still fell to them to buoy their mother's oft-frustrated spirits, to keep a relative order in the household, and even to bring income into the family.

They finally escaped their household by attending separate state colleges. It was the first time they lived separate lives. For eighteen hard years, they had done everything together: gone to the same schools, seen the same friends, endured the same miserable home life. When it came time to choose colleges, their mother—for the first time they could remember—asserted parental authority. "You just can't go to the same school," she said. "It's time."

Amy knew deep down that she was right. Though she was terrified at being alone for the first time, Amy also remembers the relief of not being viewed as a twin first and a person second—nobody staring, studying every similarity between Abby and herself. It was, she recalls, the best experience, but also a strange one.

Still, their dorm room phone bills ran into the hundreds of dollars those first couple of months away from each other. They hardly talked to their mother. Amy remembers her father calling only once during her entire college career.

Whereas Amy had taken care of the house, now the roles were reversed. On visits to each other, Abby, who was getting straight A's, helped Amy organize her work. She showed her sister how to outline her papers and made a schedule so Amy would not leave assignments to the last minute. Competition never entered the picture, however—even though Abby started to shine in her dramatic arts program.

After college they moved back to San Francisco together. Then late one weekend night they were riding with a friend who ran a red light and smashed into another car. Blood and glass flew everywhere. Amy, who was injured more seriously, required physical therapy for a year; it took a second year to recover her sense of taste and smell. The process of therapy turned her on to the healing sciences as a potential career path, and she quit her job as a paralegal, becoming a full-time aerobics instructor while she trained to be a physical therapist.

Perhaps as a result of the accident and her long convalescence, Amy suffered a nervous breakdown once she had recovered physically. She became agoraphobic—unable to leave her home. At the same time, she was terrified of being alone. So she invited a constant stream of people over to hang out. As long as her sister or some friends were there, she could sleep in the other room. Soon, one of her brother-in-law's friends became a fixture. He would visit the city from Sacramento, go to bars, and then crash on Amy's couch. They became romantically involved. She joked that with all those bars, he managed to meet the only girl in San Francisco who never left her apartment: "Aren't your parents going to say, 'Find a normal girl'?"

But they didn't say anything like that, and soon the couple was married. Amy began a slow recovery process and now leaves the house on occasion. Soon she hopes to really start her career as a physical therapist. Abby, meanwhile, has transformed her flair for dramatic arts into a knack for public relations. She has been working her way up in the corporate communications world and is now regional spokesperson for a Fortune 500 company.

Like Jan and Jacek, Abby and Amy cannot point to genetic differences to explain their divergent outcomes. Was it the accident that led to Amy's less fortunate outcome, or was she well on her way to a nervous breakdown anyway? After all, she did battle anorexia during her early adolescence. And why did Abby begin to excel in college when she moved out on her own? The respective roles of Amy and Abby have a tinge of inevitability. Maybe that inevitability comes from the extreme duress under which they grew up. The sisters were being squeezed so hard by their parents that they necessarily diverged—they had to divvy up household roles in order to survive. Amy took care of the house and Abby took care of Amy. They were like a tube of toothpaste squeezed so hard that it squirts out opposite ends. By contrast, had the family had the financial ability to, say, hire a housekeeper, the girls would not have had to assume the stressful roles they did. Even in explaining twin differences, we cannot take anything for granted without considering the family's economic resources and its place in the overall pecking order of society.

The Gorilla in the Room

Anytime a book deals with family differences, there is an eight-hundred-pound gorilla in the room: genetics. The first thing most people say when they hear about sibling differences in success is "It's all in the genes." After all, while siblings share (relatively) the same family environment, they only share about one-half of their genes. Why look hard for a conspiracy theory, then, when a fairly plausible answer is sitting there right under our noses? Many trees have been wasted in the vehement debates between the genetic proponents and the behavioralists, but the truth is that the nature-nurture issue is fairly irrelevant when it comes to success. In a complicated society where there are many routes to success (and failure), personality traits and ability, which may betray large genetic components, are by no means a road map to glory.

Besides, despite what numbers of scientists might insist, if you study the subtleties of the research, you know that it is impossible to gauge the extent to which nature and nurture affect success (or other traits, for that matter). There are a number of practical, nuts-and-bolts obstacles to this kind of research, and the problem of trying to separate heredity and environment leads to larger philosophical and ethical issues about how we study ourselves. I am going to take a walk through the research and tackle that gorilla.

Swimming in the Gene Pool

Of all the identities we carry around with us, of all the group affiliations that make us who we are, perhaps the most powerful and least publicly discussed is our family of origin—that is, our parents and siblings. The vast majority of us do not choose our race, our sex, or our nationality (though theoretically we can, whether through passing, surgery, or emigration, respectively). Similarly, we cannot choose the family into which we are born. Yet, while race, gender, and citizenship are the subjects of fierce political battles in government, in the marketplace, and in daily life, the status we occupy through chance of birth to a given family is the most depoliticized identity of all.[2]

This fact, combined with the obvious biological connections that link most siblings, makes the family unit the societal institution that "naturalizes" inequality—that is, normalizes it, makes it seem as a given, like mountains and stars, unalterable by our actions. That is, by virtue of the fact that success and failure often run within families, we come to accept a certain degree of inequality. The fact that, say, both my sister and I are on welfare confirms society's collective suspicions that there is something inherent, hereditary, and likely *genetic* that predisposes us to be dependent on the state. Like congenital diseases, inequality runs in families, and therefore in the genes—so they say. Simultaneously, yet paradoxically, the fact that radical differences can emerge in the adult status of brothers or sisters *also* naturalizes inequality. Well, we may reason, if Bill Clinton made it and Roger did not, Bill must have been luckier in the family gene pool since they otherwise had the same upbringing. However, what we may forget is that being brothers does not mean that they had the same life experience while they were growing up. Quite the contrary. Just take a look at identical twins, who share their genetic endowments completely.[3] If the assumption is that Bill and Roger Clinton had more or less the same environment growing up, then that assumption is multiplied tenfold for identical twins. But this shared-environment assumption does not hold up under closer scrutiny.

In the public imagination and in many scientific realms, twins are held to be the gold standard for understanding the dichotomy between nature and nurture. Separated-at-birth jokes permeate our culture. (Heard the one about Al Gore and Gomer Pyle? Katherine Harris and Ozzy Osbourne? Elvis and Godzilla?) The humor in these jokes reflects our underlying assumption that if we could separate twins at birth, we could truly know the relative effects of nature and nurture. Namely, if we raised them apart, the extent to which they resembled each other would reflect the degree to which genetics determined our fate and the extent to which they differed would reflect environmental influences. Too bad we cannot run the ideal experiment: fertilize clones and implant them in randomly selected, different women, eliminating the common environment of the womb as well.

Such separated-at-birth instances are exceedingly rare in history, and in fact, have never been systematically studied on record. True, there are many reports of twin studies that claim to have determined the genetic basis of everything from earning power to the love of chocolate, but each is flawed in some way. For instance, some twins are not separated at birth but rather live apart only after a number of years. In other instances, they are raised apart, but not very far apart. One may go to live with an uncle or aunt or with a neighbor in the same town.[4] Even when the separations are not planned, similarities in environments may appear. Take the case of Tamara Rabi and Adriana Scott.[5] American families adopted both girls shortly after their birth in Guadalajara,

Mexico. Neither even knew she had a twin sibling. One was raised Jewish, the other Catholic. It was not until they were both attending college in Long Island, New York, that they reunited. It happened because mutual acquaintances recognized the similarities between them. When they finally met, the resemblances were uncanny—both physically and personality-wise. As they adjusted to having a doppelganger, their connection flourished. Eventually, they landed jobs together as dancers for a company that hires out performers to liven up private parties. So far they are occupationally and educationally identical, despite their different social upbringings and having been out of contact for twenty years. Tamara and Adriana would seem to make a good case for the power of genes. But they provide an even more powerful testament to the influence of environment and social sorting. While adopted by different families, both turned out to live on Long Island—hardly what we might expect from a "random" process of adoption placement. They both went to local colleges where their social circles overlapped enough so that they were drawn together by mutual friends (the small world phenomenon). And they both ended up with the same part-time job on account of their relationship and their mutual decision to audition together (and it probably didn't hurt that they were twins, since that may add to the exotic appeal of the party dancers).

The few studies that do claim to have located twins that live in very socially distinct households report that the siblings display uncanny resemblances in the most bizarre ways. One set of twins, psychologist Judith Harris reports, both drove the same model Chevrolet, smoked Salem cigarettes and drank the same brand of beer; another set both wore wire glasses, cultivated short moustaches, read magazines from back to front, and flushed the toilet before using it.[6] While anecdotal, of course, these sorts of resemblances nonetheless appear to make a strong case for the hidden power of genes. If not DNA, then what else could explain shared traits when one twin was raised by his Jewish father in Trinidad and one by his Catholic grandmother in Germany? Not so fast. How many cases are there of twins who were reared apart and barely resemble each other? These are the cases that do not make it into books and for which we have no statistics.[7]

But there is something that is even more troubling. In examining twins who do capture our attention, we selectively focus on traits that match up in the pair. This is what researchers call "sampling on the dependent variable." For example, if neither brother smoked, would we note that as a similarity? Probably not, since it would be unremarkable. Think of all the thousands, perhaps millions, of details that make up who you are. Chances are pretty good that when you meet someone, there are things you have in common. In fact, that is the entire premise of small talk. When we meet someone at a party or on an airplane the first thing we do is seek out the commonalities in our lives if we want to get to know them.

We are quite good at finding common ground between total strangers and ourselves. So it is no wonder that when faced with a long-lost twin we notice some eerie similarities. We are defining what we are looking for after we have found it.[8] The lesson for us here is that matching people is often like the case of the blind men and the elephant: one man feels the animal's leg and says it is like a tree, another, its trunk and declares it is like a snake, yet another, the elephant's ear and claims it is like a fan. Similarity or difference on randomly selected traits does not tell us much, if anything. In order to make claims about the power of genes (or environment), we need to rely on systematic studies where what we are looking for is defined in advance of the looking.

Another place where this tendency to define what we are looking for after we have found it occurs is in evolutionary psychology, another branch of sociobiology. In his book *How the Mind Works,* psychologist Steven Pinker argues that in order to understand human "nature," we must do a bit of reverse engineering. That is, we must do what, say, Sony does when RCA releases a new product: the company's engineers run out to buy one of the new gadgets, then take it apart in order to understand why it was built the way it was. Pinker tries to do this with human nature. Of course, the problem with doing it with humans is that since we do not really know what we are ultimately designed for— if anything—it is pretty hard to work backward.

Survival and reproduction seem like obvious end goals. But even these come into conflict with each other and present their own paradoxes. What about when we sacrifice ourselves for a relative, such as a child? This might feel "natural," but do we do this because our "selfish" genes want to live on and prosper over and above our own personhood? If this is the case, then what in evolution explains homosexuality (and the failure to reproduce), altruism, or the kamikaze attack of a stinging bee? Sociobiologists tell us that certain individuals, like worker bees and gay uncles, have evolved to help out the propagation of their relatives' (or hive's) genes; that is, it is not really our own individual genes that are important to pass on, but rather, the gene pool. Of course, this is a slippery slope. Where does our gene pool end and the enemy's begin?

Even if there were a clear story about what motivates us—that is, what we are designed for—there would still be major problems in relying on evolutionary (or Godly) adaptation to explain current social dynamics. The social world is so diverse that in order for evolutionary theory to explain why we do what we do and who succeeds in doing it, the theory must universally apply to a variety of very distinct settings across time and space. A better analogy for what makes us tick (and want to succeed) comes not from the Sony engineers' "reverse engineering" but from the movie *The Gods Must Be Crazy.* In it, an Englishman throws an empty Coke bottle out of a plane window. It lands in the middle of the Kalahari Desert where a Kung! Bushman finds it. He takes it to be a gift from a god. His family finds it useful as a toy and a kitchen utensil, among other things. Finally, it creates such jealousy, possessiveness, and conflict that he decides to rid his family of it by returning it to the gods. The message is that the way something is perceived—whether a Coke bottle or a certain "innate" skill—has everything to do with the social context. An assignment for Pinker's sociobiological engineers would be to come up with a device that could be parachuted into any society (without accompanying instructions) and its purpose and usage would be immediately understood—and would be understood the same way the world over. (Even a wheel can be used to steer a car or roll a cart.)

This generalized engineering is essentially what we are asking evolutionary psychology to do when we want an account of how biology and natural selection leads to particular social arrangements—for example, the rank orderings of who succeeds and who does not. If there is a fundamental genetic-evolutionary reason for natural selection, then it is tantamount to saying that what makes someone succeed in rural China is the same as what makes someone succeed in downtown Chicago. The sociobiologists may counter that unique evolutionary lines have adapted to varied circumstances, so that Chinese farmers are a separate bloodline that adapted to be patient agriculturalists, while Chicago commodity traders are a unique tribe that evolved to take financial risks and act aggressively. The problem with trying to make localized genetic arguments is that the world of human affairs is much too messy and chaotic for that. First of all, bloodlines are not all that separate. And if they were, immigrants, who generally are among the more successful in their locale, should fail miserably when they arrive in a new society that prizes different evolved skills. Likewise, when a country rapidly industrializes, do the winners and losers completely flip? If it is the same skills that make the immigrant succeed in both societies and the rich succeed in both epochs, then we are back to a universalized evolution of generalizable skills. And it may, in fact, be the case that certain skills, like diligence and stamina, are good everywhere. But many more shift in their value from place to place and time to time. Take the relative value of brains and brawn, for instance. The benefits of brains in U.S. society have been on an upward trajectory for quite some time. Brawn used to promise a pretty good living. Not anymore.[9] Even within a family in a single generation, genetically innate skills can lead to unexpected outcomes.

Take the case of Victoria and Diane (not twins). Early on in childhood, Vic (as she was called) showed musical talent and was strongly encouraged to play various instruments. Among the many instruments she can play, the flute emerged as the one at which she would specialize. From then on, much of the family's life revolved around Vic's flute playing; their mother would take Vic back and forth to practices, performances, auditions, and so on. (Not surprisingly, as a girl, their mother had musical talent but her family's circumstances didn't allow her to develop it, so she wanted to compensate with her own daughter.) Victoria did everything right and received encouragement not just from her mother, but from her instructors as well. Eventually she gained admission to the Berklee College of Music, a very prestigious music school in Boston.

Victoria's sister, Diane, and their father were less involved with these activities, and so they did things together (like attend sporting events) somewhat by default. Because music was so clearly Victoria's domain, Diane focused on doing well in other things—school, for instance. She achieved good grades and went on to college. Today, Vic and Diane are both quite geographically and emotionally close to their parents; each lives within fifteen minutes of them. However, in one key way, their life outcomes have diverged: Diane is successful in her career as a computer programmer while Victoria's musical career never amounted to much. Faced with fierce competition of a different magnitude than she experienced back in small-town North Carolina, she eventually dropped out of Berklee. She then applied to "regular" colleges to finish her studies. But she had always done the minimum required academically in order to focus on her music and as a result really struggled with college. Her struggles do not appear to be due to lack of aptitude; instead, she seemed to not have had much direction and could not stick with much of anything. She attended many colleges and finally graduated after eight years. She now sometimes teaches flute, but by no stretch of the imagination has she achieved what everyone thought she would when she was younger.

Did genes cause Vic's relative failure vis-à-vis her sister? Genes probably caused her to go down the path of music, as musical ability is an area that may be more genetically determined than most other skills. But the consequences of that ability matter differently from situation to situation. Vic had a natural gift, and she had a parent who supported, and even pushed, that unique talent. But she ended up less successful than her sibling largely due to the social structure of the music industry in modern U.S. society. At one time, there was lots of work for many flutists across the country. But technological changes—such as the mass distribution of music across the nation—have created a winner-take-all market in the industry.[10] Why pay to listen to the eighteenth best flutist when you can hear the number-one-rated musician on compact disc? Why watch your local minor league baseball team play when you can tune in to the New York Yankees? Chicago economist Sherwin Rosen calls this the superstar effect: the rewards for the so-called best have skyrocketed, while those for the rest have suffered. Victoria's talent was unfortunately in a realm that especially suffers from the superstar effect. In contrast, the field of computers still has room for many winners.

Twin Similarity and the Influence of Genes

In light of the general impossibility of designing a true, separated-at-birth twin experiment, some scientists, called behavioral geneticists (a branch of psychology), have tried to estimate the genetic components of social characteristics (such as success) by comparing siblings who are fraternal twins (and therefore share about 50 percent of their genes)[11] with those who are identical twins (and therefore share 100 percent of their genes). Put simply, the idea is that the difference between how similar the identical twins are and how similar the fraternal twins are is an accurate indicator of the genetic component.[12] The assumption is that both sets of siblings shared the same family environment, the same age, the same womb. The only difference is the extent of the genetic similarity between them. If genes determine success, then identical twins should be much more similar on socioeconomic measures than are fraternal twins. This is indeed the case, but there is a simple alternative explanation: identical twins also share more similar environments.[13] Of course, on an intuitive basis we know that this is true: identical twins occupy a unique social space in society.[14]

For example, Jacek sums up the specialness of his and Jan's relationship with the simple example of orange juice in the refrigerator: if there were only a little bit of juice left, one twin would instinctively leave half for the other. Acts such as these, he claimed, were totally reciprocal and—even more astonishing—totally unconscious. They describe the legendary twin ability to know and adjust to each other's moods and even thoughts. Like two pistons in a car, one fires while the other rests, and through this unspoken coordination, they are both better off. Fraternal twins rarely talk about their siblings in the same way.[15] This makes the comparison specious and the estimates of genetic influence biased.[16]

The best we can conclude is that the lives of identical twins are determined by both genetic and environmental factors. The social consequences of genetic conditions may vary from place to place, from epoch to epoch—just as they do for Vic's musical talent. If I told you that we lived in a caste-like society in which skin color alone determined what occupation you worked at (not unlike the situation in the South prior to the Civil War), most people would say that it was not genetics, but rather social forces (slavery, segregation, and so on) that determine who "makes it" and who does not. But of course, under those same conditions, being a slave is also hereditary; those born to slaves are themselves slaves. Likewise, if racial inequality were maintained through separate reproductive (marriage) markets distinguished by skin color, and those with darker skin were relegated to worse occupations, then we could be fairly certain there would be a high degree of genetic heritability for occupation. That is, genetics determines skin color and skin color determines occupation so that, indirectly, genetics determines occupation.[17] The point is that we could easily switch the criterion to hair color, eye color, height, or anything else for that matter and we still would find a genetic component, but that would hardly be news. The real story is how the criterion gets selected in the first place and whether or not it seems fair or arbitrary.

Twin Differences and the Influence of Environment

Identical twins are not only the "gold standard" for the influence of genes on social behavior, they also provide a natural experiment, so to speak, for understanding the influence of environmental differences. To this end, twins are used to rule out genetics in order to understand the influence of specific environmental influences. Twin difference methods (as they are called) enjoy a considerable legacy in economics—specifically in attempts to understand the relationship between education and earnings. Estimating the "true" economic value of staying in school has been difficult. The problem is that individuals who finish high school (or college) might earn more because they actually learned something and got a degree, or they might have earned more anyway because people who stay in school (take your pick) are innately smarter, know how to work the system, come from better-off families, can delay gratification, are more efficient at managing their time, or all of the above. In other words, someone who graduated from Yale might not have needed to go to college to earn higher wages; he or she might have shined through without having paid four years of tuition.

How to test this?[18] With identical twins, of course.[19] Since they share the same genetic endowments and are generally raised in similar environments, some economists assume that any differences in schooling between twins are random, the result of chance differences (like getting pregnant or having an inspiring teacher) and therefore are more akin to the experiment of assigning kids to have different education levels and seeing how they turn out.[20] However, what if the random event (like getting pregnant) has its own influence on wages? How do we know that the twin who did not go on to college earns less because she did not go to college and not because her work patterns are burdened by early motherhood? Second, this approach assumes that these twins are *exactly* alike in every way. But what if there are differences between twins that are not random? What if, instead, there are real systematic differences between twins that affect how they do in school and in life? In other words, what if the twin who got pregnant had always taken more risks (for whatever reason) and thus it was almost preordained that if one of the twins were to get pregnant, it would be her? Then it could be the case that some underlying difference really affected their life outcomes and not random chance, pregnancy, or schooling.[21] This dilemma exposes the outer limits of what we can know about pecking orders in families. We simply can never be sure we know what is really causing sibling differences—even when we completely factor out genetics. We already saw the ambiguity with respect to the ultimate causation at work in the case of Jan and Jacek. The same sort of indeterminacy is at work with identical twins Bill and Rich.

These brothers were born to parents who had achieved much upward mobility through education and who thus held similar expectations for their sons. Their focus on achievement was intense. They also took great pains not to treat the boys differently (dressing them in matching knee socks and knickers); however, while they went to great lengths not to favor either twin, at the same time they expected each of them to find individual ways to shine. This presented something of a catch-22: how can you excel when you are expected to be identical genetically—and in all other ways?

Up to the sixth grade, at least, convergence was the norm. Their mother dressed them identically, and Bill believes this actually made them closer to each other since they were seen as a package deal at school. In fact, he felt an enormous pressure to live up to the social expectations of twinness, of being the same, when deep down, he felt different from his brother. But in seventh grade they began to diverge. The fact that they could finally select their own clothes to wear rather than being dressed alike provided their first realm for self-expression— a small but significant wedge that opened up some space between them. It was the next year, however, that would prove pivotal in their life paths. While both kids had loved football, Bill decided to try out for the high school varsity team, despite being only an eighth grader.

"Go away, kid," the former all-American college-star-turned-coach told him at first.

"No sir," Bill persisted. "You can cut me if you want, but I'm going to try out for the position of nose tackle."

"Nose tackle!" He gagged on his coffee. "I won't have to cut you," the coach grumbled. "You'll quit yourself." Convinced that prepubescent Bill would not be able to hack it on the defensive line, he let him have a run. The other linemen welcomed him, since it meant that he would essentially act as fodder for the offensive line drills. Nose tackle is probably the most physically demanding position, since it requires crouching for the entire game, absorbing blocks from multiple offensive linemen in order to allow other defensive players to make plays.

Only thirteen, Bill gave it his all. He ran wind sprints; did hours of deep knee bends; stayed late at the tackling dummies. The coach was half right: he would not have to cut Bill, because he made the team. In fact, Bill became only the second person in the state to earn a varsity letter for five consecutive years. The following year, Rich tried out for the team as well. He opted for tight end—where there was a lot more competition. At one point, Rich dropped a pass during practice—after absorbing a devastating hit from his brother. Bill leapt up, whipped off his helmet, and let his brother have it.

"What's the matter with you, moron?" he screamed into the face-mask of his twin, still lying on the ground. That sort of talk was fairly common during practice, but since it was brother against brother, twin against twin, everyone else stopped what they were doing and listened up. The coach cut Rich the next day.

That was the beginning of different roles and different lives for the boys. While Bill made athletics his calling and was popular among the jocks, Rich studied harder, joined student government, and ran with a more academic crowd. The twins still shared some things, including a paper route and a 1954 Plymouth Savoy. (Bill got it on even days and Rich on odd days.) But for the most part their daily lives and their twinness were much different than before.

After high school their paths once again seemed to flirt with each other's. Rich went to Drexel to pursue a degree in engineering; but after some difficulty adjusting to college, he dropped out to join the Air Force. This made his parents doubly unhappy given their emphasis on education and the fact that it was the early 1960s, not a safe time to be in the service with war looming in Southeast Asia. But he was not sent abroad. Bill, by contrast, tried a couple of different colleges, dropping out to bum around Europe for a while. He eventually finished and joined the Army as an officer (perhaps motivated by his continual need to outdo his brother). When he was commissioned, his supportive brother took leave from his post in Alabama to come and give Bill his first salute. Bill was thrilled to have Rich crack a deferential salute to him—even if military tradition dictated that he had to pay for that first salute. He presented his twin with a crisp dollar bill that Rich still keeps today. Unlike Rich, Bill was sent to Vietnam. Bill *wanted* to go; he was gung ho to see action, and his Army affiliation saw to it that he did.[22]

Vietnam ended any remaining closeness between the brothers who had known each other since before birth (as Rich liked to say). Bill came back, and both brothers married and had three kids. But then Bill started to show signs of what his family termed post-traumatic stress disorder. His family fell apart. He divorced the mother of his three children, much to the chagrin of his parents. Given what he, at least, perceived as their special bond, Rich decided to intervene.

Their final meeting took place in the lobby of the Atlanta Hilton, of all places. Their accounts of it differ. According to Bill, he phoned up to Rich's room and quietly gazed into the window of the gift shop as he waited for his brother to come down and meet him for dinner. Suddenly, he heard screaming coming from the elevator bank.

"What the hell do you think you are doing? Just what the hell do you think you are doing?"

Bill turned around, thinking that someone was chewing out a bellboy or a pickpocket. It was, in fact, his brother who had gotten off the elevator and was walking toward him, hollering nonstop.

"Well, what the hell do you think you are doing?"

"Well, let's not talk about it out here," Bill said under his breath. "If you'd like to talk, calm down and go in and we'll have dinner and talk about it."

They hurried to the hotel restaurant, where Rich continued berating his brother. Finally, Bill had had enough. He got up and slammed twenty dollars down on the table. "When you want to hear my side of the story, give me a call."

(In Rich's version, Bill was doing the yelling before he stormed off.)

Twenty-one dollars down, Bill never spoke to Rich again—despite receiving a written apology, which he claimed was not sincere and consequently dismissed. Bill remained career military, rising to the rank of colonel. Rich returned to college after his stint in the Air Force, and worked as a successful engineer for thirty years until beginning a comfortable retirement.

Their parents blame their own parenting for the rift. Bill blames Rich. Rich blames Vietnam. Maybe they are all right. The point is that small differences can generate large ripples. Who knew that making a varsity football team in eighth grade would be the start of different career paths? Why did it matter so much to Bill that he show up his brother, both on the field and in the military? Though they only had good intentions, their parents can take some blame by treating the twins identically, yet paradoxically expecting them to make a unique mark upon the world. But no matter how you look at it, having a twin is like having a control group shadowing you your whole life. Bill and Rich are both at a loss to explain the origins of their differences. But they certainly cannot blame genes.

Identical twin differences drive home the point that we cannot think about sibling pecking orders as distinct from the societal forces swirling around the family. In Jan's case it was education and citizenship; for Bill it was Vietnam. Nowhere is the larger structure of world society more evident in twin differences than in the case of identical twins April and Liwayway. If the case of Jan's and Jacek's life trajectories can be likened to a butterfly flapping its wings in Bialystok and causing a hurricane in New York, the noteworthy event in other instances is more like a huge meteor that smacks the earth, causing major climatic changes. This was the case with April and Liwayway, when a shooting star of sorts struck the Philippines in the form of an American GI.

April and her sister were born in Manila, conceived in an affair that their biological mother was having. Their mother had already had four children with her husband, who was abusive and alcoholic. The husband knew that the twins were not his and was thus not pleased with their presence—to say the least. Evidently, their mother tried to get an abortion, but was told that it was not possible. The kids are not sure exactly why, but ascribe this situation to the fact that she was in denial for a good portion of the pregnancy and that a twin conception made a late-term abortion impossible in the Philippines during the early 1960s.

After their birth, their father's alcoholism and abusiveness intensified as he faced the daily reminder of his wife's unfaithfulness. After three years, April and Liwayway were presented with a chance to escape this difficult situation: their oldest half sister had married a U.S. soldier. When his tour of duty in the Philippines was up, they were to move to the States. They thought that they could afford to adopt *one* of the twins; both might have been possible, but a real financial strain. When they presented the idea to the three-and-a-half-year-old girls, the toddlers were given the opportunity to choose their own life fates. April, apparently excited by the idea of adventure (or was she just having a good day?), sprung like a jack-in-the-box at the chance to move. Her sister, meanwhile, wrapped all four limbs around her mother and wailed that she did not want to leave.

The twins do not know what explains these different reactions; but unlike the case of Jan and Jacek, where it is not entirely clear whether the specific events are causal or merely reflections of differences that would have reared their heads anyway, it is fairly safe to say that the rest of their life courses can be traced to this momentous decision of a three-year-old to leave her biological mother behind. Not quite separated at birth, the sisters embarked on radically different lives: different families, different countries, different economic positions, and even different birth orders (April was raised as a firstborn and her sister as the youngest girl). Other than their own genetic connection (and the genetic connection of the two "mothers" who raised them), there was almost nothing that was the same about their lives. They did not even stay in touch for more than a dozen years.

From the moment that they landed on American soil, April's biological half sister became her "mother," and her "mother's" husband, the GI, became her "father." The new family settled in Louisiana, and two "siblings" (April's biological half nephew and niece) were soon born. Eventually, her "mother" was able to sponsor many of her family members from the Philippines; and since the alcoholic husband had finally driven himself to the grave, the rest of the family was ready to make a move.

April thus met her twin again when they were both eighteen. Upon their reunion, the twins initially got along, but problems quickly emerged in their relationship. First of all, a major language barrier separated them as April spoke no Tagalog (in her "mother's" efforts to communicate with her husband and raise her children as American, Tagalog was never spoken at home) and Liwayway had no English training prior to arriving here. There is a critical age more or less around the onset of puberty after which someone who learns a language—even when totally immersed in it—cannot learn to pronounce it like a native-born speaker (without special speech training, that is).[23] This is why, for example, Henry Kissinger still speaks with a heavy German accent despite having lived in the United States since he was a boy of fifteen.[24] Like Kissinger, Liwayway just missed this window.

What's more, jealousy soon (and understandably) erupted as Liwayway became increasingly resentful of the lifestyle that she had been "denied" for the past fifteen years. By age nineteen, this sibling ill will boiled over into a major fight and the two women have not corresponded since. April thinks of her sister as a spoiled last born, despite the fact that Liwayway lived a much more impoverished life in a developing country. Liwayway desperately wants a relationship with April—particularly since she recently learned the secret of her family, that she had been conceived out of an affair. This adds one more way in which their childhoods differed: April knew the truth shortly after she had settled into her American life. Liwayway grew up thinking that—other than the absence of her sister—she had a "typical" family. The shock of finding out the truth has left her feeling a particularly strong version of immigrant isolation—especially since her one "true" sister eschews any relationship with her.

Liwayway now lives in Texas, speaks limited English, does not work, and is married to a Philippine-American mechanic whom she met shortly after arriving in America. They are not very well off financially and have a limited social circle since there is not a large Philippine-American community in their town. Recently, however, Liwayway has found happiness with the birth of her two boys (sequential, non-twins). April, meanwhile, lives the life of a high-powered female advertising executive—rich, single, and childless.

The purpose of this chapter was to explore the nature-nurture debate by illustrating how difficult it is to make sense of sibling differences. As we have seen, even in the special case of identical twins, where genes are factored out of the equation, there is great difficulty.[25] For now, it is worth asking what we know about what predicts which twin will try out for varsity in eighth grade, or choose to go abroad to study English, or leave her family behind to start a new life in America.[26] The answers to these questions are much the same for the rest of us—outside influences, family transitions, and even birth order. These dynamics form the grist of the next few chapters.[27]

THREE

LOVE *IS* A PIE

Birth Order and Number of Siblings

An only child, Ivan Majeski spent much of his early childhood caught between the German and Russian armies, roaming the forests of Eastern Europe, surviving off of berries and scraps. When the war ended, things got a little better, but not by much. He spent ages ten through twelve in a displaced persons camp. There, at least, he was fed three meals a day by the Red Cross and received his first formal schooling. After these two years in limbo, his parents received approval to emigrate to the United States. The rest is a fairly typical immigrant success story. While his parents worked in low-wage jobs in Chicago—his father in nonunion construction and his mother as an attendant in a hospital—Ivan made up for lost time at school. He had learned to speak English very quickly, so after school he helped his mother at the hospital, often acting as a translator for her. The doctors and nurses took a liking to the teenage boy and began to show him the ropes. Long before Ivan graduated from high school with honors, he knew what he wanted to be: a physician.

He completed college and medical school and then postgraduate training in family medicine. Soon after he had opened his first practice in a small Illinois town, he fell in love with Jessica, a native-born schoolteacher. Because she had never known her own parents (they had died young and she had been raised by a spinster aunt), family was very important to Jessica; after she married Ivan, she left behind her own career to bear children and work as his office assistant. For his part, Ivan also wanted family—and lots of it. The loneliness of having been an only child imprinted in his mind, he wanted to have as many children as he could. So they got busy right away. In rapid fire, Jessica gave birth to eight children and then after four years, number nine. The first few were born in the county hospital, but eventually they quite literally starting popping out everywhere: one was born in the backseat of an automobile, with an older, unlicensed sibling gunning the car down the rural highway while another sibling pinched off the umbilical cord until they reached their dad's office; three more were born in the family bed, delivered by their father in the middle of the night. Jessica would have kept firing them out, but after eighteen years of fecundity, her body yielded no more. She endured a couple of miscarriages, and then did not manage to ever get pregnant again. They never managed to reach double digits.

Inevitably, Ivan's medical practice began to double as a nursery; Jessica breast-fed as she filed medical records and answered phones. Before long, the older kids turned into workers, helping with the various tasks like so many little elves. Understandably, the family soon became known as the Majeski nine, the largest family in the area. They occupied a strange position in the local class hierarchy. As an orphan, Jessica had grown up poor; Ivan spoke English with a heavy accent; they had more children than any of the town's poorest families; and their melding of work and childrearing in the office setting confused residents' conservative sensibilities. At the same time, Ivan was a well-respected doctor who had treated most of the families in the county. Doctors occupy a unique position in the American class structure: they are masters of highly technical knowledge, yet they often communicate in an intimate, even conspiratorial manner with their patients. Many patients tell their doctors things not even their spouses are privy to. To top it all off, doctors offer a product that is universally valued: health and longevity. Hence their almost-universal popularity, power, and status— compared with, say, lawyers.[1]

Doctors in America occupy the very upper rungs of the class structure, and Ivan wanted to make sure his family stayed there. He sent all nine children to private school, even though it meant they had to drive forty minutes each way every day. He constantly emphasized high

culture—forcing his kids to study violin and take fencing lessons, buying family horses, and so on. Nonetheless, the kids themselves often
felt embarrassed by their father's accent and their mother's unorthodox
childrearing methods. They were also different due to their Eastern
Orthodox religious tradition, which Jessica had adopted, and which
distinguished them from their austere Lutheran neighbors.

For the first three children, these pangs of self-consciousness were
less chronic. After all, they lived a good portion of their childhood
in a fairly normal-sized family—first three, then four and five—still
well in the standard range of children for Illinois in the 1960s. But as
the Majeski population swelled, community social norms seemed to
exert less and less constraint on the family. Long before there were
such things as SUVs and soccer moms, Jessica bought an old minibus
and carted her brood to and fro, often breast-feeding one or two children as she drove—the older children futilely ducking their heads as
they passed friends' houses. Their house sank into disrepair. They went
through VW buses like they were plastic toys; the old ones collected
first in the driveway, and then on the lawn, like spent cigarette butts.
Most importantly, the kids began to run roughshod over the house.

The parents had intended to fix the hole in the second floor of their
home; and they always meant to repair the abandoned vehicles in their
yard. But with six, seven, eight, and nine children, they never got
around to it. The same is true for childrearing. The first few were regularly read to at bedtime; they got help with their homework; they could
turn to their parents for succor and comfort. The later children were left
to fend for themselves. Meanwhile, the older ones were asked to check
on the middle ones' homework since Jessica was busy tending to the
babies. To make up for her lack of time to give as much individual
attention as she once did, she signed all the kids up for an endless number of classes, piling ballet on top of violin (even for the boys), science
class on top of riding lessons, fencing on top of soccer.

By the time the younger ones had reached middle childhood, whispers abounded about the quirky family that had clothes and toys piled
two feet high on every inch of floor space except for the aisles that had
been cleared—as if by snow shovel—to facilitate getting from room to

room. By the time little George—number nine—was born, the eldest kids had distanced themselves from the household, sleeping over at friends' houses, working summer jobs far away, acquiring their own cars, and forging their own paths. The middle group, however, was still burdened with helping to care for the youngest ones, while they themselves lacked for parental (and older sibling) attention. While Ivan continued to make a decent living, the pie was being sliced thinner and thinner by the year. Even with the reduced "sibling rate" that the family received at a private day school, educational bills piled up like the clothes in their living room. Ivan and Jessica took out a second mortgage on the house and worked out a payment plan with the school, doing all they could to prevent their lifestyle from feeling the burden of the cumulative financial pressures.

When Ivan had an accident at work, however, the strain became too much. Had the family not had nine children, the downward mobility that followed the accident would not have mattered so much, since there would have been more savings on hand, and, more importantly, there would have been no kids left in the house to support. But when Dr. Majeski had his fall—both literally and figuratively—there were still four children living at home depending on his income as a physician, which was soon about to end. That part of their story will be taken up in the next chapter. It is worth mentioning here, however, that Samantha, the second-to-last, is the Majeski who ultimately seems to have suffered the most, and who experienced the most downward mobility among the siblings. In contrast, George, the baby, distanced from Samantha by a few important years, is now flourishing as a doctor himself.

Among the rest of the siblings, the eldest three—Karen, Sarah, and Ivan Jr.—are economically successful today. Karen is a writer who has just had her first novel published (she also teaches writing at a commuter college); she teaches out of pleasure more than need, since she is married to an insurance executive who brings home a six-figure salary. She is the mother of two girls. Sarah became a chemist for a large pharmaceutical company in New Jersey, where she lives as a divorced mom of two boys, earning six figures herself. Ivan Jr., meanwhile, became an attorney in Chicago. He married a coworker and together they enjoy the perks of being a "Dink" (Double Income No Kids) couple. They are the richest of all the Majeskis and have generated a bit of resentment among the younger siblings, who harbor unmet expectations that they would help them out financially. (Of course, the siblings blame their sister-in-law instead of their blood brother, even though Ivan Jr. is theoretically just as much to blame as his wife.)

The next two siblings—who experienced the crunch in the middle, but who were not living at home when downward mobility struck— did not fare as well. Julie and Jennifer are both school teachers who have had trouble putting down roots. While they make a decent wage, they have quit or been laid off from their positions several times and are constantly on the move in order to find new work—from rural school district to rural school district across the Midwest. They have chosen to entwine their respective paths and thus always teach in the same district and live together as roommates. They will not "abandon" each other to live independently or take jobs far away from each other, so tension arises when one has a boyfriend and the other does not, or when one wants to leave a job due to a personality conflict while the other does not.

The next two siblings are even worse off, having endured the crunch of the middle as well as witnessed their father's fall from grace firsthand. The two boys, Jason and Jack, both "pursued" fantasy careers that did not pan out. Jason wanted to fly planes for the Navy, but never qualified as a pilot (or made it through college, for that matter, which is a prerequisite for becoming an officer). As a result he spent three years in the service as an enlisted sailor—not a moment of which he regrets. However, while he got to see much of the world, he did not acquire skills that were easily translatable to civilian life. After his tour of duty, he pursued his dream of becoming a pilot in the private sector by spending every cent he earned (from odd jobs and day labor) on flight school. But it was too expensive for him to log enough hours to move up the certification ranks to fly commercially, and the family simply no longer had the resources to help him out. Further, no airline was willing to take Jason on and train him to fly. As a result, he lives with his brother Jack, smoking pot, working here and there, and flying small planes for fun.

Always glamorous and popular in high school, Jack wanted to be a male model or actor. He had been featured throughout his adolescence in various local ad campaigns. But making it in small-town America is quite different from making it in the urban world of high fashion and show business. He did move to Los Angeles for a time and tried to make a go of it, but as is fairly typical, he found more work as a waiter than in his desired profession. After little more than a year, his money gone and his willpower wilted, Jack returned to Illinois to live with Jason (and share his bong, too). At least they are living on their own. Samantha has never even made it out of her parents' decaying home, is plagued by depression, and seems trapped with no hope of escape. (We will return to her case in more detail in the next chapter.)

The five Johnston children were raised in a high-pressure environment with an emphasis on achievement. Despite—or perhaps because of—this environment, Kristen, the second-youngest child, seems to have been the sibling most picked on throughout their childhood: she was always quieter, more insecure, and did the worst academically, so she was always the most vulnerable to her father's and older brother's attacks. Having to cede the position of the "baby" of the family to her younger brother, Rob, who was born just sixteen months after she was, Kristen spent much of her childhood trying to find a role for herself. She tried to join her older siblings in nurturing baby Rob, but was taken to task any time she attempted to play this role. Whenever she tried to show him how to do anything—from going to the potty to riding a tricycle to reading—there were three older, more experienced siblings who were more than ready to jump in and tell her she was doing it "all wrong." Her oldest brother was the harshest critic (the next two are girls). Before long, her father added himself to the chorus of critics. Rather than admonishing his other children for teasing Kristen, he became the leader of the pack.

When Kristen brought home her report card from school, her father always readied himself to read it by cupping his two hands over his head in a cone shape. "Just a minute," he would say, her grades sitting

in his lap as he adjusted his hands. "Just trying to fix my dunce cap."
She got B's and some C's—respectable in some quarters—in a household where A's were expected and achieved by the other kids. Did the
grades cause the label or did the label cause the grades? It does not
really matter, for once the dynamic was in motion, it spiraled out of
control. Though the family acknowledged her as a talented artist, she
also became the family dunce—a scapegoat. This perception of her
became what sociologists call a "master status," a perceived characteristic that colors the way everything else about a person is viewed. It
becomes the first thing that someone thinks of when that person comes
to mind. Examples of master statuses include being completely bald
(particularly for a woman) or having hair down past one's buttocks
(especially for a man); being a Kennedy, HIV-positive, or disabled; or
having won the Nobel Prize in literature. Most of us do not have a master status that marks us; but if we do, it means that all or many of our
actions are interpreted through that label—whether or not it even
holds water. Such was the case for Kristen: she was "the dunce."

By the time she reached high school—a time when kids make peer
choices that may have far-reaching consequences for their trajectory—
her self-esteem had been so eroded by this labeling that she fell in with
the wrong crowd. She had a series of boyfriends, none of which gained
the family's approval. Then she was raped in her junior year, and the
event served to reinforce her family's view of her "bad choices" in men
and how she spent her time. The only person she told in her family
was her eldest sister, Cora. When Cora then relayed the information
to their mother, her response was, "How could you let this happen to
yourself—to the family?" It was another occasion in which Kristen had
brought shame on the family, where she had failed to live up to the
expectations set by her siblings. Though they enrolled Kristen in some
counseling, their mother was so upset that she refused to hear another
word about the incident spoken at home.

After high school, Kristen's trajectory diverged radically from those
of her siblings. While almost all of them went to Ivy League colleges
and graduate schools, Kristen attended a local commuter college for a

while, and then dropped out. While the others all pursued careers as professionals in various fields, ranging from banking to sports management to law, Kristen has often turned to her sisters for support. After she dropped out of school, she moved to Los Angeles to live with Cora for a while. Cora describes Kristen's first stay with her this way: "I had no idea of the extent of her problems. I would go to work; I would come home and she would be sitting on the couch where I left her, because she had been crying all day, and she would still be crying, and the house was a mess. I was just like, My God! You are so lazy!"

Once her initial, judgmental reaction had passed, Cora began to realize that her sister was quite troubled and in need of help. She got her to see a psychiatrist and helped Kristen get set up in an apartment (with a roommate), less than a mile from hers. Kristen soon landed a job as a waitress and seemed to be benefiting from the thousands of miles she had put between herself and her parents. Things seemed okay, for a while. But then Kristen found a new boyfriend—Brett, the brother of her roommate's boyfriend—who introduced her to heroin. Soon the four of them were shacked up, and Kristen had lost her waitressing job. To make matters worse, the new man physically abused her.

Finally, Kristen sought a restraining order to protect herself. She asked Cora to drive her to the courthouse to "take care of something." As it turned out, she wanted to be present at the hearing, though the social worker's testimony was all that was needed. In fact, most of the time, women do not appear at these court dates, since their very purpose is to avoid the man against which they are seeking the order. Kristen, however, wanted to be there and wanted her sister to be there, too—for purposes of family drama.

After all that, however, the couple eventually made up, and Kristen moved back in with Brett. She soon became pregnant with his child, even while continuing to be abused. The couple then moved to Denver, and Kristen's family heard little from them until Thanksgiving, when she brought Brett back East to the family turkey dinner. Rob remembers that Brett wore a bow tie, in an attempt to effect normality. After another long stretch of time, Kristen showed up on Cora's doorstep once again, with her son, Jerrold, in tow. Brett had kicked them out. Cora's heart dropped when she saw her sister. She was bone thin, with drug-induced acne all over her skin.

"My God!" Cora gasped.

"Just don't tell anyone," Kristen pleaded, as she handed her son to Cora to hold. "Especially not Mom."

Within two weeks Cora found a crack vial in her nephew's diaper bag. Not too long after that, it was a heroin needle and spoon. A couple nights later, Cora returned from work to find a totally distraught Kristen, her baby sleeping by her side. "You got to get me to the hospital," she pleaded. "Please, you got to get me to the hospital."

"Okay, honey." Cora felt her sister's forehead. It was cool. "Let's calm down and have a glass of wine."

"No, I got to go."

"Okay, we'll go," Cora told her. "As soon as Carl gets home." They packed up a few things as they waited for Cora's husband. As soon as he arrived, they buckled the baby into his car seat and got under way. At the hospital, Kristen immediately plopped down in a wheelchair. She was given some paperwork that Carl filled out for her. When they had completed all the Medicaid forms, Cora turned to her sister. "Looks like this is going to take a while," she said. "We'll take Jerrold home and get some dinner."

"What are you going to get?"

"I don't know, probably some Chinese food."

"Oh, save me some fried rice!" she yelled out. Kristen seemed to snap out of it, just like that. Still, she and Jerrold spent the next nine months living back with Kristen's mother, going to a day treatment program. That only lasted until she fell in with another drug-using man. When she split from this new guy, Kristen returned to Brett in Denver. They soon had a second child together but later split up again, seemingly for good.

Today, as far as anyone knows, Kristen is still a drug addict and often homeless—still picking "bad" men, who give her the kind of abuse that she received from the men in her home. She was last heard from three years ago. Like her family, I could not locate her to be interviewed for this book.

What is common about the Majeskis and the Johnstons is that, in both cases, the kids on each end of the age spectrum flourished while the kids in the middle—particularly the second-to-last born—floundered. For Samantha Majeski, the causes seemed more socioeconomic—the strain on resources as the number of children piled up. For Kristen Johnston, the dynamics seemed more social-psychological. But the cases are not all that different, once we scratch the surface. The bottom line is that it is not birth order per se that matters; it is really family size that matters and that affects kids differently.

As I was working on this book and casually told people that it was about sibling differences in success, most people immediately assumed it was a book entirely about birth order.

"What does it mean for me that I'm the middle child?"

"I'm a firstborn male; that's good, right?"

"I know that it's because I'm last born that I earn the least money. My parents always favored everyone else first. When it was my turn for money or whatever, their cup ran empty."

I have already talked about how and why modern (capitalist) society tends to rely on explanations focused on individual differences—specifically, psychological or genetic explanations. Nowhere does the tendency to psychologize manifest itself more prominently than in the case of birth order. Many of the people in my study talk about various personality differences that they think led to their family's local pecking order and their place in the wider world. These may run the gamut from attention deficit disorder to shyness to organizational ability. Why these differences? Genes. Being left home alone accidentally as a baby. Having been dropped on the head at age two. There are almost as many explanations as there are siblings. The most common, however, is birth order.

The problem with thinking of birth order as the *Tyrannosaurus rex* of variables is that, like astrological signs, it is interpreted by most people post hoc—that is, after being told about someone's birth position. Do a little experiment: take ten people you know well enough to have an opinion about their birth order, but who you do not know well enough to actually know what it is. These could be people you work with, friends of friends, or even celebrities or historical figures. Write down what you think their birth positions are. Now find out what they really were by asking them, or looking up their biographies in an encyclopedia or on the Internet—whatever means will get the job done. To make it simple, you can just guess whether or not someone is firstborn; however, each only child must be discarded from the list.[2] Chances are you will do only slightly better with this method than if you flipped a coin. That's not because birth order does not matter at *all* (see below), but because its impact is relatively small compared with other factors, including random luck.[3]

But even if we give birth order devotees the benefit of the doubt and assume that birth order does have a dramatic impact on who we are, it still may not affect our success or failure in life.[4] The reason is simple: there is room out there for all types. If firstborns do indeed tend to be aggressive or more organized, then they may find their niche as managers. If secondborns tend to be more creative and outgoing, they may thrive in the marketing and sales departments. Today's economy is so multifaceted that there is potentially something in it for everyone.[5] So, on average, the links from birth order to personality and from personality to success are probably too weak to matter much at all. Go ahead and burn all those birth order books that promise to explain everything about your life. It does matter—a bit—but it matters a lot more for economic reasons than psychological ones. More specifically, it matters because it relates to how the pie of family resources gets sliced.

Size Matters

One problem with understanding birth order is that it often gets confused with family size.[6] In other words, what's more important: coming third, or having two other siblings? I have found that the size of your family matters a lot more than what order the kids popped out.[7] Sociologists repeatedly find that kids who grow up in smaller families generally do much better in terms of success than kids from large families, though the impact of family size itself varies by birth position (more on that later). The detrimental impact of a large family makes intuitive sense: if all else is equal, if the same-sized pie is cut into more pieces, then each kid gets a smaller slice. This view of the importance of family size is known as the resource dilution theory. The resources that get diluted as a family grows in number include money, space, and, perhaps most importantly, parental time and attention. Paying for private school, college, or extracurricular activities is a lot harder to do when there are six bills rather than two. Correcting homework, tutoring, or even just being there when a kid has a tough day is more difficult when three others are tugging at your pant leg or crawling over your back.[8]

A complementary theory about the importance of the number of kids in a family is called the confluence model. This paradigm posits that a small family with, say, two adults and one child has a "higher," or more advanced, intellectual climate than one with six kids and two parents. I doubt that anyone who has visited a house with a large number of small children is surprised by this assertion. Whether they are teenagers or toddlers, when there are a lot of them, chaos tends to carry the day. This is not to say that there are not families of twelve that march in perfect lockstep and military order—or, for that matter, households with just one or two kids that look like federal disaster areas. In the confluence model, however, the essential factor is the average age of the household. Kids are going to learn a lot more by socializing with mature people than with other six-year-olds; they can do plenty of that at school.[9]

Given these intuitive accounts, it should come as no surprise that researchers have found a very strong tendency for those from larger families to do worse in school (and in life) than those from smaller families. For almost as long as sociologists have been studying who gets ahead, they have found that kids from large families do more poorly than those from small ones. There is, however, one exception to this: last-born children from very large families seem to fare quite well.[10] It may be no coincidence that these kids tend to be born after a much larger gap in time. (Can you say "accident"?) Because of this, they have many siblings around who are considerably older and, thus, can act as quasi-parents. The family may have recovered a bit financially as well. In other words, spacing is almost as important as size is.

With these nice, neat theories in place and observations to back them up, it would seem that family size would be the most bankable social fact around. However, in social science there are always naysayers. In this case, some researchers have argued that there actually may be no detrimental effect of coming from a large family at all, because families who have ten kids may just be fundamentally different from families who have two kids. It could be these underlying differences—not the number of kids itself—that matter. For example, perhaps parents who have ten kids tend to be more religious than those who have only two, and it is this religious orientation that hurts them in a largely secular educational system and economy. Or, it could be the case that parents who have lots of children have poorer planning abilities, lack "self-control," and pass these qualities on to their kids, irrespective of how many children they actually end up having. To drum up even more stereotypes, it could be the case that those parents with larger families are just plain dumber than those with fewer children. So, how can we know for sure that it is size per se that matters, and not just something else that happens to go along with size? In fact, one recent study argues that the impact of family size is all a mirage.[11]

We can certainly envision a draconian experiment in which we randomly assign parents to have a given number of children. Then we could see which kids, on average, do better and which do worse. While there are cases in history where fertility has been under tight control of a central authority for the purposes of population control (such as the case of China's one-child policy) or for population expansion (such as Germany's Third Reich), the ethics of such policies are debatable. Certainly, reproductive freedom is ultimately more important than knowing the true effect of family size, and randomly assigning families to have various numbers of children is not ethical—to say the least.[12]

To truly understand the impact of the number of children in a family, we need to find a natural experiment: something that affects the number of children a family has but which does not have its own independent impact on the outcomes of the children in that family.[13] One factor that meets these requirements is the sex mixture of the children. Though aspiring parents have for years been trying to control the sex of pregnancies, their efforts have largely been for naught.[14] While slightly more boys are born than girls,[15] which sex a *particular* family gets is pretty close to random, at least for the first few children.[16] So, to use the language of medical research, we can think of the sex mix of the first two kids as an assignment to a "treatment group" or a "control group."

The key is that families with two kids of the same sex are more likely to go on and have a third than those with two kids of the opposite sex. As it turns out, no matter what most people say on surveys (or when their kids are born) many parents desire at least one of each sex. Among those with the first two children being the same sex in my 1990 census sample, 49.6 percent went on to have a third child. This figure holds for families that have two girls and those that have two boys (despite conventional wisdom about favoritism for boys). Meanwhile, among families with opposite sex children for their first two, only 42.3 percent had additional children. So, while the sex mix is not equivalent to the draconian experiment of assigning families to have different numbers of children, that seven-percentage-point difference accounts for enough variation in fertility to gain a little leverage on the problem. The key is that it is random who gets which mix.[17]

So my research strategy boils down to comparing children from families in which the first two were of the same sex with those in which the first two were of the opposite sex to see who fares better.[18] As it turns out, the results of my study of the U.S. Census show that having more siblings does matter, but not as much as most previous researchers have thought and only for kids in the middle of the pack. Here, then, is where birth order really comes into the picture. In general, middle children suffer more than firstborns. When we look at the impact of a third child separately on firstborns and later-borns, we find that firstborns face no significant reduction in the chances of going to private school;

likewise, they are at no greater risk for academic failure. By contrast, later-borns who end up having more siblings are about one-third less likely to go to private school than are those who do not have another sibling.[19] They are also several times more likely to fail at school (i.e., be held back a grade or more).* My "natural" experiment tells us about the difference between coming from a family with two children and coming from a family of three or more. It does not tell us about the difference between one and two or between three and four (or seven and eight, for that matter). So the best we can do is attempt to generalize what I have found to these other families. Thankfully, the transition from two to three is a lot more common—and therefore more important to know about—than the difference between, say, seven and eight.

One way of thinking about the effects of birth order, then, is to think of it as relating to family size. If a family has four children, where the spacing is sixteen years between the first and the last, we can think of the firstborn as having experienced four years as an only child, four years in a family of two children, four years in a family of three children, and six years (up to age eighteen) in a family of four. The last-born child is born into a family of four but sheds siblings as each grows up and moves out; thus, she spends the last four years of her childhood as an only child. The middle two, however, never get to experience only-childhood. They are always caught between the costs and commitments of an older sibling and those of the youngest. (Hence the success of George Majeski and Rob Johnston and the failure of Samantha and Kristen.)

In order to examine differences other than those associated with the transition from two to more children, I looked at birth order effects on their own—as distinct from family size. Most studies that have examined birth order merely compare individuals from different families, asking them how many kids were in their family and what birth order

---

*Keep in mind that as defined in these data, the mean value on "being held back" is very low, so the dramatic, manifold difference is largely due to the small denominator. (See the appendix for how this variable was calculated.)

they were. By comparing brothers and sisters from the same family and limiting the comparisons to groups of families who share the same number of kids, we can be sure we are not mixing up the effects of family size with the effects of birth order per se (and also factor out the ages of the kids themselves). When we do this, we see that the Majeski pattern is fairly typical. In terms of parental investment, the cup starts to run dry as we go down the line. (Parents, evidently, are poor financial planners.) Firstborns typically do better than secondborns who do better than thirdborns. Parental resources, it appears, are allotted on a first-come, first-served basis. On the other hand, when we look at the outcomes of the kids themselves, we find a slightly different pattern: the middle kids do worst.[20] The Majeskis also support this conclusion—those in the middle failed while those on either end succeeded. Samantha, who was the last of the "middle children," did the worst of all.

Likewise, Kristen really felt the crunch in the middle—particularly given the already-large family that preceded her birth and the quick addition of a younger sibling. Psychologists Nazli Baydar, April Greek, and Jeanne Brooks-Gunn followed more than four hundred children, some of whom had at least one sibling born after them and some of whom did not experience the birth of an additional sibling. They found that the type of interaction between the mother and the child under study significantly changed with additional births. As sibship size grew, the parenting style became much more controlling and authoritative. One can imagine that with the burden of a new infant, a parent just does not have the time or energy to patiently reason everything out with the elder child (who, to make things worse, might also be in the midst of the terrible twos).[21] As a result, the researchers find that after a few years, the children who experience the birth of a younger sibling do worse in terms of verbal development. This negative effect is particularly exacerbated in families with low income and in cases where the age difference between the children is small.[22] This might help account for the treatment of Kristen. She was definitely stuck in the middle, with a younger sibling nipping at her heels.

Born to What?

Birth order, it would seem, is the red herring here. Family size and the crunch at the middle are what really matter. That said, we have to keep in mind that if birth order—or even family size—alone were to explain a lot about society, we would be experiencing massive upheavals in American society for the simple reason that the numbers of only children, firstborns, and later borns in our population have drastically changed over the last few decades. In 1950, the average number of children per American family was almost four (3.7). By 2000, it had dropped to 2.1.[23] For our purposes, that means individuals in 1950 had only a one in four chance of being firstborn (or an only child). Each firstborn was outnumbered three-to-one. But in 2000, the number of firstborns and only children more or less equals the total with older siblings. If people voted by birth order, the party of the firstborns–only children would be ascendant. According to the best estimates, the average family size in America will continue to decline and could sink as low as 1.5 by 2020, which means that only children and firstborns will by then outnumber later-borns by a margin of two to one. (Many other developed countries are already at this point; Italy, for example, has one of the lowest birth rates in the world at 1.2.) The experience of having older and younger siblings used to be relatively common. In a few years, however, the experience of siblings will be considered relatively rare.

What implications will this have? For one, there may be less of a sense of family as "tribe" or "clan" in the future. In the interviews, one of the consistent findings was that those respondents from large families referred to their family as a powerful institution; it seemed to exert great influence over their sense of self, over their conscious identity. For example, despite the fact that many of the older Majeski siblings distanced themselves from their family by moving away and coming home infrequently, practically all nine of the offspring referred to the Majeskis in the first person plural—as in "Well, you know, we Majeskis like to take risks"—or in the third person plural: "Majeskis can sleep through any sort of noise." Though these kinds of references tended to be more common for younger siblings than for older ones, this kind of pattern was repeated by most of the large families in the study. Smaller families almost never referred to themselves as a clan or tribe—that is, as a group with a cultural identity all its own.

This pattern seems kind of ironic in light of the fact that it is among larger families that the household or kin effects on the success of children are the weakest. Not only do children from larger families do worse on average than those from smaller families, but they also experience more randomness. In other words, parents' class status affects their offspring more weakly in large families than in small ones. Likewise, siblings resemble one another less in larger families. For example, sibling similarity in income levels is approximately 24 percent stronger in families with three siblings or fewer than in families with four or more children. For net worth levels—which may be more directly related to family dynamics such as gifts and bequests—the degree of sibling similarity is 59 percent greater in smaller families (three or fewer children) than it is in larger families.[24]

This pattern makes sense in light of the resource dilution theory and the confluence models discussed earlier. When there are only two kids, parents can control their environment a lot better and, therefore, they can imprint their values (and their class status) more easily. To top it off, the family itself becomes a morass of competing influences when the numbers increase; when more cooks are added to fix the proverbial soup, the result may be a mishmash. As a result, community conditions, peer influences, and random chance all seem to play a greater role the more siblings there are. To see what I mean, contrast the situation in figure 1 below for two siblings, where there exists only one social connection, to that with four siblings, where there are six relationships, and finally to a situation where there are five siblings, when the number of ties jumps to ten.

What all this means for the class structure of American society is that as families get smaller, there may be less socioeconomic mobility, not more. Parents will be able to more carefully control the environments of their offspring and thereby reproduce their own class status.

Figure 1:

Exponential relationship between group size
and family organizational complexity

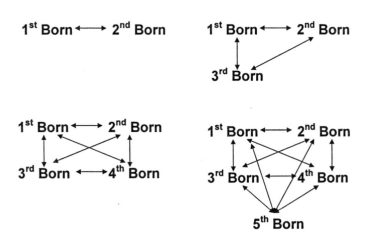

Of course, this depends not just on the overall average number of kids
that families are having, but also on the distribution. If the most dramatic declines in family size occur among the economically disadvantaged segments of American society then we could have more equality
of opportunity.[25] In other words, those children who were doubly disadvantaged in the past due to, say, low income and numerous siblings
would, in the future, only suffer from a smaller pie, not one that is also
sliced into more pieces. But if it is the case that the most dramatic
declines in family size occur among those who are already the best off,
economically speaking, then inequality of opportunity may increase.

The family does not live in a vacuum, however. What we do as a society affects these relationships between family size and sibling differences. To the best of our knowledge, if we provided equal access to
higher education—that is, if we helped finance the college education
of anyone who wanted and was able to go—sibling differences in educational success would be reduced. Further, the relationship between
family size and sibling disparities in educational outcomes would diminish. Good evidence for this comes from a study of the GI Bill. Economists Jere Behrman, Robert Pollak, and Paul Taubman studied the

resemblance in educational attainment between brothers who, because they were veterans, were both eligible for college financing through the GI Bill after World War II. They compared this generation with their children and found that the GI Bill (read: equal access) attenuated the negative relationship between family size and sibling similarity.[26] In other words, the way we structure the larger "game" affects how siblings have to compete with each other. There is nothing inevitable or innate about birth order or family size effects. As with most other social factors that matter, their impacts depend on the choices of the wider society.

In the meantime, the choices of individual parents may affect the outcomes of their children. In 1984, Judith Blake, the president of the Population Association of America, in her annual address to America's demographers said, "If people believe that they can trade off child quantity for child quality they are, indeed, on the right track." Blake further concluded that family size is a more important factor than socioeconomic status, because by the time a family is formed, family socioeconomic status has been largely determined whereas the final family size is still a decision to be made. A couple can more easily influence the quality of their children through family size decisions than by trying to change their socioeconomic status. She concluded with a piece of advice: "If the intellectual growth of your children is important to you, the model predicts that you should have no more than two [children]. . . . Because the larger the family, the lower the overall intellectual functioning." It may not be quite that simple, but it looks like she may have been on to something important.

FOUR

DEATH, DESERTION, DIVORCE

When Bad Things Happen to Good Families

Escape from Disaster

Debra and Andre were raised in a very tight-knit household for most of their childhood. Their parents were upwardly mobile and made it a point to send their children to private high schools so that they could maximize their social advantages. Both kids seemed to rise to their parents' expectations, achieving good grades, participating in extracurricular activities, and becoming active in the community. Debra elated her parents in her senior year of high school when she gained admission to Princeton University on full scholarship. During Debra's first year at Princeton, however, an affair of her father's came to light, which quickly led to their parents' divorce. It was a very painful time, in part because family values had always been spoken of highly in their home, and their father had been a hero to both children. As many researchers would have predicted, both kids' grades dipped for a period of time during and after the divorce.[1] But in the case of Debra and Andre, timing made all the difference. While Debra's grades at Princeton slipped for a time, she had already made it to the Ivy League and had the rest of her college career to make up for a bad semester or two. In addition, she did not have to witness the breakup firsthand, except for a couple of difficult visits during school holidays.

Her younger brother, Andre, however, had to face the reality of the broken family every day during his critical junior and senior years in high school. Like Debra, his grades slipped markedly, but for him, this academic dip made all the difference in the world. He did not get accepted to the colleges to which he applied and instead had to enroll in a local community college. Once at the commuter school, he continued to get bad grades and soon dropped out. He now declares himself to be turning his life around and is slowly working toward a college degree, but his trajectory will forever be different from Debra's Ivy League path that led to a job in investment banking.

Since we cannot randomly assign some parents to wed and some to remain unmarried, some to stick it out and others to divorce, or some to drop dead and some to live on, an alternative approach to understanding the effects of death, desertion, and divorce relies on comparing siblings who experience family transitions at different points in their life. Doing this, we find that when tragedy strikes a family, often the eldest siblings have been safely shepherded through the gates of the family household, and it is left to the younger siblings still at home to bear the full brunt of the tragedy. While such events are horrible to all, their imprint often seems to be the most long lasting and damaging for those who experience its aftermath up close while growing up. It is these siblings who not only have to deal with their own grief surrounding unfortunate circumstances but who also have to deal with the negative emotions of their remaining parent.

This dynamic can be seen in the case of Edwin and Jaime. Their parents married after dating for only a relatively short time because their mother became pregnant with Edwin (as practicing Catholics of Mexican background, abortion was out of the question). Though it would be approximately twenty years until they finally separated (and approximately twenty-five until the divorce was finalized), the marriage was somewhat strained from the beginning. Their parents fought a lot, and their father frequently seemed very angry; he did not deal well with anything that went wrong in his life and seemed quite unapproachable to both sons as they grew up.[2]

The same year that Edwin left for college (on a partial baseball scholarship, which his father actually expressed approval of), the rest of the family moved to Venezuela for their father's new engineering assignment. Their mother had always struggled with English in Texas, consequently staying home for much of the boys' childhood, enjoying a very limited social circle and a narrow range of activities. (She mostly tended house, hung out with other Mexican-American mothers, and watched Spanish-language daytime television.) But when they moved back to a Spanish-speaking environment, she flourished—taking courses at the local university and then getting a job. While as the member of a minority group in the American context she had felt compelled to cling to Catholic doctrine for a sense of identity, in Venezuela she was surrounded by nonpracticing, Spanish-speaking Catholics. The pressure to conform to tradition lifted, and it was in Caracas that she finally realized that she did not have to stay married to someone who was so angry and bitter, and so she left her husband, taking Jaime with her.

This decision set the stage for a bitter custodial fight between Jaime's parents. His father was extremely angry and spent four years both fighting the divorce proceedings (i.e., not signing papers for months at a time) and trying to convince Jaime to come live with him. It was a terribly ugly scene, and a long-lasting one. And it affected the boys differently. Jaime experienced severe adjustment problems. He has been on antidepressants and in therapy regularly, and goes through fits of severe anger at everything (including, especially, his mother, at whom he yells and screams). Despite a high IQ, his high school grades were not good, and he has drifted quite a bit since graduating. While Edwin has also struggled with a lack of focus and direction, his problems have not been nearly as severe as Jaime's. As of this writing, Jaime is still living with his mother and trying to find a program where he can learn automobile mechanics. His brother, meanwhile, made a neat segue from baseball to marketing in college, and so far has been twice promoted in five years at his Chicago marketing firm. Despite his fractured family, he feels his future is bright. Unfortunately, Jaime, the youngest, could not escape as Edwin did. So while both boys endured their parents' unhappy marriage, only Jaime had to directly suffer through the divorce.

Timing is everything.

For the Anderson family it was not divorce but parental death and remarriage that hurt. The five Anderson siblings grew up in a very close-knit nuclear family until the death of their father from lung cancer. Shortly before his diagnosis, Mr. Anderson—an independent plumber for many years—had decided that he wanted more stability in his work life, so he quit his own business and went to work for the Oregon state government. This turned out to be a stroke of luck since when he fell ill, he received both disability payments and high quality medical treatment. Back in the 1960s, however, even "high quality" treatments for lung cancer were largely ineffective. He endured cobalt therapy for about six or seven months. This radiotherapy burned the hair off his chest and left large seared marks across his skin. Yet it did little to stave off the progression of the cancer, and he died nine months to the day after his initial diagnosis. By the time of his death, he had withered from a robust (even slightly chubby) weight of 210 pounds to a mere 128 pounds. When he died, the oldest child, Frank, was twenty-two years old and the youngest, Patrick, was twelve; hence, the aftermath of his demise affected each sibling differently. Their mother went to work as a dispatcher for a home-heating-oil company. It was there that she met her next husband; they were married three years later. Her two husbands could not have been more different. Whereas her children's father never missed a Sunday at church, never swore, and did not touch alcohol, Bert, their stepdad, drank until he passed out every night, used foul language, and was generally nasty.

To escape this confusing and painful family atmosphere, the middle girls, Kimberly and Mary Ann, married immediately after high school graduation. Susan, the oldest girl, moved to New Mexico to live with and help take care of her paternal grandfather. Frank, the oldest brother, joined the Army for a time and eventually set up a career as a financial consultant. It was Patrick, the youngest, who had the worst time of it, having had no escape—by virtue of his age—from the abusive second marriage. By 1969, he was so "lost" and had such low self-esteem that he was using and selling drugs. He grew his hair long. Wore tie-dye. Smoked pot. And, got caught.

"What is this?" his mother demanded one day when she found it in his closet.

"I don't know what it is," he responded, avoiding her eyes.

"No, you tell me what this is."

Patrick suddenly got the impression that she really did not know, and so he turned to finally meet her gaze. "Tea," he said. "It's tea."

"It is not."

"Well, then, fine, what is it?" His tone got challenging, even belligerent as he now maintained eye contact.

"You tell me," she shot back.

He said nothing.

Finally, she broke the silence. "If you are going to make these choices," she stuttered angrily, "then you are not going to stay here." Then she softened her tone a bit and amended her dictum. "If you are going to stay here and make these kinds of choices with your hair and with your clothes, then you are going to pay money to live here."

Apparently she understood that Patrick had pot. So at age fourteen, for about six months, he paid twenty dollars per week to live at home. He got a job working in a fast-food restaurant after school and really tried to shift the direction in which he was heading. But his efforts did not take root. He soon gave up his job. He still scrounged together the twenty dollars each week (usually by selling pot), but he spent all his time hanging out late at night, hitchhiking, and, above all, skipping school. Whenever his mother tried to enforce some discipline, he retorted that he paid his rent and that she should therefore leave him alone. The monetary system that she had hoped would instill order and discipline to his teenage life backfired and, instead, gave him autonomy and an excuse to disobey her parental commands.[3] At one point he ran away from home for a week, even deducting the amount from his rental "bill." Things deteriorated so badly for him that he did not graduate from high school. (He never did, something his family is unaware of to this day.)

He drifted for quite a while, until he was twenty and joined the Army (to emulate his older brother who had become his replacement father figure, albeit from a distance). Luckily for Patrick, most of the American involvement in Vietnam was over by then. However, after one week in basic training, he realized that he hated the military, that the military did not particularly like him either, and that he had made a grave error in judgment. But unlike school, where he could drop out at will, the Army gave him no choice but to finish the three-year tour he signed up for. Whether he liked it or not he finally had to finish what he had started, for once in his life. It was, he claims, the best experience he ever had. After being discharged, he hoped that this newfound "stick-to-it-ness" would transfer back to school. He enrolled in a community college with the idea of getting a GED and then a college degree, trying to take advantage of the GI Bill to make up for lost ground. But almost as soon as he found himself in a classroom setting, Patrick felt those old, uncomfortable feelings of doubt and restlessness creep back. School, he decided, just was not for him. Instead, he decided to stick with his eleventh-grade education and make the best of it.

He moved down to New Mexico to be near his sister Susan and to help take care of his paternal grandfather. The two men developed an extremely close relationship, and it was only then that Patrick began to develop a healthy sense of self-esteem. When his grandfather died several years later, he left the vast majority of his estate to Patrick, instead of disbursing it equally among the siblings. This caused some problems within the family, particularly with Susan, who remains hurt about it to this day (citing all *her* years of taking care of her grandfather). She believes that somehow Patrick took advantage of the old man. As a result, the two have not had a relationship to speak of for the past two decades.

But for his inheritance, Patrick would likely have been—in his own estimation—homeless after his grandfather passed away. So his case illustrates two phenomena. The first is that he was most detrimentally affected by his father's death because the consequences for him were not just personal—the loss of a loved one—but also structural. He experienced his mother's grief and financial stress firsthand whereas the others had ways out. He also had to endure a harsh stepfather who his elder siblings were spared. However, the fact that he escaped an even worse fate is again testimony to the importance of economic resources. In general, families with the means to bring the black sheep up to par with the others will do so. In Patrick's case, economic help did not come from his nuclear family, but rather his extended family. All the same, had his grandfather been poor himself, Patrick would have been in dire straits. Instead, as it turns out, he fixed up his grandfather's duplex and was able to rent out the bottom floor for a goodly sum and live on the top floor, virtually cost free.

Sometimes family trauma does not strike in a single blow, but is chronic and cumulative. The same pattern still holds, however: the eldest kids escape the least scathed if the situation progressively deteriorates. For years Emma and her younger sister, Carole, begged their mother, Lauren, to leave Harrison, their alcoholic father. She never did, even though the situation got worse and worse. Harrison's own father had been a womanizing alcoholic who had abandoned his family, though in those days, around the 1910s, divorce was often not made official. Harrison and his two sisters were left with no means of financial support.[4] As the only male left in the family, Harrison was expected to work outside the home. So he did. Starting at age six, he had a paper route, and later got a job as a drugstore clerk. One hundred percent of his earnings went to help support his mother and sisters.

His own children speculate that this arrangement led to a misogynistic attitude toward women. His misplaced resentment at his sisters was heaped upon his wife, Lauren, whom he had married in 1934. Although he eventually became a pharmacist, he took up drink, just as his own father had. Unlike his father, however, he became an episodic alcoholic: most of the year he would be sober, but then he would go on a drinking binge during which he would get drunk every day for about a month before drying out again. At first, things were not so bad. He entered this Mr. Hyde–like state for only one month a year—always around the holidays when, not coincidentally, his mother would come to stay with them. But soon, the months of drinking came more and more frequently, until he spent about a third of the year wet.

What's more, the periods in between the binges got nastier and nastier as time went on. Emma and Carole never discussed his drinking or how terrified they were of their father. On occasion, though, they would silently conspire to do things like water down his whiskey bottles or hide them—or even pour them down the drain when he was passed out on the living-room sofa. Though he was highly critical of his wife's appearance (which he alternatively considered too frumpy or too seductive), her manners, her housekeeping, her cooking, and anything else he could think of, he never disappeared and abandoned his family like his own father had (though the kids wish he had). Instead, he became increasingly dictatorial with his wife and daughters.

Things got progressively worse, and Carole, as the younger of the two by seven years, bore the brunt of the worst behavior. When she was in high school, she had a midnight curfew, which she dared not disobey. But even when she arrived early, the door would be locked and chained, and she would have to wait patiently until her father fell asleep and her mother could sneak down to let her in—even in the dead of winter. This high school experience stands in contrast to that of her older sister, Emma. One day, many years later, Carole came across a photo of Emma going to a school dance all decked out, with a corsage from her date. There in the background of the picture were her parents, smiling and also dressed up, Harrison's arm around Lauren as they chaperoned their eldest daughter's date. This photo floored Carole since nothing could have been further from her own experience of her parents during high school. Emma, meanwhile, remembers civilized family outings as not having been so rare in her experience. She had even enjoyed the benefit of a baby grand piano in the house and accompanying piano lessons—quite a luxury indeed, especially for the time. Sadly, by the time Carole was old enough, the piano had fallen into disrepair and lessons were out of the question.

In addition to the progression of their dad's alcoholism, another reason things deteriorated was that many buffers seemed to fall away as time marched on. As was common in the first half of the twentieth century, the family lived with extended kin. First, Lauren's mother lived with them after her own husband passed away. Then, later, Lauren's brother moved in and out for a few years. He himself was also an alcoholic, but a jovial one, and some of both girls' most cherished memories involve Uncle Howard acting silly to entertain them. However, when

Emma left home for college, only Carole and her two parents were left in the household. The resentments, anger, and alcohol seemed more intense in such a barren fishbowl.

When her parents fought, Carole could hear every word. One time, Harrison had brought home the gun that he carried for his new job as a pharmaceutical salesman. (He was issued it because he traveled from doctor's office to doctor's office with a trunkload of narcotics.) Lauren was terrified and demanded that he get rid of it. Carole describes the ensuing anxiety like this:

> I had never seen a gun and I overheard my mother say, "What are you doing with this? What are you going to do, kill us all?"
>
> And you know, here I am, this kid, and I go to school with the worry that I am going to come home and my father is going to kill us all. I remember being in class [the next day], and the teacher came up to me and she kept asking, "Are you okay?"
>
> "Yes, I'm all right," I said.
>
> But she said, "I don't think you're okay. You're very pale."
>
> And I repeated, "No, I'm okay."
>
> Well, she made me go to the nurse because I looked so bad, and of course I never told anyone what was happening, and I remember walking home very slowly from school. I was terrified because I thought we were going to all be killed by my dad. I never told anyone this until I told Emma years later.

Increasingly, when Harrison was drinking, Lauren would crawl into Emma's now vacated bed across the room from Carole's. Especially during those nights, when her mother would whisper across the room to ask if she was still awake, Carole begged and pleaded with her mother to get a divorce, but her mother still refused. She always claimed that she could not manage without Harrison or his income. Carole did not understand this logic since she managed the house all by herself and also worked at the post office, for a decent wage. But her mother was deaf to these arguments. She was fond of quoting an old Irish saying: "What can't be cured must be endured." And that always signaled the end of the conversation. She would never leave her husband, though she cried herself to sleep in her daughter's bed almost nightly.

The cycle of drinking and conflict and withdrawal went on like this until Carole left home. Then, according to reports from their mother, it quieted down, and Harrison grew silent and distant (though the girls did not always trust their mother's spin on domestic issues). Finally, a few years later, Harrison—who smoked in addition to his drinking—died of throat cancer. By then, the respective dice of the daughters had long been cast. Emma, not surprisingly, ended up more successful and well adjusted. She married a wealthy man she met in college and together they built a minor real estate empire. Carole, meanwhile, bore many more scars of her youth. She never finished college and now works as a real estate agent, where her everyday task is to do what she learned to do so well in childhood—trying to mask a displeasing interior with a relentlessly positive spin.

Those Left Behind: The Cinderella Effect

In *The Nurture Assumption,* Judith Harris retells the tale of Cinderella. How amazing, she marvels, that Cinderella meekly took so much abuse from her stepmother and stepsisters—presumably for years—but then was able to confidently charm the prince off his feet at the royal ball. She then lists the premises that one needs to accept to suspend one's disbelief and swallow the fairy tale:

1. Cinderella was able to go to the ball and not be recognized by her stepsisters;
2. Despite years of degradation she was able to charm and hold the attention of a sophisticated guy like the prince;
3. That the prince did not recognize her when he saw her again in her own home dressed in her workaday clothing;
4. And that he never doubted that Cinderella would be able to fulfill the duties of a princess and, ultimately, of a queen.[5]

Harris argues that these assumptions may not be so preposterous if we accept that people cultivate multiple selves. Namely, Cinderella may have learned to adapt to her situation from an early age so that she acted meekly and dressed shabbily in front of her stepfamily, reserving a more glamorous self for the outer world. Outside the cottage, Harris argues, Cinderella might have learned from her peers that she was, in fact, quite pretty and may have gained a very confident demeanor from her peer interactions.

Harris is talking about personality. How does socioeconomic success fit in? While it is true that in Cinderella's case, her beauty and charm ultimately led to great power and wealth (through marriage to the prince), it was necessary to invoke some magic to even have the opportunity to allow her "natural" advantages to shine through. After all, if it were not for her fairy godmother's wand, which turned a pumpkin into a carriage and various household animals into horses, drivers, and footmen, then she would have still been home, dressed in rags. It is one thing for burdened siblings to learn how to act differently when they sneak out of the house at night, but it is quite another for them to be able to sneak all the way out to the ball—and to be dressed to the nines to boot. Put another way, it is one thing to escape one's meek household existence to rebel—smoking, drinking, having sex, anything else that parents might disapprove of—but it is quite another thing to sneak out of the house to college or a great job. Family responsibilities and roles are not shed so easily without the right kind of fortune or serendipitous opportunity. Fairy godmother, where art thou?

So, if the eldest has managed to escape the household *before* the shoe (or glass slipper) drops in the form of parental death, desertion, or divorce, then he or she is usually better off than those left behind. But being firstborn among those who remain is no advantage in the case of parental absence or demise. Like Cinderella, the eldest often has to take on the job of surrogate parent when there are other, younger siblings around. They, more than the others, have to bear a burden of premature adult responsibility—usually conditioned by gender roles. This can be a positive, character-building experience with long-term benefits for some, but for most it proves overwhelming and ultimately damages their chances for later socioeconomic success.

Such is the case with the Majeski nine, whom we met in the last chapter. They had long been labeled eccentric Eastern Europeans by their small community of German Lutherans (even though Mrs. Majeski was herself born German Lutheran). That outsider status became intensified after a series of unfortunate events befell Ivan Majeski. One afternoon, the doctor took a fall on the stairs in his office, and hit his head on the way down, topping it off by smashing headfirst into the concrete floor with his full body weight. His wife, Jessica, found him unconscious in a pool of blood. He underwent emergency surgery to relieve a subdural hematoma (a blood clot on his brain). When he finally awoke three days later—surrounded by all nine of his children—he could eat, move, and talk just fine but had trouble remembering anything that had happened within a week or two of the accident and suffered from mind-splitting headaches. All this went on for over a year. Samantha, the second youngest and the youngest girl, bore the brunt of his convalescence, relieving her mother as soon as she got home from school each day. For reasons having to do with age and gender roles, George, the youngest, escaped these sorts of responsibilities.

The family made do on Ivan's disability insurance for a while—but bills soon piled up like the clothes on their floor. After about six months, Ivan was well enough to go back to his practice part-time and, after another half year, to resume full-time hours. But he never seemed to be the same. He moved more slowly. He forgot things. Then one day, representatives from the state medical board and the county prosecutor's office showed up at his practice and told him to shut it down, pending an investigation. A teenage junkie from a nearby town had died from an overdose of Dilaudid, and evidently the prescription (which he had filled in Chicago) bore Dr. Majeski's signature. This was big news. Ivan maintained that his prescription pad must have been stolen. The investigation proved inconclusive, but the Illinois state medical board determined that either way—whether he had written it himself or allowed his prescription pad to fall into the wrong hands—he was no longer fit to practice medicine. He claims that he was unfairly prosecuted and punished in order to serve as an example to other doctors, but it does not really matter: either way, his career was finished.

Jessica stepped in and took a job as a librarian. The remaining four kids at home chipped in with their own earnings (two were working part-time and two were still in high school). They took another (third) mortgage out on the home. But the real cost was psychological. Dr. Majeski's story had dominated the local news for over a year. The publicity was awful for the youngest children: Samantha and George bore the brunt of the family humiliation at the private day school they attended (now on credit). This fall from grace seemed to affect Samantha and George similarly at first. Both suffered from low self-esteem and severe depression for several years. But then their paths diverged. Not knowing what to do with himself, George joined the Navy reserves, following in one of his elder brothers' footsteps. Later, after he finished college, he decided that he would restore the family honor by becoming a doctor himself. He studied hard and aced the medical boards, gaining acceptance into the state medical school. Samantha, though, was mired in the nurturing role she adopted shortly after her dad's accident. Today, George is a successful physician, while Samantha lives at home, ostensibly taking college classes in computer science but really spending most of her time helping to manage the house—trying to rescue it from its cumulative state of disrepair, tending to her father, and taking over the roles that her mother filled before she took the job as a librarian.

In this case, gender and birth order worked together to doom Samantha. She was older than George and hence was expected to bear the brunt of responsibility. Plus, George defined his role as an avenger. Samantha nursed their father, while he avenged his father's fall. Male-male identification surely played a role here. Finally, George was the youngest of all; we already know that the youngest from large families generally excel vis-à-vis their siblings, in part because they garner the attention and supervision of all their older siblings. Since George was four years younger than Samantha, she was already in preschool by the time he was born. She was attending kindergarten when he was one. In short, the breakneck pace of childrearing had slowed to a trickle, and as a result, he got to spend lots of time alone with his mother's undivided attention for the first few years of his life. This cemented their unique bond, which was accentuated by the fact that Jessica knew he was the last child she would have.[6] This bond endured through most of his childhood and gave him a protected, privileged status with his mother—and it paid off.

When the Collinses' dad deserted their mother, Brian, the eldest, seems to have taken on the role of "father," trying to discipline the children, tell them what to do, urge them to excel, and so on. This also involved protecting his siblings, particularly from verbal and physical abuse regarding their racial identity: one night, a mob of teenagers—some of whom were Brian's peers, who he had thought were his friends—came to the house, yelling "Nigger" and threatening violence. Brian protected his siblings by shooting one of the perpetrators with his BB gun and chasing the rest away with his Louisville Slugger baseball bat. But his responsibilities didn't end with physical protection. He also had to manage the household finances, making sure the mortgage and utilities got paid, file tax returns, and balance bank accounts. To top it off, he contributed substantially to the family income from a young age, holding down after-school jobs from the age of eleven. By the time he was sixteen, Brian earned enough to cover a substantial portion of the total household budget. He even helped his mother file her divorce—when it finally came to that. (He was, in fact, the one to push her to get a legal divorce in the first place.) And then, ironically, their father—who throughout the marriage could not have been bothered to show up at home all that often—began to stalk their mother. It fell upon Brian, again, to take action and help his mother through the process of getting a restraining order.

Today, Brian speaks freely of the difficulties of those years and of the burdens he had to assume. Unfortunately, even after things settled down and their father had moved away once and for all, he seems to have been unable to part with this role, and much tension has arisen between himself and his siblings. In fact, the others now report disliking him intensely, finding him very abrasive and generally unpleasant to be around. He, of course, now believes that his siblings are ungrateful for all that he did for them; he still maintains the façade that he knows best about everything. He is also struggling somewhat in his career as an independent contractor and is markedly less successful than his other siblings, all of whom are professionals in the financial industry (perhaps trying to make up for the financial insecurity of their childhood).

Of course, in the Collinses' case, had they had economic resources to buffer their father's absence, Brian might not have turned out all that different from his younger, more successful siblings. Had they enjoyed substantial wealth, he would not have had to take on a breadwinner role. His mother might have been able to hire an accountant and a lawyer instead of relying on Brian. In the Collinses' case—as with others—we cannot predict the emergence of sibling differences solely on personality, gender, or birth order grounds—they are contingent on the position of the entire family in the economic hierarchy of America.

Like illness and injury or divorce and desertion, death often forces the eldest child still at home into this role of pseudoparent. When the oldest Byrne sibling was thirteen and the youngest was three years old, their father, who worked on the railroad and also bartended one night a week, was killed in a car accident. The family was suddenly thrown into crisis; their father, a joyful, active, vital man, had been a major light in their lives. Their mother, who had always been much less demonstrative, grew even more remote as she worked two jobs to keep the family afloat. The family was also buoyed financially by their father's life insurance policy, compensation from the railroad, and the money they received a few months later from the government because the construction of U.S. Interstate 95 displaced them from their home. The family relocated from the row house in which they had lived to a larger home in the suburbs. While this move would seem to mark significant upward mobility, in the Byrnes' new middle-class bedroom town, there was not nearly as close-knit a community as there had been in the row houses of Baltimore. This difference may have been due to class differences among the residents, or it may have merely been the result of the Byrnes being relatively new to the neighborhood. Either way, while the schools were ostensibly of better quality in their new digs, the kind of social support from friends and neighbors that they had enjoyed in the immediate aftermath of their father's demise was largely absent there. Finances always remained tight, and the lives of the six siblings were quite stressed by this fact. It fell to Brenna, as the eldest, to take care of the house and the younger children, and she rose to the challenge, cooking the meals for the younger siblings, packing their lunch boxes, and acting as "parental" disciplinarian while their mother was off at work.

However, soon a forward-feeding, vicious cycle emerged: the more she precociously took on this role, the more heavily her mother leaned on her, upping the implicit (and sometimes explicit) demands on her time. Brenna's grades slipped as she found little time to do her own homework—she was too busy correcting her siblings' work. Her mother did not allow her to have much of a social life, either. She was trapped in a Cinderella-like existence in which her mother would come home from work and pass a figurative white-gloved finger over the various surfaces in the house to inspect the thirteen-year-old Brenna's cleaning efforts.

"You can't go out," her mother would announce if she found a mess anywhere during her daily inspection.

Brenna internalized her anger and resentment and did what many teenagers in her situation would do: she often sneaked out of the house at night. She also took up smoking and drinking to rebel. Finally, when she was seventeen, her anger boiled over. One Friday night, her mother—making her usual criticisms of the state of the house—grabbed Brenna's hair and dragged her over to see a stain on the couch.

Brenna finally spoke up. "I've had enough of this shit!" she yelled, before grabbing a hunk of her mother's hair in retaliation.

Mother and daughter collapsed into a heap on the floor. When the struggle was over, Brenna announced, "I'm outta here." She got up, brushed herself off, and straightened her skirt. Then she left the house—for good. In order to make sure her escape took root and stuck, she got married right after high school. Ironically, having forsaken her original career ambitions, she now finds herself economically dependent and tending house to four children, just as she was when she lived back at her mother's home. The younger siblings, meanwhile, went on to college and have all achieved moderately successful careers as professionals. Obviously, Brenna's story is one of parental death and one of birth order. But it is also one of gender, since had she been male, the same expectations of housework would likely not have been placed on her thirteen-year-old shoulders.

The burdens placed on the eldest do not *always* result in negative outcomes, however. Occasionally an elder sibling matures substantially in the pseudoparent role, and the experience serves them well during the course of their own life. This only seems to be true, however, when that elder sibling is able to break free of that role, once and for all, and when that break takes place in time to make a difference to her life course. Often this opportunity for freedom occurs when a parent remarries and takes over some of the duties (financial or household), freeing up the elder child to focus once again on her own life. Such was the case for Bridget.

Bridget was thirteen and Colleen was five when their mother died of a rheumatoid heart condition. She had been sick for approximately three years before her death, so the children remember her primarily as a figure convalescing in her bed, not as someone who was very active or involved in their lives. During her illness, their father was called up into military service, to fight in the Pacific during World War II, so the girls and their mother moved from Connecticut to their grandmother's house in New York City. Their mother spent most of her time in bed at home, or in the hospital for a week or two at a time when things got worse.

During this time, Bridget became responsible for most of the household chores and day-to-day activities, though there were a few other people (such as neighbors) who also helped out here and there. The tasks were not trivial. These were the days before modern amenities, so Bridget had to do all the washing by hand; she had to clean out ashes from their coal stove, and bring new coal in to keep the fire going; she had to cook everything from scratch (no TV dinners back then, of course); she had to raise Colleen; and she had to nurse her dying mother, to top it all off. She was so overwhelmed and so young, she wonders how she got through it all. One time her mother told her to take Colleen out for a stroll in the pram so that she could get a break from the noise. It was winter and though she had bundled the young child in blankets, she stayed out too long, enjoying the quiet stroll once her sister had fallen asleep in the stroller. She walked for a few miles through the icy weather and city slush. When she arrived home, it turned out that her sister had a severe case of frostbite. The image of infant Colleen's frozen blue fingers and toes still haunts Bridget.

Shortly after their father returned from the war to take a job as a traveling salesman at a printing company, their mother died. Things actually got easier then, since "casserole ladies" began appearing at the door to help out.[7] Still, with all the work to be done, Bridget had no time to grieve for her mother. Within a few months of her death, their father began dating various women, conscious that he would need a new partner and that the girls would need a new mother figure—particularly Colleen, who was already becoming a handful and who was constantly demanding attention. On at least one occasion, Colleen, then five-and-a-half, went berserk and attacked a neighbor who had come over to help out with the cooking and the cleaning.

A year later, during Bridget's freshman year of high school, their father married Roberta, who was rather shy, substantially younger than their mother, and who, a few years before, had been at a convent, preparing to be a nun. With Roberta in the family, Bridget gained a bit more freedom. Now Bridget had enough time to develop typical teenage friendships and participate in extracurricular activities. She was, in fact, very physically active and competed in many sports. After high school graduation, she left home for good; after college, she became a teacher at a series of high schools and community colleges, married relatively late in life to a very religious man several years her senior, and had five children. For her, the key to leading a fulfilling life was getting out of the house while she could—not getting totally enveloped in the task of raising Colleen. This escape might not have been possible had Roberta not arrived on the scene.

Colleen, on the other hand, had already departed quite a bit from the straight-and-narrow. As early as she can remember, she got into trouble;

as a result, her stepmother frequently called her a "bad" child—and she ultimately came to believe it was true. By age eleven or twelve, she was beginning to do rebellious things—like sneaking out of the house and associating with people whom her father and Roberta did not like. Then her father was transferred to Kansas City, Missouri. Colleen, then fifteen, rebelled more than she ever had before; she cut school, periodically stole the car, came home late, experimented sexually, and so on. Roberta, now with two young children of her own, was at her wit's end, and their father finally had Colleen arrested for "incorrigibility." She was sent for a time to live with Bridget, who was then just out of college and student teaching in Omaha, but she soon proved too much for Bridget, too, and so she was sent back to Kansas City. Since she still did not behave, she was sent to a home for wayward girls, from which she escaped after a few months (with the help of a much older security guard, with whom she had cultivated an affair). She lived for a few months with the guard, then began a relationship with the milkman (really!), who at her behest drove her to St. Louis, where she could begin a new life. She was on her own and would not depend on her family again. Sadly, without a high school diploma, she has had quite a tough go of it. She is currently destitute, and over the years has spent more nights than she cares to remember in homeless shelters.

Bridget turned out okay despite—or perhaps because of—the enormous responsibility placed on her young shoulders. The key here, however, was that she was able to shed the Cinderella role before she got stuck with it forever, thanks to her father's remarriage to Roberta. On the other hand, why did Colleen end up having such a marginal economic existence? It is hard to say whether her "incorrigibility" resulted from the stresses and strains of her mother's death, from being raised by a sibling for much of her early childhood, from the additional transition of gaining a stepmother, or because of some innate personality attributes. The answer is probably all of these. But keep in mind that had the family had lots of money, none of this might have mattered, for the widower father would have been able to "buy" the care he needed for his children. He would have, for example, had other avenues to deal with Colleen's rebelliousness—perhaps opting for boarding school over having her arrested.

For Better or Worse?

I have given death and divorce fairly equal weight in this chapter, but that is quite a misrepresentation looking from the present into the future. The total proportion of marital dissolutions has remained constant for much of the last 150 years, but the proportion of marriages that end from death and the proportion that end from divorce have flip-flopped in that time period.[8] In the middle 1970s, the crossover point was reached such that more marriages now end in divorce than end in the death of one of the spouses.[9] Remarriage has followed a similar, steady state equilibrium as well. Today, second marriages make up 46 percent of all conjugal unions.[10] Though spouses may learn much from their first (bad) marriages, the divorce rate for second (or third, or fourth . . .) marriages is actually higher than it is for first marriages.[11] This means that the stories told here can become even more complicated as parents shift in and out of multiple partnerships and the children may experience not just one major transition in their household structure and economic circumstances, but two or even several.

With continual advances in reproductive technologies, the severance of romantic love and relationships from reproduction and childrearing is likely to continue, rather than abate. In other words, no matter who wins various battles in the culture wars, family breakup is likely to be here to stay.[12] Unfortunately, the highly moralized and politicized debate around the long-term consequences of divorce has largely treated its effects as uniform for all offspring.[13] As we have seen from the above stories, nothing could be more naïve. For example, in their best-selling book, *The Unexpected Legacy of Divorce,* Judith Wallerstein and her colleagues claim that divorce—almost universally—damages children's self-esteem and developmental trajectories. Based on interviews with about fifty offspring of divorced parents,[14] they conclude that adult children of divorce suffer from higher rates of depression, endure low self-esteem, and have difficulties forming fulfilling, lasting relationships of their own.[15] She does not examine the socioeconomic consequences of divorce on her subjects, but one can only guess that given the other symptoms she documents, her view would be that their educational and occupational achievements were negatively affected as well.[16]

Such a dire view of family separation stands in contrast to other research, which finds that children from divorced households generally do not do that much worse than other kids. For example, in *For Better or for Worse: Divorce Reconsidered,* psychologists E. Mavis Hetherington and John Kelly found that the children of divorce, for the most part, do adjust well to the new reality (especially since a majority of parents in their sample appear happier a few years after the split).[17] The authors note several mediating factors that help determine whether kids thrive in the postdivorce environment. For example, when parents communicate to each other through the children, rather than directly to each other, unnecessary stress is placed on the offspring. Likewise, continued parental conflict leads to detrimental outcomes for the children (surprise, surprise).[18] Also, when roles become reversed and children have to "play parent" this can also lead to depression and anxiety among the kids.[19] Along the same lines, we have seen that such stressful demands (put disproportionately on the eldest and on females) often lead not only to depression and anxiety, but also to compromised chances for socioeconomic success later in life.

These are merely two examples among thousands of studies on the subject of marriage and divorce (not to mention two books by Mr. and Mrs. Al Gore);[20] however, the problem with all family structure research is the same as the problem with most research on family size: selection bias.[21] Since we cannot randomly assign families to divorce or stay together, we cannot know for sure what the effects of divorce per se are and what are the effects of say, a bad marriage, or of being born to the type of parents who would even contemplate divorce (say nonreligious ones who are not particularly into commitment).[22] Saying kids from divorced families fare worse than kids from intact families is one thing; saying that divorce *caused* those worse outcomes is quite another matter entirely.[23] Going from simple observation of differences to staking out the position that divorce is bad for kids is equivalent to making the strong claim that had these unhappy parents stayed together, these kids would be better off. It may be true in some cases, but is not likely to hold universally.[24]

So, in contrast to the two absolutist positions—claiming either that divorce is generally harmless or that it is almost always severely damaging—I argue that the way divorce affects kids depends on when it occurs during a child's life and what role it places that child in.[25] As we have already seen from cases like Debra's and Andre's, most children whose parents divorce when they have already left the nest fare better than those who endured the separation (and its aftermath) close up. The one important caveat is when divorce signals relief from a highly conflictual, abusive, or even violent situation.[26] In that case, the findings flip: kids who endured that situation for longer (i.e., the eldest) are the worst off. Also, though marital dissolution more commonly leads to downward mobility, it can sometimes result in an improved socioeconomic situation, particularly when accompanied by remarriage to a more successful partner—thus adding further complications to the divorce debate.[27] Transitions that result in *better* economic situations imprint differently on siblings, just as those that result in downward mobility do. Such stories of upward (and horizontal) mobility are the subject of the next chapter.

FIVE

MOVIN' ON UP, MOVIN' ON OUT

Mobility and Sibling Differences

Just as family trauma and downward mobility generate differences in sibling success depending on when it happens in the particular history of a given family, the same is true for positive (and neutral) family transitions such as upward parental career trajectories, remarriage, immigration, and the overall rising tide of the economy and society. It is not so simple, however, that we can say that positive transitions have the opposite impact of family trauma on siblings. True, changes that result in a better climate, more money, and happier parents generally advantage the kids who experience those benefits the longest (i.e., the youngest), but the formula is not so straightforward, as we shall see below. Their impact depends on factors internal to the family—such as gender norms, birth order, and spacing—as well as forces that are external to the household—such as class, race, and nativity. First, I will deal with upward economic mobility.

In chapter 3, I mentioned that birth order matters more for socioeconomic reasons than for psychological ones. While the main relevance of birth order is its relation to family size—in that the pie gets sliced into more (and thinner) pieces with the addition of each child—there is a countervailing trend at play as well: the pie often grows in size as the family does. Most families that remain intact experience some upward mobility over their history. This is what sociologists call a "career" effect (referring to the careers of the parents). In fact, from a social engineering viewpoint, family economic trajectories seem poorly designed: A couple decides to start a family together. They probably rent a home for a while before they save up some money for a down payment on a house or apartment. When they first buy a home, they are told to push themselves to the max in terms of what they can afford. The monthly payments on their thirty-year mortgage may seem almost unmanageable. When their child is born, the costs increase; with a baby comes the expense of diapers and another mouth to feed. But, more importantly, if both parents work in today's society, they face a choice of having one drop out of the labor market (thus losing that income) or hiring a babysitter or seeking out group daycare (since, unlike in most European countries, it is not free here).[1] If they have a second or third child, these costs really pile up. But hopefully one or both parents can manage to hold their act together at the office and will begin to make progress up the career ladder. If all goes well—and the economy does not tank—then the financial pressures should ease up after a few years, largely as the result of two factors. First, while inflation causes some costs to increase, if the family was lucky enough to be one of the two-thirds of American households that owns their home, then their housing costs—which generally take up the largest slice of a household's budget—will remain more or less fixed. If the family secured a fifteen-year or, more commonly, a thirty-year fixed mortgage, the monthly payments are exactly the same in year thirty as they were in the first year, but, of course, inflation has made that figure seem a lot less daunting. Added to this is the fact that hopefully the parents' incomes have outpaced the inflation rate. This was certainly the case for the majority of American households in the period between World War II and the Oil Shock of 1973, though since 1973 the record has been more mixed.[2] In recent decades, the upper half of American households have seen their incomes rise with regularity, but the lower half have been stagnant or even lost ground—except during a brief period in the 1990s.[3]

In some cases, then, the upward career paths and rising earning power of parents can offset the growth of expenses with the addition of children (and put them in a very nice position when kids start to move

out and become independent).[4] For those families who still experience
the American dream of upward mobility, the socioeconomic changes to
the household can imprint differently on the children by their birth
position, particularly when the spacing between children is large, as
was the case for Mathilde, Margaret, and Arnold.

Mathilde, Margaret, and Arnold's father was seventeen years older
than their mother; the marriage was the second for both parents. But
while their mother had been married for only two years when her first
husband died in an accident (and she had borne no children with him),
their father had been married for approximately fifteen years to a woman
named Ada, who had died from typhoid fever in 1930 along with their
oldest daughter, thirteen-year-old Agnes. Two children survived their
mother: eleven-year-old Eleanor and four-year-old Anne. Their father
remarried one year later, and the woman he married (Mathilde, Margaret, and Arnold's mother) was Ada's niece (somewhat scandalous even
in Oklahoma in 1931). A year later, Mathilde was born and, three years
after that, Margaret.

The four girls always considered themselves "real" sisters, though
Eleanor, the only one who could remember Ada, was always somewhat
resentful of her stepmother/cousin and felt that her life would have
been much better if her own mother had not died. Most available
research supports her claim (see chapter 4). Eleanor, who eloped at
eighteen, was also much older than the others, and was already married
by the time Mathilde and Margaret could first remember her. (She
resided nearby, though, and Mathilde and Margaret lived with her and
helped her take care of her two children.) Anne, who could not really
remember Ada and grew up somewhat uncertain of her place in the
family, battled low self-esteem her whole life, and even had a period
where she underwent electroshock therapy. Despite this, Mathilde always felt closer to Anne and, in a more maternal sense, Eleanor, than
she did to her "full" sister, Margaret. Mathilde and Margaret each grew
up feeling resentful of the other—and more than a little competitive—
though they grew a little closer as adults.[5]

When Mathilde was a senior in high school and Margaret was a freshman, Arnold was born—a happy accident, as the family members report. From the start, everyone loved Arnold and was very proud of him; by all accounts, he was always a "self-starter": motivated to do well in his studies and be active in the community. Because his parents had wisely invested the capital and assets that had accumulated during his father's marriage to Ada and had worked to make them grow over the years, the family was also much wealthier during Arnold's childhood than it had been during the previous children's, and so he received more material things than Mathilde and Margaret and Anne (and, certainly, Eleanor) had enjoyed. Further, with his sisters out of the house, Arnold was essentially raised as an only child (though there were a number of cousins and other relatives around his age, too). But his position as a (virtual) only child, coupled with the substantially better financial situation his family enjoyed during his youth, benefited him enormously: he could afford to enroll at Harvard when he was accepted there, and this set the stage for remarkable upward mobility. At Harvard, exposed to new ideas and new people, he continued to excel. He then returned home to Oklahoma to attend law school, and has been a successful local and state politician, including several terms as mayor and state senator, ever since.

Remarriage

The transition from single parenting to (re)marriage often triggers upward economic mobility. Monica and Julia remember their mother as a critical, stern woman who often had angry outbursts. They forgive her, though, since they know it was tough for her as a single mother who was constantly worried about money. Nonetheless, tensions often ran high between the three women in their Denver home. There was a lot of screaming in the household, and both girls suffered from extreme anxiety. While Julia chewed her fingernails down until her fingers appeared to be bloody stumps, her sister manifested even more serious neuroses. When puberty hit, Monica became anorexic, a disorder she attributes to her financial worries about the cost of consuming anything.

In the middle of Monica's sophomore year of high school, their mother moved them to Knoxville, Tennessee, where she had wanted to return ever since she had graduated from the University of Tennessee. This transition seems to have been fairly difficult for Monica, and she reacted by quitting many of the things that she had always been good at—especially drawing and other creative activities. "At first I was excited to go," Monica recalled. "But once we were there, I flipped out. I called my father and told him I wanted to go back and live with him. I remember lying in my room in the dark, listening to Elton John, crying for no particular reason. I spent all my time lying in the dark. . . ."

Though she had always been labeled "the reader" in the family, Monica struggled to find her way after high school: she dropped out of several colleges, had a nervous breakdown at one point, and has relocated around the country several times. Finally, at age thirty-five she has found some stability, working steadily as a hairdresser for the last five years in Minneapolis. Around the same time that Monica turned eighteen and left home for college, their mother remarried—to a wealthy doctor. The family moved to a much better neighborhood, and Julia finished school in the "rich" high school. Best of all, their mother relaxed about money. She quit smoking. She stopped yelling. She got more sleep and was generally more pleasant to be around. So, after three high school years of a more relaxed and wealthy existence, Julia applied to private colleges across the country.

"Go to any school you like," her stepfather told her.

Her mother even objected, but he insisted on paying the full tab for her education (an offer that was made to Monica as well, but too late to make a real difference). Four years later, Julia graduated from the University of Southern California with very good grades; like many twenty-somethings (including her own sister), she struggled for direction for a couple years after college. Luckily, she had her stepfather's wealth as a safety net to fall back on. He paid for a postgraduation trip around the world, a stint as a freelance photographer in Spain, and then financed her move back to the United States to pursue an M.B.A. at the prestigious Thunderbird school of international management. She now works in the marketing department of a Fortune 500 company and is being transferred to Paris to work as an account executive.

Of course, life does not always follow the straightforward equation that more money—later in the family's history—is necessarily better for the younger ones who are around to enjoy it for longer. For example, Donald, Derek, and Charlotte were lucky enough to be born to a father whose prospects were good. He had attended the Naval Academy and married a woman who had been a "Navy brat" herself (that is, her father had been in the Navy, too). The three kids grew up on numerous Navy bases as their father, who worked as an engineer, worked his way up the military ranks. (He finally retired as a rear admiral.) As a result, the first two siblings had a very different upbringing than the last, since the first two were children of a military man without much rank, and Charlotte was a child of a very high-ranking officer—thus, a military "princess." This turned out to be very relevant to her childhood; over time, she became quite dependent on her father's rank for status and a sense of identity. The family moved at least once every two years, and sometimes much more frequently than that, so they were all frequently the new kids in school. As is the custom in the military, their father's rank extended a certain status and renown to them on the military base itself, but their own friendship networks were continually disrupted and thus they never enjoyed a settled or consistent childhood.

When Derek—the secondborn boy—started to get into "mischief," his parents' scolding was put in terms of how he could hurt his father's career. By the time Charlotte came into her teenage years, her dad was already so powerful that no one would challenge his authority over a family matter. Donald and Derek were raised in what they called "dress military" (i.e., lower ranks), living in the barracks (albeit the officers' quarters) on base while much of Charlotte's childhood was "upper military." At one posting, the family lived in a mansion on a hill over the base. A little later, when they were stationed in Italy, they enjoyed the luxury of private drivers and a service staff in their home. But the biggest perks were not material; they were the inherent status that accrued from being the child of one of the highest-ranking officers on base.

Sadly, in Charlotte's case, all this privilege backfired. It made her less independent. Now Charlotte finds herself with three children to raise on her husband's rather modest income as a struggling restaurateur. A would-be entrepreneur who had impressed her with big talk of the glamorous life, her husband didn't bank on the difficulty of getting a restaurant off the ground, and the couple's finances are now virtually devastated. She has been diagnosed as clinically depressed. She never attempted to develop a career of her own—having always anticipated being taken care of by men in the manner to which she had grown accustomed. She now regrets this life choice—or lack thereof—but she does not know what she can do to better her situation. Perhaps all the maid service she enjoyed growing up contributed to a sense of "learned helplessness."

Geographic Mobility

It is also worth noting that a postmarriage transition does not always have to result in significant upward economic mobility to have a salutary effect on the remaining siblings. We can see this in the case of the Shallenskys. Lynnette, Zachary, and Neal Shallensky's parents' marriage was very shaky; the couple endured multiple separations. During their last reconciliation, Neal was conceived, but they finally divorced soon after he was born. The children saw their father with decreasing consistency as they grew up; he is now a rather pathetic (isolated, depressed, lonely, socially strange) figure with whom they barely have contact. When Lynnette had one year of high school left, their mother quit her job as a pizza waitress and remarried (to a man who had a very rural background, several kids of his own, and no high school degree). Soon the reconstituted family left the Midwestern city in which they lived to start a salmon farm in an isolated, rural area of the Northwest.

The family was still struggling economically, but so were many of the people around them. Lynnette was resentful of this and never considered the farm to be home (having lived on it for only the last nine months of high school); Zachary, who had become involved with a "bad group of kids" and had been getting into lots of petty trouble in their old location, used the move to engage with a new kind of crowd and straighten himself out for the last two years of his high school career. Neal, who barely remembers living anywhere but the farm, grew up rather isolated, developing into a nerdy, bookworm type. To some degree, he considers himself to have grown up as an only child, since he was so far removed from Lynnette and Zachary's childhood experiences.

He claims that when he first encountered the fish and other animals, "it was just fucking cool and fun and more like a hobby, and then the hobby grew. I never felt like [working the farm] was something I was being mandated or obligated to do. It was just like they [his mother, stepfather, and stepsiblings] were fucking working, what was I going to do, sit by the whole time?" All that "fucking" labor paid off as his work ethic got him into an Ivy League college (despite his frequent use of foul language) and inspired his career as a marine biologist. In contrast, his siblings attended less prestigious schools and have pursued less prestigious careers. In Neal's case, he benefited from the stability and the work ethic of farm life that resulted from his mother's remarriage and relocation. His siblings were too well-formed as individuals by the time that transition took place for it to have the same effects on them. The story might have been very different if Neal's parents were never able to cut their marital losses and start over again on their own. Again, there is no universal outcome for remarriage (or divorce), except to say that chances are it will affect the kids differently based on their age, birth position, and gender.

Race also gets into the picture and combines with gender to affect how mobility matters. The biracial children of a white mother and black father, the Terrys, lived in a very wealthy suburb of Chicago that was almost entirely white. Nonetheless, neither Andrew nor Hannah seemed to have difficulty with the fact that their skin color did not match that of their friends. Active in the PTA, their parents did the best they could to raise awareness about other cultures in their elementary school, and the youngest Terrys were generally accepted by their peers. However, when Andrew was in the fifth grade and Hannah was in the fourth, Mrs. Terry began to feel smothered by the "perfect, stultifying" world of her suburb, and convinced her husband that it would do the family good to move to the city.

However, city life introduced a number of different elements into their lives that they might not have encountered had they stayed in the suburbs. On the one hand, it was exciting and stimulating in a way that the suburbs had never been. The Terrys went to museums, concerts, exotic restaurants—Mrs. Terry was always trying to get her children to expand their horizons, and she exposed them (and herself, for she was hungry for culture) to as many new and interesting things as she could think of. On the other hand, as Andrew and Hannah grew into teenagers, they were confronted with challenges to their racial identity that they had not faced in the suburbs. Though they certainly may have had to face other obstacles regarding their racial identity had they stayed in their old neighborhood, the race relations that they witnessed in the city gave their coming-of-age a particular edge. It was in junior high school that both Andrew and Hannah first really felt it hit hard. As Hannah says:

> When we moved into the city, there were a lot of black kids in the school. And I was too white. I was called Oreo—like black on the outside, white on the inside. There was a scenario that my mom and I can joke about now but was a pretty big deal at the time, where my mom did my hair. She French-braided it, combed it into two braids with a part in the middle, and a black girl came up to me at school and said, "Who did your hair?" with an attitude. You know, I was proud of it, so I was like, "My mom did it," and she looked at me and moved her neck back and forth and she said, "Not bad for a honky." So I went back to my mom. I didn't know what that was and I said, "Mom, there was a girl who said my hair didn't look bad for a honky." And she just looked at me and said, "Excuse me?" and I said, "That's what she said!" And she said, "We don't say that around here." She explained to me exactly what it meant.

Andrew adds:

> That was really our first contact with other black kids. And when you
> go from a school where you are the only black kid to one with like half
> black and half white, basically you just sort of naturally fall in a crowd
> with the black kids. Because they accept you before the white kids do.
> So as we got more and more black friends, we just got more and more
> into, you know, black popular culture I guess. But it is sort of unspoken
> between us [him and Hannah], how we both primarily only dated other
> black people. And then musicwise, too, we went that route as well.

Over time, though, embracing their African-American identity
came to mean different things to Andrew and Hannah. Both claim that
they never felt alienated from their mother and siblings because of their
race. However, by high school, both were struggling with what it
meant to be "black" in their new environment. Andrew went through a
period of withdrawal from his mother (certainly not abnormal for teenagers under any circumstances), and became heavily involved in music.
He started rapping in various clubs with friends, and became so good at
it that he entered—and won—several local competitions before he was
out of high school. However, his grades suffered considerably from all
the time he put into working on his rhymes—not to mention the fact
that he felt that getting good grades made him seem too white, too
much like his old suburban persona. Though he is very intelligent and
had previously always been a conscientious student, by the time he
graduated from high school the only place he was accepted for college
was a school that was unaccredited. He tried it out for a while but, dis-
satisfied with the quality of life there and increasingly determined
to make something of his music, he dropped out after two semesters.
Today he works odd jobs to help finance his dream, but he is primarily
supported by Hannah, who married an heir to a pharmaceutical fortune.

Hannah, too, went through a period of wanting to fit in with her
peers, but tired of "the constant struggle to be cool" after about a year.
By her sophomore year in high school, she had met a group of girls who

would become her closest friends. A few of these girls were white or Latina, but the majority of them were African-American, and becoming friends with them allowed Hannah to feel that she could be "a good student *and* black, and it wasn't too white to do that; there was no contradiction there." So while she watched her brother increasingly devalue anything but music, she saw her own grades steadily rise. Her mother was thrilled. When it came time for Hannah to attend college, she had several options to choose from, and she ultimately selected Howard University, the prestigious, historically black college in Washington, D.C. As Hannah says: "I felt like I was coming full circle. Going there was my way of not only going to a great school, but also claiming my blackness proudly—on *my* terms." At Howard, Hannah blossomed even more, and she was introduced to a variety of ways by which to embrace both her African-American ancestry *and* her white family. She went on to law school, specializing in international law, and now practices in Washington, D.C. Thanks to her own hefty income and her marriage to the pharmaceutical heir, she never has to worry about money and has begun to set up trusts for her two children.

Though Andrew and Hannah were raised in the same family, their respective stories regarding race make clear that race can be experienced in very different ways. In fact, they are a perfect pair to illustrate this point, because their stories are so different despite both coming from a family with a lot of resources. Certainly Andrew's life would likely be very different right now if he did not have his sister to support him while he tried to make it big—and, for her part, it is not likely that she would have married the scion of a wealthy family if her own family had not provided her the resources to move in circles where she could meet such people in the first place. But we have already established that family resources matter. The larger point here is that even *within the same family* things like gender and race can matter substantially, affecting life trajectories and eventual outcomes because of the way they affect the dispersal of family and community goods, both tangible and intangible. These differences can become accentuated when something like geographic mobility throws the kids into new and challenging environments.

Immigration

There are also times, as was particularly the case in the latter half of the twentieth century when immigration was on the rise, when the family actually changes its entire society. We have already heard of the case of April and Liwayway, identical twins who lived in different societies for thirteen years of their childhoods, but the situation does not have to be so dramatic as siblings being whisked off to live with another family. All it takes is a family migration in the middle of childrearing years, and a birth order difference becomes almost guaranteed by the societal differences that the siblings experience. For example, George, the elder son of a Japanese mother and an American father, spent most of his childhood (up until his teenage years) in Japan. He enjoyed it very much there; he was always very studious and excelled at school. He was less talented in the social realm, however, and this was probably made worse when he and his family moved to America, since the new environment exacerbated his shyness. In contrast, Martin, eight years younger, barely remembers Japan and is very "Americanized." He has always been considered more successful with girls, more attractive, more athletic, and generally more popular—but less talented academically. Though the two brothers were never very close, as adults they have forged a closer bond. George, now extremely successful in the computer field, has helped Martin get jobs, and Martin sometimes gives George advice about women. Yet they remain separated by their very different cultural orientations, despite the fact that they are both from the same family.

The effect of immigration may mark siblings differently even if they do not experience it themselves but rather indirectly through their parents' decisions. Take Marion. She is a fifty-year-old woman whose mother, YiYi, is Chinese and whose father, Louis, is a white American. Louis was a representative for a sales company, and he met YiYi while on business in Taiwan, where her family had lived since the Communists had taken over China in the 1940s. Though there was a substantial language barrier at first, the two were quite smitten with each other from the onset, and within three months they were married. At first, Louis arranged for the couple to remain in Taipei, where YiYi's family lived, but when YiYi became pregnant with Marion two years later, he decided that it would be best for his growing family to move to America, and YiYi reluctantly agreed. They moved to Columbus, Ohio, near Louis' parents and siblings and, though Louis and YiYi did not have additional children until Marion was a junior in high school (when Marion's sister, Yvonne, was born), Marion was raised among a large extended family, including several cousins almost exactly her age.

There were strains, though. In particular, as she grew, Marion was increasingly embarrassed by her mother. YiYi's broken English, though more than adequate for her needs in her new country, made Marion cringe, and she was hypersensitive to the cultural differences that existed between YiYi and the rest of her family on her father's side. By the time she became a teenager—a time when even the smallest things about parents often bother their children—Marion had mentally detached herself from her mother, and "did everything I could to be totally white." She made sure that she appropriated none of YiYi's Chinese idioms in her everyday speech (though she occasionally relaxed this when she was alone with her parents), she avoided as many occasions to be seen in public with her mother as she could, and she took care to adorn herself in direct opposition to her mother's style; she dressed and made herself up very conservatively, rather than imitate YiYi's what she termed "loud and flashy" taste. She did well in school (though never in math, which she felt was too much of an Asian stereotype, and never to such a degree that she could be seen as a drone), ran with a white circle of friends, and dated only white boys. She never mentioned her mother, or her Asian ancestry (though she did not deny it if asked, either). Her main concern was just fitting in, and this lasted even after she went away to college.

However, around the time she hit thirty, Marion started to relax about her heritage enough to make overtures toward her mother. In part, she attributes this to her sister Yvonne's influence. Growing up in a time when Asians had become fairly "normal" in suburban American life, Yvonne had the latitude to be much more accepting of her Chinese background than Marion. Yvonne seemed to be able to incorporate both parts of her ethnic background with little difficulty, which inspired Marion. For the first time, Marion decided to accept YiYi's invitation to accompany her on her annual trip to Taiwan, and the voyage was an eye-opener for her:

> That experience with my mother helped me to understand her and her family—ultimately, *my* family—and it just helped me in general. I got to know my mother a little bit better—where she is coming from and why she does the things she does. It really enlightened me as far as our relationship goes, and it really helped me understand more about myself. . . . I started to embrace my ethnicity more. Now I am proud of the fact that I come from a multicultural background, and I want to pass some of that on to my own kids.

Though Marion's newfound openness to her ethnic background did not influence certain other life decisions she made consequently—in particular, her decision to marry a working-class white man (because "I'm just not attracted to Asian men")—she looks back at the first thirty years of her life with some regret. She is sad that she denied "half of me" for so long but, after some reflection, also notes that "I'm not sure what else I could have done. It's like I had to be one or the other, and it was my mom on one side and everyone else in the entire world on the other. I wanted to be with everyone else. It felt natural. And, you know, it's not like being so different was really going to help me in any way." By the time she was thirty, however, the effects of these cultural pressures had been imprinted on her. She chose not to excel in order to avoid a stereotype in high school and college, and continued this pattern after school. She worked for a while as a sales rep for a fashion company, but then was laid off and drifted for a while. She has only worked intermittently for most of her adult life. Yvonne, by contrast, who grew up in a much more accepting, politically correct period, had no fear of the "model minority" identity: she majored in math and then went on for an MBA. She now works as an analyst for a major investment bank.

The Times, They Are a-Changin'

To even complicate matters further, changes not only occur in the size, economic status, and culture of the family, they also happen in society as a whole. Transformations in the educational system and occupational opportunity structure generate what demographers call "cohort effects." For example, if I was born in 1970 and therefore came of age before the computer industry boom I might experience a vastly different outcome than my younger brother who was born in 1975 and went into computer science right when it was about to take off. My career choices would be much more likely to match those of my father's, since the economy as a whole was more like it was in his day. Indeed, the economy and the distribution of job opportunities can—and do—change rapidly enough to generate such intra-family differences, as does the educational system. In 1995, for example, the proportion of the population that had completed a bachelor's degree (or more) was 23 percent; by 2000 it was 26 percent.[6] In fact, one study by sociologist Robert Hauser finds that birth order differences in educational levels attained can be wholly accounted for by such global trends that manifest themselves as within-family differences.[7]

Sometimes these within-family differences can result from the rising educational tide; sometimes they have to do with more specific periods in American history. We already saw how an increased level of immigration made for very different cultural contexts for Marion and Yvonne. Then there is the case of Dennis and Greg, raised in a very strict household dominated by their demanding and often critical military father. Dennis, the eldest by eight years, came of age in the early 1960s and was the model of preppy obedience. He remembers a rather stable childhood in which the family did not move around that much (at least relatively speaking, given that their father was a career Marine). His primary focus during high school was on meeting his goals in terms of grades and athletics. And meet them he did: he excelled academically while also becoming the star running back for his high school team (and was named all-state). Already his father's favorite, Dennis then cemented that position by gaining admission to the Air Force Academy and becoming a fighter pilot.

Greg, in contrast, came of age in the late 1960s, and dressed and behaved according to the customs of the day. Issues like Vietnam dominated the news and the dinner table. During high school, grades and sports were further down on the list for Greg, who was busy contemplating his own identity in light of the turmoil of the late 1960s. He was constantly criticized and picked on by their father, who saw him as lazy, fat, and not nearly as good as Dennis in anything he did.

Mostly Greg just absorbed his father's criticism and occasionally shot it back at him. (If anything, his father's words only backfired, pushing Greg further into the counterculture.) But one night, when Greg was still in high school, Dennis, who was home on leave, joined the rest of his family for dinner. His father, as usual, was laying into Greg about how he dressed (in tie-dye and sandals) and for his "poor" table manners. Finally Dennis had heard enough. "Lay off of him already," he said sternly, certainly uncharacteristic of his usual tone with their father. "Give him a break, why don't you?"

The fork, carefully making its way to his father's mouth, stopped in midair. "What did you say?" he asked, the utensil not wavering a bit.

"Give Greg a break," he repeated, this time looking down at his plate. "Let's just have dinner."

"Yes, lieutenant!" their father snapped back, now dropping the fork with a clang onto his plate. He turned and marched upstairs.

Despite such occasional moments of revenge, Greg's adolescence was marked by constant and unflattering comparisons to his older brother, while Dennis' adolescence was marked by relatively straightforward achievement and approval. Not surprisingly, Greg's confidence took a big hit, and he has spent the better part of three decades working at a series of part-time jobs, sometimes struggling to make ends meet. He became alienated from his family and remains somewhat distant still, even years after his father's death. In contrast, Dennis continued to experience success; he retired from the Air Force to go into the military contracting business, and he lives a comfortable upper-middle-class lifestyle today.

Conclusion

The types of family mobility I outlined in this chapter are varied, so there is no simple formula as to who benefits from such a transition. There is no Cinderella effect; there is no crunch in the middle. In general the younger siblings benefit from improved economic conditions more than older ones do since they experience them for more of their childhood; however, this can backfire if changes are too extreme (as it did for Charlotte). A new social environment such as a transition from urban to rural living (or vice versa), from one country to another, or from the halcyon days of the early 1960s to the tumult of the latter half of the decade also generate sibling differences. However, these changes are less clearly tilted toward benefiting younger over older children.

What all of these changes in family life uniformly illustrate, however, is the false dichotomy between personality and social structure. Whether it is a changing economic situation, a new neighborhood, a new country, or altered social norms in society as a whole, siblings experience these transitions differently. The result is not only sibling differences in success, but very different personalities as well. Would Charlotte have been so helpless had her father never attained the career heights he did? Would Andrew have differed so much from Hannah had their parents not moved, had there not been a gender difference between them, and had there not been a different impact of race by sex? It seems they hit the trifecta. Would Marion have made the life choices she did if not for her mother's status as an Asian immigrant? Would Yvonne have been so different had there not been such a large age gap between her and Marion? Ditto for Dennis and Greg. Would the two brothers have turned out so differently had the Sixties not intervened? In all these cases we see the neat line between society and family break down. Alas, the home is no haven in a harsh world—it both creates and reflects that world.

LEGACIES AND ROLE MODELS, FAT AND SKIN

Gender Dynamics in the Family

COAUTHORED BY KAREN ALBRIGHT

Everyone in a family experiences that family differently. That is a truism beyond dispute. While there are many potential fault lines in American households, one of the strongest is gender. When offspring vary by gender, siblings often experience the "same" family very differently, and this can lead them toward substantially different life outcomes. We have already seen how it falls disproportionately to elder females to assume the "Cinderella" role when trauma strikes a family. But life need not be so dramatic to engender such different roles and outcomes.

The story of Linda and Adam illustrates how powerful the psychological effects of differential gender treatment can be. When Linda was ten and Adam was eight, the family moved from Milwaukee to a small town in northern Michigan to start a new life. Finances were tight and both their parents worked long hours at a number of jobs to make ends meet. Though both parents outwardly encouraged a large degree of independence in both children, in practice, their father, Peter, was often very hard on Linda. Though she never doubted that he cared for her, and though they had many warm moments together, he criticized her often, particularly when she would try to express an opinion about current events or even discuss something she had learned at school.

"What do you know about it, anyway?" she remembers him saying many times over the years. "You don't know what you're talking about. Get your facts straight before you speak up."

Not surprisingly, Linda found this sort of reaction discouraging, and over time her confidence suffered. She became quieter and more hesitant about speaking—even about her own worth. By the time she was ready to apply for college, she was pretty firmly convinced that she did not have much to offer. Though she wanted to go to college—and her parents encouraged her to apply—she felt that she would not stand a chance at a four-year school, even though her grade point average was solidly in the B range. She decided instead to attend the local community college (though, in keeping with the outward and "equal" emphasis on independence that her parents espoused, she moved out of their home and got her own apartment). After graduating with her associate's degree, she took a retail job at the local mall, where—much to her surprise—she quickly worked her way up to become manager of the store.

In contrast, whenever Adam ventured an opinion, he was typically rewarded with lots of positive feedback from their father. Though Adam and Linda had tested similarly in motor skills and other cognitive developmental measures, what really set the two siblings apart was Peter's enthusiasm for Adam's interests and the fact that he valued Adam's strengths much more than he did Linda's. While Linda typically performed better in writing and art than Adam did, Peter did not think that those subjects were as important as math and science, where Adam excelled. It also did not hurt that Peter had much more interaction with Adam in general—the two played soccer together and did "guy things" like hauling firewood out of the woods—and their time together included helping Adam with his studies.[1] Peter took care to reinforce his belief in Adam; he encouraged him to speak his mind, to inquire when he did not know something, and to consider himself a leader. The lessons and attention paid off: by the time he got to high school, Adam had been allowed to skip a grade; after graduation, he attended Stanford, and is currently earning a doctorate at Johns Hopkins. A simple story of gender favoritism, right? Yet the distinction between the way in which the siblings were raised seems to have escaped even them. Today they both attribute their markedly different paths to differences in personality alone. As Adam says, "I think there was just always a big difference between my sister's personality and mine. She always had a little bit of low self-esteem and she never really aimed at a high goal for what she could achieve. It was always like 'let's go just a step below that' rather than going for a higher level of success. I don't know why."

Indeed, it is hard to identify destructive familial patterns when we are surrounded by and desensitized to them, particularly when they are spread out over time and/or not acknowledged as damaging.[2] However, this is not to say that all families are always biased toward their sons.[3] Instead, we must look at differential treatment in the context of each particular family. As developmental psychologist Susan McHale and her colleagues point out, problematic gender bias occurs only in families that have both the opportunity for differential treatment by gender (because they contain both sons and daughters) and choose to implement such treatment (usually when the father has traditional sex role attitudes).[4] These two criteria hardly hold true for all families—though when they do, it can make a real difference in the social experience of a family's children over the course of their lives.[5]

For example, a number of researchers have reported that parents tend to restrict their sons less than they do their daughters, assign them fewer household chores to do, react with less hostility to signs of their emerging adolescent sexuality, allow them more independence, and criticize them less.[6] Further, fathers tend to spend more time with their sons, and report feeling both closer to and happier with them than they feel with their daughters.[7] Fathers of sons also tend to be more involved with their children's activities, including their schoolwork, than are the fathers of daughters.[8] (Mothers are generally assumed to give equal attention to boys and girls, so there is apparently a net gain for boys.)[9] In fact, parents are less likely to divorce when there is a son in the family.[10] Though this may be simply due to the fact that fathers can more easily relate to their sons' experiences—having been, once upon a time, boys themselves—such an explanation can hardly be comfort to a daughter who feels rejected by her father and who may be missing out on useful guidance as she negotiates the complicated terrain of adolescence and beyond. In some cases differential treatment can be relatively benign; in others it has long-lasting economic consequences.

Take the case of the Maadsens, whose son, Charles, is due to inherit the family business, despite the fact that he has three older sisters, one of whom, Evelyn, has already proven herself to have a solid head for business. Evelyn graduated from business school with honors and has excelled at every internship she has had. In addition, she has declared an interest in continuing the family legacy.[11] Charles, on the other hand, is currently struggling through his own stint at business school. While he has displayed no flair for business, his parents nonetheless consider him the front-runner for the job. As his father says: "It makes sense for Charlie to take over eventually. It's been passed down to men in the family for years, since my great-grandfather started the whole enterprise. I love my girls, don't get me wrong. But they are already busy with their kids, and they are just going to get busier. Charlie's a fine young man. When he's ready to do a good job, I know he will make his mother and me proud. I don't think he is ready right now, but that's just as well, because I'm not ready to retire."

Charles may indeed one day shape up and do his father proud, and Evelyn, who is now considering starting up her own business, may get over her disappointment at not being entrusted with carrying on the family legacy. Or not. No matter how it turns out for the Maadsen siblings, one thing is clear: because he happened to be born a male, Charles has an advantage that he never would have earned on merit alone.

So who benefits more from so-called male advantage? Boys. Yet this "advantage" doesn't always pan out. Charles might find the pressure of carrying on the Maadsen family name too much to bear, or he might find that it is not as lucrative a career as he had imagined. Indeed, the fortunes of a given family business can shift over time, resulting in a less-than-ideal family legacy.

Look at the Heissners. When Bethany, Pamela, and Raymond were growing up in Idaho in the 1980s, the two girls often resented the extra attention that their parents—particularly their father—paid to Raymond and his activities. Take, for example, sports. Both Bethany and Pamela played basketball on their high school teams. As Pamela says, "We weren't always the best players on the team, but we were pretty good, and we always started." Pamela also played softball in the spring, and ran track for a couple of seasons. Raymond, on the other hand, was not a particularly gifted or enthusiastic athlete. The youngest of the three siblings, he halfheartedly played Little League baseball until he aged out of the system at twelve and thereafter abstained from sports completely—with the exception of one season on the high school's junior varsity basketball team. However, that one season was enough to demonstrate to his sisters that their parents were more interested in his athletic career, limited though it was, than in their daughters'. As Pamela recounts, "They went to every single one of Ray's games. *Every single one.* He didn't even start! Or even play that much of the time. Maybe they were trying to encourage him; I don't know. But I can count on one hand the number of times that my mother went to one of our games, combined. And my father didn't come once."

As Bethany puts it, "I've realized that my dad's a product of his own time and place, too, and that's just his way." Though both sisters insist that they didn't feel unloved by their father's seeming disinterest in their athletic achievements, one particular memory still stings. About six months before the 1988 presidential election, the Heissners' home was visited by none other than Vice President George Bush. Here's Pamela's view of that day:

> It was a huge deal. He [Bush] came because at that time our farm was the largest working, family-owned farm in the state, and he was on the election trail. And we were thrilled. I was maybe fifteen at the time; Beth was seventeen, and Ray was twelve. All of us dressed up and were on our best behavior, and we all got to shake his hand. He made small talk, asking us what we liked to do. The thing that I will never, ever forget is that, after he talked with my dad for a while in the living room, he noticed that we had a basketball hoop in our driveway. And he asked if any of us kids would like to shoot a hoop or two. Well, Beth and I would have been the obvious choices, since we were the ones who actually played. But what does my dad do? He bragged about Raymond and put him out there, so Raymond got to play basketball with the next president, while Beth and I had to stand around and watch. I still feel upset about that. I was really hurt. It was just so blatant.

Given such a story, it is perhaps not surprising to learn that the Heissners, like the Maadsens, decided to place the responsibility for the continuation of the family business squarely on the shoulders of their only son. According to Bethany, she and her sister "always knew it was going to go to Ray. There was never any mystery about it; they were completely open about it. You know, 'It's a man's job.' And for the most part we just accepted it; it was just the way it was."

However, as it turned out, the "advantage" that Ray had because he was a male didn't wind up to be such a blessing, after all. By the time Ray took over, the farm was already going through some tough times (like many other farms throughout the country), and things just got worse over the years. With the farm's value substantially decreased and its future increasingly uncertain, Ray found himself working extremely long hours, constantly stressed, and forced to sell off a number of acres in order to keep out of the red. With his ambivalence regarding both the raising of genetically engineered crops and the increasingly prevalent reliance on "factory farming," the future of the farm is still precarious at best. His sisters now worry about Ray, describing him as "old before his time." Meanwhile, without the responsibility of the farm pinning them down, both have been able to develop other interests and have flourished. Bethany, married to a prominent pediatrician in Boise, spends much of her time engaged in local philanthropic pursuits and tending to her three children. Pamela—who moved to the Northeast for college and eventually settled in Maine—invested her savings wisely and made a killing in the stock market during the 1990s, liquidating her portfolio just before the crash. She is currently in the planning stages of building a small, private school for developmentally challenged children.

The Beauty Myth

Another burden that falls disproportionately on females is that of physical attractiveness. It is still far more important for women than for men to be considered physically attractive, and this can play a major role in determining the differences between women's and men's life chances. Because whole books can—and have[12]—been written about this subject, I am only going to touch on one part of it here: a woman's weight. How much a woman weighs is an increasingly central measure of physical attractiveness in our culture. And, as a number of scholars have found, how much she weighs can have quite an impact on her life outcome.[13] Compared with women with body mass indexes in the range recommended by doctors and insurance companies, women who are obese encounter substantial discrimination in the labor market. An obese woman might get passed over for a promotion at an advertising firm because she is not deemed "attractive enough" to sell her firm's ideas to potential clients. Or she might get fired from her job as an airline stewardess because she deviates from the height and weight chart on which most airlines still rely.[14] Or, more likely, she might just not get the benefit of the doubt from her superiors at work, and over time be passed over for promotions or lose the job itself. Of course, women who are downwardly mobile might put on weight as a result of their growing disappointment in their socioeconomic trajectory. Who knows?

However, the burden of a woman's weight does not take its toll exclusively in the labor market. It is the marriage market where weight most makes its presence known; it is here that the majority of the economic deficit associated with obesity in women is found.[15] Since overweight women are viewed as less attractive in our society, they marry less frequently than average women; and when they do marry, they tend to find themselves coupled with men who are less successful in terms of income and status. Therefore, these women have substantially lower total *family* incomes than do their thinner sisters. For men, on the other hand, being heavy is no obstacle to marriage; in fact, heavier men are more likely to be married. Further, though some evidence exists of wage penalties for obese men, it is generally less consistent than the evidence for an "obesity effect" among women.[16]

We can see two of the many ways that weight can play out in women's lives by comparing the experiences of Jill and Erin. First, let's take a look at Erin. Though not considered particularly striking or beautiful,

Erin was generally treated as attractive throughout her childhood and her adolescence, and did not particularly struggle with her weight until she was a senior in high school. From that point on, however, she started to gain weight steadily, until she was about sixty pounds heavier than her "ideal" weight. Boys stopped flirting with her and started cracking jokes about her weight gain under their breath as she passed by. When she went out at night, the boys looked through her to concentrate on her (thinner) girlfriends. This made dating difficult: those who knew her were put off by her weight gain, and the new people she met did not seem to consider her datable.

The pattern continued even in college, where Erin had hoped people would not be as concerned about her size. By the time she graduated, she had lost the same thirty pounds twice, to no avail, and had developed sexual relationships with about ten men, only three of whom would deign to be seen with her outside the bedroom. However, after graduation Erin took a job as a bank teller in her college town and, four years later, met Travis there when he opened an account. He was a year younger—a truck driver without a college degree. When he asked her out, she was elated and charmed; when he asked her to marry him, she was relieved. She had already watched most of her girlfriends get married, and she had been wondering if she would ever be a bride herself. Today, fifteen years after their marriage, she is frustrated. Travis still drives a truck, and she is still a bank teller; neither makes very much money, and they have three boys. Though she says that she still loves him, it is "almost like brother and sister. I feel responsible for him; he doesn't know as much as I do about business and things. In some ways I guess I feel like I married down, but no one else asked me, and I have to say I don't know if they ever would have."

If Erin's experience is a fairly straightforward story about how overweight women typically fare poorly on the marriage market, Jill's experience serves as an example of how excess weight can take a toll on a woman's confidence, which in turn can lead to diminished chances in *both* the labor market and the marriage market. Jill always felt in the shadow of her older sister, Jennifer. The two grew up in various places around the world as a diplomat's daughters, and everywhere they went,

Jennifer was considered prettier and had a steady string of dates. Jill, on the other hand, spent the majority of her time from age eight on (around the time her mother first pointed out to her that she was "turning into a chubbette") struggling with her weight. Though she could often be quite entertaining at home, in the privacy and security of her own family, she typically clammed up when faced with anyone from the "outside." She already felt too self-conscious to draw any more attention to herself, so she kept her quick wit and wickedly ironic sense of humor to herself. Trying to pretend that she did not hear any of the jeers or taunts that neighborhood kids threw her way, she stuffed her feelings with junk food when she felt particularly lonely.

Over time, the differences between Jill and Jennifer grew even more pronounced. Jennifer graduated from Brown and then moved to Boston to start a career as an interior designer. By age thirty-five, she owned a successful business, had married an editor at a well-known publishing house whom she had first met through her old Brown circle of friends, and had borne two children. Jill also went to Brown, where she gained even more weight. By the time she graduated, she topped the scale at three hundred pounds—more than twice what her doctor told her she should weigh for her height of five foot five inches. She kept mostly to herself at Brown, getting good grades but not doing much else. When she graduated, she hardly had any contacts of her own, so she relied on her father's connections, and got a job as a fact checker at the *Washington Post*. Today, ten years after she started, she is still there, and has not yet enjoyed a single promotion. Though her work is solid, her bosses hardly know her, because she forces herself to disappear into the woodwork. She still turns to food as a comfort (she has gained more weight since leaving college), and she has never married.

Here's a strange fact: the "obesity effect" is most profound for *white* women.[17] For example, economist John Cawley found that obesity lowers wages for white women by somewhere around 7 to 9 percent (as compared to nonobese white women), which is "equivalent to the wage effect of roughly one year of education, two years of job tenure, or three years of work experience." In contrast, he found no evidence that weight lowers the wages of black women at all.[18] For a variety of social, political, and historical reasons, there are fewer social and economic penalties for overweight black women. However, we should not take this to mean that black women's life outcomes are somehow less dependent on physical attractiveness. Instead, a comparably important measure of beauty for black women is that of their skin color. Indeed, despite some gains made with the Black Is Beautiful mantra during the 1960s and '70s, lighter-skinned African-Americans are still more likely to be considered physically attractive than are their darker peers,[19] and black men are much more likely to prefer lighter-skinned black women as their mates.[20]

Scholars have a number of theories about why this is so. Some say it is simply because lighter-skinned black women more closely approximate the Eurocentric ideal of female beauty that dominates Western culture. Others say that it is because of the higher status that lighter skin has historically represented: as the controversial sociologist E. Franklin Frazier has argued, during slavery "mulattoes" (individuals classified as black but who also have white ancestors, and who are today more commonly referred to as "biracial") led a much more privileged life than blacks without apparent white blood.[21] They were more likely to be house (rather than field) slaves, were more likely to have some education, property, and jobs with higher status, and were more likely to eventually obtain their freedom.[22] These individuals were also much more likely to intermarry; over time, their (similarly lighter-skinned) descendants occupied the highest tier of black society. Thus, according to this theory, light skin not only more closely approximates whiteness, it also signifies a potentially long history of higher status—something that tends to be attractive to almost everyone in our culture, no matter what color you are.[23]

Similarly, some argue that lighter skin not only signifies higher social worth historically, but also represents the promise of greater earnings in the future. Even today, light-skinned blacks enjoy higher adult socioeconomic status than do darker African-Americans, and several studies have shown that differences in social origins are responsible for only a small portion of that difference.[24] More specifically, sociologist Mark Hill finds that as little as 10 to 20 percent of the "color gap" in adult

African-American attainment can be attributed to differences in class background. The rest, he argues, is due to color bias—otherwise known as discrimination.[25] In other words, darker-skinned people are more likely to be discriminated against when they seek jobs with higher status or income than are their lighter-skinned counterparts, whether that discrimination is conscious or not.[26]

Of course, the theory of color discrimination and the history of color and privilege in the African-American community are not mutually exclusive.[27] It may well be that *both* of these dynamics help explain the colorism that is still prevalent in many communities today.[28] The point is that the burden of physical attractiveness can play itself out in a number of ways within different communities and, on the marriage market especially, women are more vulnerable to deviations from what is held up as beautiful. Just as overweight white women are more likely to be in a disadvantageous social position because they deviate from the cultural ideal of thinness, black women who happen to be born with darker skin also have less cultural cachet to work with. Because black men are more likely to view light-skinned women as more desirable, upwardly mobile black men are more likely to choose them for their mates, thus leaving darker-skinned black women at a considerable disadvantage. The latter are more likely to marry downwardly mobile men who have less social status, or men who are darker-skinned themselves and thus have more difficulty finding and keeping a high-prestige job.[29] Thus, in any culture, those deemed more physically attractive often have very different life outcomes than those who are not—even when they come from the same family.

Take the case of Stacey and Samuel, two African-American siblings who had very different experiences with interracial dating. Stacey and Samuel's parents had worked very hard to be able to afford the steep tuition at a private high school outside of their neighborhood school district in Baltimore, and they were proud that both of their children graduated with distinction. Both siblings, in fact, were quite high achievers during their high school years. Both earned good grades, were involved in athletics and various student clubs, and were also popular with their peers. However, in the mid- to late 1980s, they were also among a very small handful of black students at the school, which helps explain why Stacey—the darker of the two—recalls her high school years very differently than does Samuel:

> No one would date me. I went to every party, and hung out with every-one, but I was always "like a sister," or "such a good friend." I was the only black girl in my class, and no white guy would touch me, even if we were super close as friends. After we graduated, some of them told me that they'd had crushes on me but were afraid to get into it, but that doesn't erase how I felt at the time. I felt so hideous, and so lonely. And there was no one I could talk about it with—my friends at school were white, the people I knew from the neighborhood wouldn't have understood, my parents didn't want to hear that everything wasn't per-fect at school, and my brother certainly couldn't relate. It wasn't until I got to college that I even found people [black girlfriends] who got what I went through.

Indeed, as Stacey suffered alone, hiding her loneliness with a brighter smile and an ever more energetic façade, the lighter-skinned Samuel did not have any problems making romantic connections. Throughout high school his popularity, his success on the football field, and his genial personality won over several girls, two of whom became long-term girlfriends. Being (a lighter-skinned) black in a sea of white faces did not seem to cramp his style at all; in fact, he remembers many girls commenting that they liked how "different" he was and admiring his dreadlocks. As long as he was careful not to be *too* different—for instance, he always avoided talking too much like his lower-income neighbors, particularly around his white friends' parents—his positive identity as a successful and upwardly mobile young man easily overrode the potentially negative connotations of being black. For Samuel, fac-ing the harsher realities of racial discrimination would not come until later, while Stacey was forced to face them at a younger age—by virtue of her gender and her skin color.[30] Today, Stacey is still struggling with self-esteem issues while working as a lower-tier federal bureaucrat de-spite excellent grades in college. Samuel, meanwhile, went on to law school and then to a major corporate firm where he soon expects to make partner.

I have focused on the burden of being overweight and of having darker skin—a cross that women bear disproportionately. However, I should mention that the increased relevance of physical attributes to the success (or lack thereof) of women can work the other way as well. Women who do fit a certain beauty ideal can get a boost in their economic status. (In much the same way that tall men tend to earn more and hold more prestigious occupations.)[31] The bottom line is that, for women, success is less related to talent and hard work, since beauty muscles into the equation too.

Maternal Role Models

There is one factor that I have found that tends to level the playing field between brothers and sisters: maternal employment. Though much attention has been paid to the debate surrounding infant day care, particularly its detrimental effects[32]—and, indeed, a number of studies have shown that children who are away from their mother for a significant amount of time during their first year of life do suffer a variety of difficulties with attachment[33]—many pundits have overlooked the fact that mothers who work outside the home during their daughters' childhoods and adolescence can actually serve as *positive* role models.[34] In fact, I find that in families where the mother worked while her children were growing up, her adult daughters and sons attain jobs that are more equitable in terms of prestige. But in cases where the mother did not work—and therefore daughters lacked a direct, same-sex parental role model in the world of careers—sisters fare considerably worse than their brothers: my data show that women whose mothers did not work outside the home when they were growing up are 15 percent less likely to have graduated from college than their brothers were; this statistic stands in contrast to a statistically insignificant 5 percent difference between sisters and brothers in families where the mother did work outside the home for at least a year during their childhood.[35] To put the impact of maternal employment in even starker terms, consider the following: if we hold education level and occupational prestige constant, sisters earn approximately $5,000 less in annual income than do their brothers. If we divide this same data according to maternal employment, however, the pattern diverges wildly. For those whose mothers worked outside the home when they were growing up, the income differential between sisters and brothers is reduced to approximately $4,500—but for those whose mothers did not work, the income differential shoots to more than $8,000.[36]

This may be in part due to the greater self-esteem that employment outside the home can provide mothers; many scholars have documented, in turn, the significant effect that mothers' increased self-esteem can have, both in the belief that they can have a positive impact on their children's development and in their efforts to do so.[37] Of course, the key here is the *type* of work involved. In cases where mothers experience adverse occupational environments—such as jobs that consist of monotonous, uninspiring work, where initiative is not valued or encouraged—the levels of human, social, and financial capital within the household are reduced, and children's emotional well-being may suffer. Look at Johanna and Caleb, on the one hand, and Danielle and Nathan, on the other.

Johanna and Caleb were raised in the 1950s in a small, tight-knit community in Oregon, where their parents had also grown up. From the start, Johanna, the older of the two siblings, was deemed "the spitting image" of their mother, who was somewhat passive and considered very feminine. Caleb, who had many of those same qualities, was nonetheless said to be very masculine: "the strong, silent type." (Perhaps unsurprisingly, he later became a policeman.) Both Johanna and Caleb liked their respective characterizations; they fit well with the somewhat narrow conceptions of masculinity and femininity that were especially dominant in the time and place where they grew up. Johanna in particular relished her identity, and felt confident in what she felt was her natural role. She grew into a pretty, popular, conscientious girl, who always knew that she wanted to get married right out of high school to her high school boyfriend. She did not want to go to college; all she wanted—and had ever wanted—was to follow her mother and father's example. They, too, had been each other's high school sweethearts and had married soon after graduation. As her mother had, Johanna wanted to help her family in and around the home, not work outside of it, and to play a supporting role in her husband's career advancement.

She did just that. One year after graduating high school, and working as a librarian's assistant, Johanna married her high school boyfriend, the only boy she had ever dated. Together they had seven children; Johanna devoted herself to her marriage and family and did all she could to facilitate her husband's professional life. Then, after twenty-four years of marriage, her husband fell in love with someone else and divorced her. Devastated and with four children still at home, she was forced to enter the workforce for the first time as an adult woman. For the last twenty-five years, she has struggled to make ends meet, barely getting by with the money she earns from a variety of low-paying jobs. Feeling deeply betrayed by men, she has never remarried, and she is bitter: the "rules" she learned about women's roles from her mother had changed without her knowledge. She has spent the majority of her adult life trying to reset her frames of reference, but is still penalized by the fact that she was caught unawares. Her own daughters, raised in a household characterized by Johanna's despair, have suffered a variety of problems and are now poised to repeat some of their mother's life choices: two married right out of high school in order to escape the negative and chaotic environment of their youth; one is already divorced, the single mother of two.

On the other side of the tracks, we have Danielle and Nathan, who also grew up in the 1950s, in western North Carolina. Before Danielle's and Nathan's births, their mother, Priscilla, had worked as an elementary school teacher in a one-room schoolhouse in the area for several years; it was there that she had met the man she eventually married, who happened to be the principal of the school. Priscilla became a full-time homemaker during Danielle and Nathan's early childhood years. As Danielle says, "That was what the majority of women did in those days, especially in our little Carolina town." But it wasn't just conformity. Priscilla had lost her own mother when she was only five, so she considered it crucial to be home with her children while they were young.

Her husband attended law school at night. When Danielle was six, and Nathan was five, and her husband had finished law school, Priscilla again began teaching in the one-room schools around the area. She did this for eight years, until she began to notice that a number of children who lived in the surrounding mountainous region did not have any access to books at all. In an effort to remedy this, she began a stint as a bookmobile driver, delivering books throughout the area to help raise child literacy rates. From this initiative developed Priscilla's full-blown career as a librarian; she went on to help found the county library and later became the head librarian. Having such an active and capable mother rubbed off on both her children but particularly affected her daughter. Danielle credits her mother's example with giving her the confidence to leave the isolated Appalachian region of her childhood in search of more opportunities and to eventually become a clinical psychologist. Her own daughter is now in medical school in California, a world away from Priscilla's North Carolinian universe but, nonetheless, very much in keeping with her efficacious spirit. Nathan, meanwhile, has remained where he grew up. However, he has similarly reproduced his parents' ambition and initiative, and his position as a chemical engineer continues the family's upwardly mobile trajectory.

Of course, Danielle and Nathan had more going for them than just an active and fulfilled mother. They also came from a family that, despite its Appalachian roots, had a significant number of resources. First, there was an emphasis on educational attainment. Priscilla worked as a schoolteacher and had completed two years of college in an era when many women, particularly in rural areas, did not attend college at all. Priscilla's husband was a school principal and then went to law school. In contrast, neither of Johanna and Caleb's parents earned more than a high school degree.

Second, Danielle and Nathan grew up with more economic resources than did Johanna and Caleb, particularly after their father became a lawyer. They were not rich by any objective standards (their father, one of the only lawyers in their small town, accepted freshly grown vegetables as payment when his clients had nothing else to offer, and such arrangements were not uncommon), but they were secure in their socioeconomic status relative to those around them, and certainly never wanted for anything. Things were tighter for Johanna and Caleb; their father worked on the railroad, and that meant that work could be variable. Though they were hardly destitute, they had fewer resources available to them than they would have liked. In fact, it was lucky—and convenient—that Johanna had no college aspirations, for it is doubtful that her family would have been able to afford it. So the bottom line is that both resources and role models matter.

Gender and Family Resources: The Case of Teen Pregnancy

The thing to remember, again, is that *resources matter* in more ways than it may initially seem. Take the issue of pregnancy, for example. Pregnancy is one of the most easily identifiable ways that gender can come into play: simply put, teenage girls can get pregnant, and teenage boys cannot. While both males and females can—and do—have sex, in our culture teenage girls still endure more detrimental and lifelong effects if they have a child than do boys. Teenage fatherhood has far fewer negative effects on males, since they are typically not the primary caregiver and thus theoretically have more time and freedom for educational advancement and status attainment. In fact, research shows that while male partners of teenage mothers may assume an important role early in their children's lives, only a very few still see them regularly by the time their children are teenagers themselves, and even fewer commit themselves financially to help with their upbringing.[38] Thus, the issue of pregnancy is sometimes pointed to as one of the causes of unequal life outcomes among male and female siblings. On the face of it, this makes some sense. Certainly Tammy's story supports this.

In the late 1960s, her world fell apart. Three days after her eighteenth birthday, her father died suddenly of a heart attack, leaving her mother heartbroken—and in a lot of debt. Their family had never been well-off, but Tammy's father, an electrician, had always made enough money to provide for his family, which also included Tammy's brother and sister. After his death, all three siblings, as well as their mother, had to pitch in to keep the family going—and the debt collectors away. Tammy's brother, Kyle, took a job working the night shift at a nearby factory (at which he is now foreman), while their sister, Maura, waitressed full-time at a local restaurant. (After waitressing for approximately eight years, she now considers herself "in semi-retirement"— married to a bartender she met on the job, she still picks up a shift or two here and there.) For her part, Tammy took a day job as a salesclerk at Macy's and worked nights as a coat-check girl at a local club. She enjoyed both jobs reasonably well, but she particularly relished the one at the club. Though she was too busy working to have much leisure and social time, that job at least allowed her to be around the excitement.

It was at the club, however, that Tammy eventually met Marcus, an attractive and charming man who soon became her boyfriend. Tammy fell in love. After dating for a few months, she became pregnant. When she told Marcus, he panicked and urged her to get a (then-illegal) abortion. When Tammy decided that she could not go through with such a dangerous procedure, he left her. Though her family supported her to some degree (as best they could, given how tight their finances and schedules were already), they also felt that Tammy had shamed the family. As is so often the case, she ended up bearing the brunt of the responsibility for the baby by herself; she has raised the child alone, on the money that she makes as a salesclerk. Tammy has struggled quite a bit over the years. Her educational and occupational possibilities were very much diminished by her pregnancy and consequent single motherhood. Though she loves her son enormously, she believes that her life might have been very different if he had not arrived—when and how—he did.

While Tammy is no doubt correct that the particulars of her life may have been very different had her son not been born, there is a growing body of research that suggests that her overall life outcome may have been much the same even if she had not gotten pregnant under the circumstances that she did. Epidemiologist Arline Geronimus has persuasively argued that many of the *apparent* long-term costs of teen childbearing are a statistical illusion. Specifically, Geronimus points to the fact that women who have been raised in socioeconomically disadvantaged families are the most likely to become teen mothers.[39] Therefore, she would ask, how much of Tammy's life outcome is due to her pregnancy per se and how much is due to the lack of resources and opportunities that she enjoyed? In an effort to disentangle these factors, Geronimus and public policy expert Sanders Korenman did something interesting. They compared outcomes among sisters who became mothers at different ages—in other words, between a woman who gave birth as a teenager and her sister who did not become a mother until later in life.[40] As it turns out, Geronimus and Korenman's data show that the effect of teen childbearing is much less damaging when family background is fully factored out. In other words, even with teen pregnancy and childbearing, family resources matter more than may initially meet the eye.[41]

Karla's story illustrates how significant this can turn out to be. Like Tammy, Karla became pregnant in her late teens. In Karla's case, however, the pregnancy occurred when she was seventeen, a senior in high school. The younger of two children in an upper-middle-class family, Karla was a member of her school's marching band, liked to play soccer with her friends and family, and often helped out after school in her father's dental practice. Most important to her sense of identity at the time was the fact that she dated the captain of the basketball team—that is, until she became pregnant, and he left her. Karla's family rallied around her and supported her eventual decision to keep the baby, even though her parents initially felt it would be better if she gave it up for adoption, so as to not interfere with her schooling. With her family's help (they hired a tutor when bed rest was ordered for the last six weeks of her pregnancy), Karla managed to finish high school on time and graduate with the rest of her class. From there, she not only went on to college, but earned her master's degree in nutrition by the time she was twenty-six. Karla's educational successes, of course, were aided immeasurably by her family: not only did her mother, in particular, serve as an inexhaustible day care provider to her daughter, the family as a whole had always valued education *and* had enough resources to help her stay in school. While her reliance on family support in raising her child meant that Karla could not do things exactly as her older brother, George—who went halfway across the country for college, and worked as a travel writer for more than a decade—did, she now claims that she "has no regrets." She is now forty-nine and a practicing nutritionist; she works for a local hospital part-time, and also treats private clients. Her daughter, Tracy, now almost thirty-two, works as a chef in an upscale New York City restaurant.

To be sure, Geronimus and Korenman do not argue that there are no negative effects of teen pregnancy.[42] Even if one comes from a family with high socioeconomic status—or at least enough resources to buffer the effects of the problems that pregnancy presents—there will certainly be costs to everyone involved. Thus, the potential of pregnancy is one of the burdens of being female, and one variable that we must take into account when we look at life outcomes for men and women. But, as with all within-family differences, how teenage childbearing matters depends on between-family factors like the levels of social, cultural, and economic resources available to a young mother via her family.

SEVEN

RANDOM ACTS OF KINDNESS
(AND CRUELTY)

Outside Influences on Sibling Success

The S45 bus winds from the Staten Island Ferry terminal all the way down the island to the far south end, where it drops most of its passengers at the Arthur Kill Correctional Facility. The bus is filled with raucous laughter and furtive whispers; high fives are exchanged and kids tug at one another's jackets; women snap gum as they clutch flowers, bags of groceries, or stacks of magazines. The route takes the passengers through a socioeconomic tour of Staten Island. I might be the only passenger to notice, a sociologist on his way to interview a subject for this book.

The houses closest to the ferry terminal are run-down. The units are pressed tightly together as if someone kept trying to pack more and more houses in, until they were jammed shoulder-to-shoulder, eave-to-eave. Ramshackle fences keep back dogs that snarl and growl as the bus roars past. The narrow sidewalks are cracked, grass pushing up through them. In this stretch of urbanity, nature seems to be conquering man's efforts to tame it.

After a while, the spaces open up. The sidewalks get wider and then disappear altogether. The homes get bigger and they stand apart. Soon we pass through the "historic" Richmondtown section of the island. It is still another half hour or so to the prison. All this seems backward—since most Staten Islanders commute to Manhattan to work, it would make more sense if the rich lived closer to the ferry terminal, leaving the poor to commute longer distances (as in Brooklyn, for instance).

But Staten Island has always rebelled against the logic of the rest of the city; it is, in fact, the only borough to have had a real secessionist movement.

This hour on the bus is just the last leg for most of the travelers who have come long distances to visit their loved ones. Most have traveled from the Bronx, Brooklyn, or Queens, having had to ride the subway for an hour or so to the ferry terminal in Manhattan, wait for the next ship to dock, motor across New York harbor for twenty-five minutes, and then wait for the S45 bus to show up (they are not timed for the arrival of the ferry). As visiting hours are on weekends, the bus service is infrequent at best. In total, most of the passengers will have trekked about three hours each way to visit their husbands (or "baby-daddies" if they are not married), their fathers, their cousins, their siblings.

I am one of only three grown men on the bus. The other passengers are the women and children the incarcerated men have left behind—the other half of the prison equation.

Despite the long journey, the mood is joyous. After all, at least they can visit their loved ones. Most New York prisons are upstate, many hours from the city—New York—that populates them. Getting transferred to Arthur Kill is a blessing for prisoners who have endured the harsher treatment upstate and the less frequent family visits. Since it is a medium security prison, most of the inmates have been on good behavior and have only a few years to go on their current "bids." In short, life is much more relaxed than it is in Sing Sing, Attica, or the Coxsackie Correctional Facility.[1]

Spontaneous picnics of sandwiches and chips break out on the bus; many children can wait no longer for lunch. Lone travelers bop their heads to hip-hop spilling out from foam earpieces. Suddenly the bus makes a sharp right turn. Razor wire blurs as we race by. Guards from watchtowers peer down. The prison is an imposing sight. I am here to see Lincoln Howard, who has spent most of his adult life inside prisons like Arthur Kill. Since the process of getting state approval to bring a voice recorder into the prison has dragged on for months, I have made repeated visits to the facility, taking notes on the bus ride home in lieu of recording his story verbatim. I cannot take notes *during* our repeated meetings, since pen and paper are not allowed. About the only thing you can bring through the metal detectors leading to the visiting room is cash to buy snacks for the inmates or to give to them through a guard.

Lincoln is thirty-eight years old. When I met him, he was doing the last of five years for burglary. He was caught stealing from a stereo shop in Long Island. He has never carried a gun, never even hurt anyone, but he is a serial offender going back to his teens. Though born in rural Georgia, Lincoln grew up in the public housing projects of New York City to which his mother moved when she was pregnant with him at age nineteen. He had a younger sister who died days after her birth. He would have had an older sibling, too, if not for the Georgia backwoods abortion that Lincoln claims made his mother go crazy from infection at age sixteen. Annie, his mother, spent most of her days man-hunting, sipping homemade hooch from a mayonnaise jar, and waiting in lines in a welfare office. She went on to have one more surviving child—a girl she bore in her mid-twenties, despite the pain of the rheumatoid arthritis that had already developed and that was further exacerbated by drinking. In short, Lincoln is the product of the worst stereotypes of the "underclass" that urban America has to offer. He, however, is very smart; though he suffered from an undiagnosed case of attention deficit hyper-activity disorder (ADHD), he always received high praise in school and the neighborhood for his abilities. Unfortunately, as he grew older, the combination of his keen intellect and his ADHD tendencies caused him to become bored and restless in the low-achieving school environment that surrounded him. Once, in second grade, he took a water-melon into class and smashed it on the teacher's desk to the uproarious laughter of his classmates. The result of this incident was that, rather than being placed in a gifted program and given medication to treat his hyperactivity, he was instead stuck in what was known as a 600 school—a special education program for problem kids.

By the time Lincoln was a teenager, he had cultivated a cocaine addiction to complement his mother's alcoholism. To support his habit, he took to stealing. He never wanted to get shot or hurt someone, so he robbed businesses rather than residences; he did not want to end up confronting someone in their own home. Furthermore, because he believed that most businesses carried insurance, his victims seemed less "real" and "personalized" to Lincoln. Even after he kicked his drug habit during one particular bid in New Jersey, Lincoln continued to steal electronics equipment and similar items, fencing them on 125th Street in Harlem. It was hard for him to stop. Certainly, as a felon without much formal schooling, it was difficult for him to get a legitimate job; but it was also true that he liked the thrill—the rush of putting on black sweats and a mask, sneaking into a store in the middle of the night, running from the cops, and negotiating for the best prices when he sold his successful scores to the shops that took his business.

Lincoln's sister, Selma, was not such a thrill seeker. Though she did not test higher than Lincoln, she was never put into the special education system. She just kept to herself and muddled through the regular track at the impoverished schools in their neighborhood. As soon as she graduated high school, she left New York behind and went to live with her grandmother in Georgia. There she got a job as a cashier at a local department store (the kind Lincoln often liked to rob), eventually working her way up to assistant manager on the night shift. Today she is raising two kids with the help of her grandmother and lives a relatively comfortable—though hardworking—life. Her only wish is that she could spend more time with her kids—and of course, that she had a bit more money. But overall, she has found satisfaction in the slower pace of the Deep South.

Why did Lincoln end up leading such a tough life? Was it simply that he was a bad seed, or was he just planted in barren soil? His sister, of course, was a product of that same "fallow" ground, so was Lincoln just unlucky? Had he encountered a different teacher in second grade who understood the nature of his problems and showed some compassion, would his life have turned out differently? Maybe not, but it is not so far-fetched to suspect that had Lincoln come from a family with high education, lots of money, and social connections—all of which could have been brought to bear on his problems in school—he might have ended up as a successful businessman rather than someone who steals from them. He may be a perfect example of the old saying that a gene for aggressiveness might land you the job of CEO if you are born to wealth and privilege, but gets you jail time if you are born in the ghetto. The random lottery of birth seems to have made all the difference.

Thirty years ago, Christopher Jencks and his colleagues authored a book, *Inequality*, in which they used siblings to examine the various factors that influenced success at that time. They said that "luck" mattered in determining who ended up on which rung in the hierarchy of society.[2] As they put it:

> Income also depends on luck: chance acquaintances who steer you to one line of work rather than another, the range of jobs that happen to be available in a particular community when you are job hunting, the amount of overtime work in your particular plant, whether bad weather destroys your strawberry crop, whether the new superhighway has an exit near your restaurant, and a hundred other unpredictable accidents.[3]

It is easy to say luck explains what happens in families; but it only gets you so far. In fact, while luck may seem arbitrary, it is actually pretty systematic. That is, unlike these nice, neat examples that Jencks plucks from the air, outside influences are more often than not linked to individual and family attributes. This tension between individual characteristics (destiny) and the randomness of outside influences (chance or luck) is the theme of this chapter. The common element of both "luck" and "pluck," however, is that together they explain the inexplicable—what is left over after we have taken into account shared family characteristics and within-family differences like gender or birth order. However, it turns out that random differences are not so random, after all.

Take sexual assault, for example. Missy has struggled with a major trauma for most of her adolescence and adult life: at age fifteen, she was gang-raped. In the aftermath of that event, she dropped out of high school (she later got her GED) and became involved in a very abusive, unhealthy marriage. After ten years she finally divorced her husband. Today she has remarried and seems to have a very stable self-image, but having missed many educational opportunities due to the fallout from her attack, Missy makes her living by cleaning rooms in a hotel. This, despite being as articulate and intelligent as her older sister, an editor for a major New York magazine. Missy tells her own story best:

It happened at a fairground where I was camping out with some other friends. I was always a horse fanatic, and any time I could be around horses I grabbed the chance.

He was several years older than me, probably in his early twenties. I was fifteen, one month shy of my sixteenth birthday. And he asked me if I wanted to go see the horses and I said, "Oh yeah, definitely."

I am a very "oh yeah," laid-back kind of person—not suspicious at all and definitely not then. But when I got to the stables, I was held at knifepoint, and this guy and five others took turns raping me. An acquaintance of mine came looking for me and saw what was happening, and they held him at knifepoint, too. They took all my clothes and shoes. My friend had to lend me his jeans. He was walking through the fairgrounds in his underwear, and I was in his jeans. The police who were assigned to the fairgrounds found us walking around dazed like that and took us into the station. I was just numb. The boys had actually done it in a horse stall, so after that, I couldn't go near horses or I would get sick. Obviously, that day was a very pivotal point in my life.

The kid who lent me his jeans disappeared two days later to Florida. He was in a living-with-relatives situation, on probation. Then he just dropped off the face of the earth. So I'm not sure what kind of push the police put on him. Somehow, somebody put pressure on him—because he wasn't a part of it; he was as innocent as I was.

So my parents had to come get me, and then I had to go to the police station and be interrogated by these officials—not just the police, but town "officials" too. They wouldn't let my parents go in while I was being interviewed. I say interviewed, but "demolished" was more like it: they told me that all my friends were having sex; that I really wanted it; that I had asked for it. They literally banned me from going back to the fairgrounds. I told them that I could bring them to the spot where it had happened. Those people were exhibitors, showing horses, and I could find them. But they wouldn't let me on the fairgrounds. Basically, in later life, I realized that it was all small-town politics, and this is a big fair for our town, and it brings in lots of money and the last thing they wanted was for this to get out. But when you're young and you've got these people telling you this stuff it gets to you eventually and I thought, "Well, God, maybe in some way I did ask for it. Oh gosh, I never should have smiled at the guy. I should have never agreed to go with him. I should have never . . ."

My sister was leaving for California at the time, and my parents instructed me, "Don't tell your sister. She won't go to California if you tell her. Please don't tell your sister." So I had to keep this secret. And I was so hurt by this, by the police department and everything else, that I totally retreated inside myself for a long time. I never spilled the beans to her until about two years ago when I casually said something about it, and she was like, "What?" And by then, to me it was just kind of common knowledge, and I've come to terms with it; it happened to me; it wasn't my fault. But she didn't know and had to deal with it at that point.

After that fateful day, I went from this naïf loving butterflies to just this big whirling mess of stuff. And I think that's where drugs and alcohol came into play, because I just wanted to numb myself. Something had already been taken away from me, I had nothing else to lose. I just really started going in bad directions. And I guess my parents were just trying to wait until I got through it. But the truth was I wasn't getting through it. What I really wanted were parents who were forceful, who would step into my life and take control. But they wouldn't, until finally my dad laid down the law, as much as he is capable of doing.

"You know, I followed you this far," he told me. "I've always been behind you, but if this is the road that you're going to choose, your mother and I are not going to walk with you. You'll walk this road alone. It's killing her. It's killing me. And we can't do it, so if you're going to choose this road, we're not walking with you."

And that was an absolute turning point for me because I was like, "What do you mean? Wait a minute. I'm only having fun." Of course, it wasn't making me happy, but I was still fooling myself, trying to get away from my pain by doing a lot of partying and just checking out.

After that, I really reexamined my friends and all that was going on and what I was doing. And reenrolled myself in school [at the adult educational facility where she got her GED]. In retrospect, I realized that I didn't really understand what had happened to me. I didn't want to talk to anyone, in fact. My parents just figured that I'd come to them when I needed them. They're so laid-back and hippie in that way; plus, they didn't know exactly what happened because I just couldn't talk about it. Yeah, actually I didn't even remember a lot of the details. I really blacked the whole thing out. I knew it *had* happened but I really couldn't remember much more than that.

And then it all came back—not that long ago. Probably seven years ago. I allowed myself to start remembering, and then it all came back in big, big, big waves. And now I remember everything. But at that time it was just too painful. I was such a softy. I was such mush. I didn't believe that people could hurt other people. My parents, they had been married forever and a day. I can't recall them ever having a serious fight. That was my world. And then that world was over.

Missy's story is instructive for several reasons. While there is no 100 percent certainty in social science, I think, had she not experienced this horrible tragedy, she would never have fallen off the track of straight-laced honor student. It was a random act of cruelness that befell her—but, then again, it was not completely random. After all, teenage boys rarely get gang-raped. So what happened to Missy was related to her gender and age. The reactions of the various authorities in her life also colored how the event played out. The town officials appeared more concerned with denying cracks in the economic and moral structure of the community than in comforting (or avenging) this injured young woman. They took advantage of her shock and numbness to serve their own ends. Missy's own parents perhaps made some ill-fated choices as well. In an effort to quarantine the negative effects of the rape, they suggested that she not tell her sister about it at all. They did not want both their kids knocked off course by this tragedy. This is understandable to some degree, yet at the same time unforgivable.[4] The upshot, of course, was that her sister, Denise, went off to college with no major trauma, and Missy was left to deal with the rape's aftermath on her own, without any sibling support.[5]

Vietnam

Sometimes world events step in and generate "random" differences within the family. The military conflict in Vietnam shaped the generation that came of age in the 1960s. Look at the twins Bill and Rich, who we met in chapter 2. Largely due to the physical and psychological fallout from his tour of duty in Vietnam, Bill—though long the dominant twin—is now less successful than his twin brother. However, in some respects, we can say that Bill brought his fate upon himself by joining the military as an officer. Vietnam was already aflame, so he knew what he was getting himself into. For Bill, then, Vietnam was not really a random influence.

But it was different for Mike. He was a typical middle-class kid growing up in 1960s California. His father owned two fast-food franchises in San Diego. Mike worked there after school and was paid like any other employee. He spent his free time hanging out with friends at other franchises in the mall. He was a good student and got a scholarship to the University of California at San Diego to study oceanography. As part of a special program, he spent his first year studying on the school's ship off the coast. When he returned to campus, it was already a week into the new academic quarter. He was a bit overwhelmed by the campus and its associated bureaucracy. Once he had settled in and started his classes, Mike was already two weeks behind.[6] By the time another two weeks had passed, he had failed to catch up in his chemistry and physics classes.

So Mike decided that instead of marring the high grade point average he had accrued in his ship-based classes of the previous year, he would just drop all his classes, take a breather, see family, and even study up so he would have a jump start on the next quarter. Little did

he realize what an effect that seemingly unimportant decision would
have on his life:

> When I dropped out, the draft board snagged me just as quick as any-
> thing. When I went down to tell them that there has been a mistake,
> I have the scholarship, you know, they wouldn't budge a muscle. They
> said that's the way it is, you know, "You shouldn't have dropped out."

So after a few weeks of training at Fort Ord, Mike found himself carrying gear through the jungles of Southeast Asia. Not surprisingly, when
he completed his two-year tour of duty, he was a changed person. One
of the consequences of his experience was that he could no longer stand
school. He just could not bear structure and order. So he never went
back and instead started his own business as a mason—a far cry from
the career in oceanography that he had planned on before he was
drafted. His two brothers, meanwhile, chugged along through college
and master's degrees with draft deferments, ending up as engineers who
earned a lot more money than Mike ever did.

Sometimes legal troubles interact with world events and lead to
unique outcomes. Ryan, for instance, began drinking early in his high
school career in Ohio. He also began driving, though he had neither a
license nor insurance. One night shortly after graduating, the police
apprehended him speeding away from a minor accident—intoxicated
and still unlicensed. Having just turned eighteen, he was afraid of fac-
ing jail time, so, in an effort to avoid it, he enlisted in the Marines. It
was an unfortunate choice, as he was promptly sent to Vietnam. Thus,
while he escaped the conviction, a worse fate awaited him.

His sister describes Ryan as a kid who felt things deeply, and who
was sensitive; his life in Vietnam bears this out. Wartime in the bush
presented him with a series of overwhelming dualities: He was a machine gunner who killed dozens of people by his own estimation, but he
wrote home every week decrying the poverty that the Vietnamese had
to endure—demanding that his family send over clothes and food that
he would distribute to the children he had befriended in the villages

where he camped. He did not trust any adult, thinking that they all turned into Vietcong each night as soon as the sun went down, yet he all-but-legally adopted Thuc, an orphaned boy of eight, teaching him English and planning his future in the United States. He was intending to bring him back with him when his tour was up. But one day young Thuc disappeared, and no villager knew (or at least spoke about) his whereabouts. After a few weeks of trying to find his erstwhile adoptee, Ryan's unit was transferred a substantial distance away from Thuc's village. At that point, Ryan gave up all hope and took to using heroin, as so many of his fellow GIs did while in Southeast Asia. He stayed an addict until well after the war, at which point he turned to drinking to numb the pain he continued to endure.

In a letter to his sister during those weeks of searching for Thuc, he penned a phrase that she has never forgotten to this day: "I didn't realize what an innocent I was until they had already made me a murderer." This same sister did not recognize Ryan when he returned to Toledo: "I don't know what he was on. He came back home a rebel. He had a phenomenal job at the [train] depot when he left for Vietnam, and when he came home he didn't go back to work."

Eventually Ryan did return to work for the railroad, as an electrician who tended to the signals. He soon married a girl with whom he had gone to high school; she had been married previously and had two kids, to which they quickly added two more. But his drinking and drug use did not abate. Then one day, when he was working on the rails, he had to twist a signal post with a special tool. It was stuck, and he put so much oomph into it that he tore three vertebrae in his lower back. He never worked again.

Home all the time on disability insurance, Ryan mixed alcohol with his narcotics (having switched to legal drugs to kill the severe physical and emotional pain that he felt). His wife, who had herself grown up with an alcoholic mother, grew increasingly frustrated with the impossible situation. Finally she left him. Ryan now lives alone on government disability checks; his health has deteriorated further, and his family members do not expect him to live much longer. His sister, meanwhile, lives a comfortable, middle-class existence as a homemaker and part-time real estate agent. She and her husband live comfortably, pulling down a combined income just shy of six figures.

Vietnam-type experiences can also engender sibling differences through intergenerational ripples; in other words, how a parent is affected by war may have a different impact on each of that veteran's children. Regina and Louise's story is a case in point. Regina, the elder of the two sisters, always felt like the misfit of the family. She felt constantly criticized by her parents, and felt very uncomfortable with herself in general, especially in comparison to Louise, who was much more gregarious, confident, bossy, and seemingly much more appreciated by their parents. Regina's mother never encouraged her to succeed; in fact, Regina remembers being actively disdained and resented by her, a memory that is perhaps unsurprising given that Regina's conception was the reason that her parents, then only casually dating, got married. As Regina herself puts it, she served as a symbol of what had gone wrong with her mother's life: "I'm not saying that she doesn't love me, because you know all moms love their babies, but one minute she's twenty-eight years old, a nurse, dating, living it up, and all of a sudden—boom!—she finds herself pregnant without a job and then wondering if her husband is going to come home [alive] from Vietnam." Regina's mother suddenly found herself for all practical purposes a single mother with a baby to raise on the checks that her husband, a Marine she didn't know well at all, was sending home from Asia. When he finally did come back, things did not get much better, as Regina found the "triangle" difficult to adjust to:

I was two weeks old when my dad went away to Vietnam for three years. So for those foundation years, he just wasn't there. And then when he did come back and was inserting himself into the family, I wanted nothing to do with him. I would scream at the dinner table because he was sitting next to my mom. I would crawl in between them on the couch because I didn't want him sitting next to my mom. I would scream from my crib because I didn't want them sleeping in the same bed together.

Eventually Regina got used to it. But her mother did not. The role of scapegoat had already been bestowed on the young Regina, something difficult for a young child to shake off. In fact, Regina had a clear sense that she was a burden and did what most kids would do in those circumstances: she tried to make herself less of one. For example, when she was in grade school, her favorite extracurricular activity had been ballet classes. Her mother, however, was exasperated at chauffeuring her eldest daughter to and from the dance studio—and made these feelings known. "You really don't want to dance, do you?" she asked one afternoon in the car ride home.

"No, I don't have to take ballet anymore," Regina answered, trying to please her mother. She quietly shed tears in the backseat, having forfeited her favorite activity. Years later, as an adult, she still replays the scene in her mind's eye. "Yeah, I *do* have to take dance," she imagines saying. "I really love this. This is *mine* and you can't take it away from me."

Meanwhile, Louise—who was born several years later, after their parents had weathered their turbulent early years and, against considerable odds, had managed to create a fairly happy and stable marriage—never experienced these sorts of limitations. She was given a horse when she wanted to ride and later a car when she was old enough to drive. Always it was Regina who paved the way, who inadvertently fulfilled the role of "problem child" only to smooth the path for her younger sister who did not have to bear the same stigma. The result is that Regina barely graduated high school, then got involved in an emotionally abusive relationship that culminated in marriage. After five painful years, she worked up the courage to get out of the marriage, supporting herself with earnings from a secretarial position. To supplement that income, she began moonlighting as a stylist in a friend's beauty salon, and found her calling. Having gotten a cosmetology degree and logging many hours as an apprentice, she now has her own clientele and feels proud of her work. She has also distanced herself from her family and feels like she is only now finally coming into her own. Louise, on the other hand, graduated from a four-year state university and now works as an administrator in a large public hospital. Louise enjoys her work, and is happily married to a man who works at the same hospital in the public health field.

Health Problems

The summer before her senior year in high school, Meredith fell and hit her head on a metal bench and then the cement ground during her cheerleading practice. She ruptured her inner ear, experienced a basilar fracture, and suffered a severe concussion. Brain damage resulted. She had to endure a year of nausea and extreme pain before she could even start physical therapy to relearn all the things she had taken for granted—walking normally, climbing stairs, and other gross motor tasks.

As a result, she had to finish high school by correspondence. Her injury also prevented her from completing college in an orderly and timely fashion; she kept starting and then being sidelined in order to undergo an operation or recover from one. Meredith attended about ten colleges here and there over a period of about seven years. Meanwhile, her relationship with her sister, Holly, grew distant. Meredith describes the transformation the following way:

> [Before my accident] we had always been pretty competitive—mainly because we really enjoyed the same things. We loved performing arts, tennis, dancing, and horseback riding. Not only did we love the same things, but we were always very close talentwise. Our teachers always threw us into competitive situations also, so that didn't really help matters. But in a way it was all really great. I really don't think I would have gotten such great grades if she wasn't there to take me on.

Leaving high school and being bedridden put a stop to this sibling rivalry, but led to a competition of a different sort, since the time Meredith spent recovering from her injury changed her relationship with her mother. Previously, their relationship had been somewhat contentious (though likely no more than the "typical" teenager). As an invalid, however, she received her mother's full attention, much to the chagrin of her sister. The two spent lots of time together and became very close, "like best friends":

> At first, I kind of resented [my mother] because she was doing every-thing for me, and I was so frustrated that I had to completely rely on her to take care of me. But then after I learned to accept that, our rela-tionship deepened, and so I still feel really close to her now. I think the whole family sees that she and I have a very unique tight bond, and it's kind of hard on them. I know Holly, especially, was always mad that I am like the chosen one or something now, whereas it was never like that before.

Her mother saw her through not only her initial convalescence but through a series of six reconstructive surgeries. After Meredith's hair grew back from surgery number five, her spirits were still sagging, and so her mother took her to get her hair styled in an effort to cheer her up. As it turned out, the hairstylist also worked for the Miss America Pageant system. As she combed and teased Meredith's hair and served as psychotherapist, she remarked on how beautiful Meredith was and how remarkable her story was. "You should try out for a beauty pag-eant," she said.

"You've got to be kidding," Meredith laughed. It was the first time she remembered laughing in quite some time.

"I'm not kidding, you know," the stylist persisted. "You know they do give college scholarships out for winning the interview section of it."

She decided to give it a go and enter the local pageant a few weeks later. She came in dead last among the seven contestants but she won the interview portion of the competition. And the hairdresser had been right: she received a scholarship for winning the "intellectual" category. She was inspired:

> I started doing several other local pageants to get scholarship money. I really didn't care to win them. I just wanted to get the money for doing

them, get practice interviewing. But then I won one of the major pageants, Miss Phoenix. I actually looked at the ladies that announced me as the winner and asked, "Are you sure you got it right?" So, then I end up entering the Miss America system. I went as far as being a finalist for Miss Arizona and then I went out to Texas and I tried the Miss Texas system. I was Miss Houston and that was fun, for two or three years I was a total pageant girl, until I aged out of the system.

With various scholarship monies in hand, she finally completed her degree at Arizona State University, in Tempe. After graduation a unique opportunity came her way. Someone had seen her during one of the pageants and asked if she would consider becoming the spokesperson for the American Association of Head Injury Survivors (AAHIS).* She had found her calling; or rather, it had found her. Before long, she was on the lecture circuit, speaking at conferences across the country. Her crowning moment was when she spoke at the international convention in Washington, D.C., before a crowd of six thousand scientists, policy makers, parents, victims, and activists. She was the keynoter. Ironically, her warm-up speaker was none other than Miss America.

Her injury shaped her career path in other ways as well. While serving part-time as the spokesperson for AAHIS, she studied acupuncture and other forms of alternative medicine and now works professionally as a healer. Today she is married to a minister and has one daughter, who is not yet two years old.

Her sister, Holly, traveled a more traditional track to get where she is. She finished (one) college in the standard four years. After that, she went to work as a graphic designer and married the owner of the firm. She has just given birth to her first child. She is certainly wealthier than her sister—but no happier. The two remain distant. Meredith hopes that the presence of "cousins" might bring the "aunts" (i.e., her and her sister) closer together again, though geography stands in the way. Meredith now lives in Scottsdale, Arizona, while her sister resides in the Minneapolis area.

*The organization's real name has been changed to protect the subject's confidentiality.

Meredith's story shows the power of two different types of random chance. First, tragedy struck when she slipped on the wet pavement and hit her head. This freak accident led to her being derailed from a "normal" academic track, despite having always obtained high grades (even if it was mostly to be in competition with her sister). Second, she was the beneficiary of a "random act of kindness." In Meredith's case the kindness came in the form of counsel and encouragement from a hair-stylist. Of course, if Meredith had not been beautiful in the eyes of the stylist, she might never have received the encouragement to join the pageant circuit. Furthermore, had she not enjoyed performing prior to the accident, she might have resisted the prodding. But she was game, and it paid off. She was able to finish college and find a calling in life. Her injury and the subsequent events triggered a life path for Meredith that would have been beyond her wildest imagination prior to her accident. Most people who suffer severe head trauma or other health problems are not as lucky as Meredith, however.[7]

The Kindness of Strangers: Positive Influences

Of course, not all outside influences are negative. Fairy godmothers, guardian angels, hairdressers, and other such provident figures can influence a person's socioeconomic trajectory, generating differences in sibling attainment in the process. However, as in the case of illness and injury, while respondents often speak of a specific person or event that triggers their pathway in life, it is not clear how meaningful the actual event was and how much that sibling would have found his or her way anyway with or without a particular mentor or other such outside influence.

Take the case of Esther. She ran away from her impoverished home at age sixteen, was put into a mental institution at age seventeen as a welcome-home present upon her return, and was released when she was eighteen years old. Essentially disowned from her family, she worked for a while as a B girl (the term for "bar girl" in the late 1940s) in order to make a living. Under the circumstances, it wasn't that bad.

She would sit alluringly at the bar all night and entice men to buy her drinks. The drinks *she* received were mostly water. At the end of the night, she would receive twenty-five cents for each highball swizzle stick that she had collected over the course of the evening. She also resided for free in an apartment above the bar, courtesy of the rich owner.

Soon, however, Esther fell for one of the men with whom she was drinking watered-down cosmopolitans. She left the bar and moved in with this man, who was a hashish dealer and card shark in Atlantic City. Within two weeks they were married at City Hall. After sex, they would lie in bed, molding the clumps of hashish into figurines of giraffes, zebras, and unicorns. Then young Esther would hang them with some thread over the bed to form a mobile of sorts, as if they slept in a crib. One day, however, the police raided the apartment and found their "artwork," in addition to another sizable stash of hashish. They were dragged into the police station, whereupon Esther's husband called his attorney to bail them both out of jail.

During the course of the legal proceedings, Esther skipped like a flat rock on a pond from the bed of the drug dealer into the arms of the defense attorney. She annulled her six-month-old marriage and, for the next four years, lived with the much older attorney, enjoying a very luxurious lifestyle as he showered her with jewels and furs. She was shuttled around in a chauffeured limousine. During this period, she met many famous people, including Jimmy Hoffa. Esther's relationship with her benefactor was less directly sexual than it was controlling—he seemed to enjoy being tortured by thoughts of her infidelity. They never even got around to actual intercourse, but they did engage in a lot of S&M–style whippings (of him).

One time the lawyer came home with a one-and-a-half-carat diamond ring that he had received as payment from one of his clients, a jeweler. The ring was so flawless that it did not sparkle, so she turned the gift down. That marked the beginning of the end of the relationship. He soon fell in love with another young woman (though she was not quite as young as Esther) whom he met while he was defending her on a charge of manslaughter.[8] Soon they were married, and Esther had to move out. He had found a new wounded sparrow to nurture back to health.

However, he did not abandon Esther entirely. Even though their live-in set up came to an end, he still served as her sugar daddy by paying her rent for about two years. Then he suggested that she earn money by working for him, managing his office. She held down this post for the next two decades, earning a decent wage and supplementing her salary with extra money that she occasionally skimmed off the top. (She had learned to forge his signature perfectly over the years.) It was through his law practice that she met another attorney (one of his assistants), whom she eventually married with her benefactor's blessing. One way or the other, then, Esther has enjoyed an upper-class lifestyle for most of her adult life, despite having run away from home at age sixteen and never having completed high school.

While Esther relied on the "kindness of strangers" (who, of course, did not remain strangers for long), her experience with mentors formed an integral part of a survival strategy she had adopted. If it was not the bar owner, then it was the hashish-dealing card shark; if not him, then the defense attorney, and if not him, then it probably would have been someone else. Of course, not everyone could pull off what Esther did; she was quite beautiful in her day and had a way of listening that made these men feel like they were the center of the world. So it can hardly be described as "random chance" that she ended up living a rather luxurious and economically secure lifestyle—especially as compared with her two younger sisters, who lived "regular" lives and who married their working-class high school sweethearts.

The seeming inevitability of Esther's story stands in contrast to that of Tara. Tara was adopted into a farming family in Iowa, after which her parents bore two biological children, both girls. Tara loved her siblings and parents dearly. Neither she nor her sisters knew she was adopted.

Then, when she was twelve, her biological mother stepped into her life.

One day, her father waved a letter in the air and announced that they needed to have a family meeting. The group gathered in the kitchen, where they discussed mostly work and family issues. Tara could always tell by the look on her father's face whether or not it was a serious meeting. If there were only two wrinkle lines in his forehead, then he just wanted to talk about school or schedules or some other mundane family matter. If three or four deep lines were etched in his brow, then something bad had happened. There was the time that the bank had almost foreclosed on the farm; there was the time that her grandfather had died; and then there was the time that her mother had wrecked the family's only car.

This was a four-wrinkle meeting. Tara's heart beat faster. She could barely swallow, though for some reason she felt a need to keep trying. "Your mother and I never told you something before," he addressed all three of the kids. Tara's mind raced from divorce, which the parents of one of her friends were then in the process of getting, to nuclear war, something she had recently learned about in school. "Tara," he said, seemingly having trouble swallowing himself, "you're adopted."

That possibility had not even crossed her mind. To this day, Tara still does not completely forgive him for not telling her alone first. But what was done was done. After the initial shock wave that shuddered through her body had subsided, he turned the letter over to her. Tara's biological mother, Grace, wanted to meet her. Grace had lived in a nearby town and had gotten pregnant when she was just fifteen. In those days (the early 1950s), unwed teenage childbearing was still rare. Often teenagers got married shotgun style. There were secret, illegal abortions. Other times, babies were given up for adoption. Since the father was nowhere to be found, and since they very much wanted a child, Tara's adoptive parents told Grace, whom they had met through acquaintances, that they would raise Tara as their own. Meanwhile, Grace was sent off to live with relatives in Chicago. By the time she wrote Tara, she had become a journalist, writing for a major daily newspaper. Though they hadn't let Tara in on the adoption, Tara's adoptive parents had secretly followed Grace's career. Her success was exactly what they had hoped for: to have Grace—who had always been bright and motivated—thrive and not be held back by her teenage "mistake."

After that momentous kitchen-table conference, Tara learned more about her mother and the circumstances surrounding her adoption from her parents. Then, when she felt ready, she corresponded directly with Grace herself. About a year after receiving the first letter, Tara finally met her biological mother. That encounter signaled the start of a very contentious, painful relationship; Tara often felt very torn between her biological mother's urbane (but highly unstable) world and the down-home comfort of her adoptive parents' lifestyle. This tension caused some problems, but they were minor compared to the anxiety that Tara had to deal with in "reinventing herself." In her words, she was not who she had always thought she was, so she spent several years asking the "real Tara to please stand up."[9]

Eventually, she decided that the "real" Tara was closer to her biological mother than to her adoptive parents. Her adoptive parents never put any pressure on her to choose a particular life path—and Tara still calls them Mom and Dad. But it was due to her biological mother's influence that she went to college, felt important enough to become a writer, and made contacts in the world of journalism herself. Today Tara is a successful author living in California, while her youngest sister works for the large agricultural corporation that eventually bought out her father. Her other sister married into another local farm family that still manages to resist big agrobusiness.

Tara's story is quite different from Esther's. Though we cannot be sure, it is very likely that had Grace never made her way into Tara's life, she would have continued along the same track as her brother and sister. Unlike Esther, the twelve-year-old Tara did not seek out mentors, role models, or "sugar daddies." Rather, a role model was thrust upon her. It was chance—but, again, it was anything but random. After all, it was not a perfect stranger, but her very own biological mother, who played the role of fairy godmother. And, as in the case of Esther, Tara also had a role in determining how her "mentor" would matter. She could have chosen not to explore a relationship with Grace. (Though how many kids that age would have such willpower as to resist?) She could have cultivated a loving relationship with Grace, but one that did not affect her career trajectory. Instead, she had a tumultuous tie to her biological mother—but one that very much shaped who she became as an adult.

Most fairy godmothers turn out not to be complete strangers, but rather people who are weakly—but definitively—connected to the person in question. In fact, sociologists have a phrase for the importance of these kinds of social relations: the strength of weak ties.[10] Weak ties (i.e., outside influences) work on most of us in equally consequential— but less dramatic—ways than they did in Tara's and Esther's cases. How do you find out about a new job opening in a factory or law firm across town? Usually not from the people you hang out with every day (such as your nuclear family and primary peer group). After all, they are in the same social network as you are; they have access to the same sources of information, more or less. No—new and potentially useful information and contacts come from the people you sort of know, but not too well. That uncle who lives in Boston. The advertising executive you met at a party last week. Or her husband who runs an insurance company in Albuquerque. You get the picture—not total strangers, but not your best friends. I mentioned at the beginning of the chapter that there is a social order to "random" influences. This is one such order.

Lest we get carried away, however, we should keep from jumping to the conclusion that knowing more people is necessarily better (since it would seem to increase the chances that we would know someone with new and useful information for our careers). This is an argument that has been made occasionally over the years, most recently and most prominently by *New Yorker* writer Malcolm Gladwell in his best-selling book, *The Tipping Point: How Little Things Can Make a Big Difference.*[11] In this book, he tells of a little, unscientific experiment he likes to conduct. He gives people a list of 248 last names from the Manhattan phone book. His test subjects are then instructed to check off each surname for which they know someone.[12] He gave this test to about four hundred people in the course of researching his book on social networks.

Gladwell reports that, although there was a huge range of checked surnames (from 2 to 118), a consistent pattern emerged: individuals who were older, highly educated, successful professionals tended to know more names. For example, a college class at City College in New York knew an average of 21 people with the last names on his list. The average for a group of health educators and academics at a Princeton University conference was 39; for his group of friends—the friends of a best-selling *New Yorker* writer—it was 41. However, more intriguing to Gladwell than the differences between the groups were the differences *within* the groups. In every group he encountered, there would inevitably be some people who scored very low and some who scored very high. These high scorers Gladwell calls "connectors." He implies that these connectors tend to be especially successful. They are social entrepreneurs who bring together various worlds of people to the benefit of everyone involved. If you want to sell a product, start a trend, or just get a rumor going, it is helpful to know a connector who will spread the word wide and far—or, better yet, to be a connector yourself.

Given the enticing argument that Gladwell makes, I decided to test his theory a bit more scientifically. I used the same approach to generate a list of 250 surnames and distribute them to the siblings involved in this study. I made some refinements on his approach, so the results are not directly comparable. For instance, I did not use the New York City phone book, which would have biased the results in favor of people who live there, but rather took a list of common names from the 1990 U.S. Census.[13] I then compared the responses of the siblings to see which siblings knew more people and whether or not this tended to fall in line with who was more successful. Of course, there still lurked the old problem of cause and effect: are people who know a lot of people successful because they have those contacts, or do they enjoy a lot of contacts thanks to their success?

Fortunately or unfortunately, the issue of cause and effect never came up in this case, because the results from my experiment were disappointing. It appears that how many people you know does not matter much. Even knowing *different* people from your siblings does not seem to have an effect. (The survey is reproduced in the appendix, so you and your brothers, sisters, parents, friends, and enemies can all take the test and see how much your social networks overlap and how much they differ.) Viewed in combination with the stories I obtained from the interviews, it seems that what really counts is knowing that just-right person. Furthermore, that person often has to believe in you in order to invest in you. There are various strategies to knowing the right person. One might entail getting to know an awful lot of people (like Gladwell's connectors do); but an equally effective way might be to develop deeper relationships with a few well-positioned people who are either powerful in their own right or one step removed from the people who can help you.[14] Of course, this all sounds very strategic, and for some people it is. But for most of us, the kind of social capital we cultivate is largely an unconscious process that fits in with other aspects of who we are and the social position in which we find ourselves.

Two themes emerge with respect to outside influences in this chapter. The first is that while appearing to be "random chance" from the point of view of the individual, many outside influences flow within deep social grooves. That is, they are not totally haphazard. For example, poor people are more likely than rich people to win the lottery since they are more likely to play. Girls are much more likely than boys to get raped or sexually abused. Teenage boys are more likely than teenage girls to get into legal trouble. Given the structure of American society, black teenage boys are more likely than white teenage boys to get into trouble with the law. And obviously, only men can be drafted and only women can get pregnant. However, underneath these social realities, there lurks another theme: the tension between the outside influence and the character of the person him- or herself.

It seems that the decision about where to assign causal weight has to be made on a case-by-case basis. For instance, Esosa was bused out of South Central Los Angeles to a magnet school, but his older siblings were not. In Esosa's case, it seems as though he was indeed the beneficiary of luck. It may be only because his immigrant parents did not know about the possibility of busing to a nondistrict high school that his older siblings were not able to attend one as well. By the time Esosa hit eighth grade they had learned the ropes. This unique opportunity to go to a better school paid off in the form of a Ph.D. from a prestigious university and a high-paying job in the computer industry. His older siblings, meanwhile, seem to bear the scars of their impoverished neighborhood more obviously. Both have endured long bouts of unemployment and poverty despite being—in the estimation of seemingly everyone who knows them—just as smart as Esosa.

Esosa's situation stands in contrast to that of Aileen and her two younger siblings, Hugh and Aubrey. Like Esosa's family, they also grew up in a poor neighborhood—in Cleveland—but unlike Esosa's siblings, all three children were tested for admission into the city's most elite public school. However, only Aileen, who had been a star student all the way through elementary and middle school, made it. So while Hugh and Aubrey attended the local neighborhood schools, Aileen was exposed to other worlds and set her sights on professional and financial success; she associated with richer kids and—according to her sister, who is still somewhat resentful of her—she acted "like she was better than everyone else." Aileen went on to be very successful in her business career; she met and married a man who was also very accomplished, and the two are quite wealthy now, living in a gated community outside Cleveland with their two children.

Hugh and Aubrey, on the other hand, who were both more "human-centered" (Aubrey's term for "less bookish") are less financially successful than Aileen, but both are doing fine, especially given the lack of opportunities in their community. Hugh left Cleveland for Galveston, Texas, where he spends part of the year working on an offshore oil rig making good money (and part of the year surfing). Meanwhile, Aubrey has always been steadily employed in various office jobs in Cleveland, some of which her sister helped her find. For obvious reasons of geography, Hugh has less contact with his siblings now, but Aubrey currently lives with Aileen and her family, as she has for several years. This arrangement seems to work well for both of the sisters. Aubrey gets free rent, while Aileen gets help raising her children. As of late, however, the living situation has gotten tense as Aubrey's jealousy and resentment increase as her "biological clock" keeps on ticking with no marital prospects yet surfacing.

While in Esosa's case, we cannot know for sure that his brother and sister would not have fared equally well if given the chance, Aileen seems to have been an overachiever her entire life. Chances are she would have ended up more successful than her siblings even if the unique opportunity of attending a magnet school had not arisen. Would Esther have thrived no matter who she met or did not meet? After all, she did manage to create a rather exciting life for herself at a tender age. Would Tara have made it as a writer even if she never found out she was adopted, let alone met her mother? Maybe the talent was in the genes and not in the connection. Conversely, would Missy have faltered if not for the rape and its aftermath? What about Mike: was Vietnam the key moment that shaped his life, or was it just one potential path among many on the road to oblivion? And, finally, what to make of Lincoln: was he just a bad seed from the beginning, or did a confluence of factors (including his intelligence, his undiagnosed ADHD, and the dire poverty of his family, but especially the decision to place him in a 600 school when he was in second grade) conspire to doom him to a life of crime and prison?

While it is hard to "prove" that any particular outside influence was the key moment without which a given life path would have been radically different, it is sometimes easier to show the converse—that some aspect of an individual's particular identity was key in generating differences between him/her and his/her siblings. This is particularly true when individuals become outsiders within their own families. While there are many reasons why people can feel like outsiders within their own families—including raw talent and drive, such as in Aileen's case, or having a different mother, such as in Tara's—there are two particular "identities" that repeatedly came up in the interviews as important outsider roles that facilitated socioeconomic mobility (both upward and downward). These were being gay or being highly religious. Being gay makes one an outsider in almost any traditional, heterosexual family, though, of course, some families are more open to sexual diversity than others. On the other hand, being highly religious makes one an outsider only when an individual comes from a family that is not also extremely pious. Importantly, the consequences of these statuses seem to vary by the class position of the family itself. When the family has lots of resources, being an outsider serves as a disadvantageous barrier and can often result in downward mobility vis-à-vis one's siblings. By contrast, when the family and community from which an individual comes is at high risk and has few resources, being an outsider often acts as a catapult to thrust him or her above and beyond the trajectories of his or her siblings.[15]

Kevin, Scott, and Jordana grew up in a very wealthy family in Massachusetts. Their mother, an artist, fell in love with another man and left the family when Jordana, the youngest, was six years old. Their father, with the help of his relatives, raised them from that point, until they were sent to boarding school as teenagers. While away at school, Jordana came to accept that she was gay. She spent much of her time from ninth through twelfth grade struggling to come to terms with this realization. As a result, she felt like an outsider to most of her peers at the elite institution; when she came out to her parents, they put even more distance between themselves and Jordana. As a result, she did not perform as well in school as she thought she could have and upon graduation, she was reluctant to rely on her parents for financial support to attend college, as her brothers had done. Instead, she followed another dream: to become a master carpenter—consequently, she is the least financially successful of the siblings, though she is very happy working at a medium-priced woodworking shop in a Boston suburb and taking on apprentices here and there on the side. To compound the financial difficulty (and, perhaps, the stereotype), Jordana's live-in girlfriend is a gym teacher, and earns a very low salary.

But while Jordana's outsider status cut her off from privilege, James' homosexuality served to get him out of a bad situation. In Birmingham, Alabama, James grew up in a family that was in perpetual financial straits, and his parents constantly fought with and complained about each other, their four children, and "the system" in general. They were, in fact, a very litigious family, suing anybody and everybody who offended them. Only when the parents were deeply enmeshed in a lawsuit—and therefore had a common, external enemy to unite them—did any semblance of peace descend upon the household. Yet,

there was a cost to these often frivolous lawsuits, for James and his siblings were terribly embarrassed by them. Some legal actions were worse
than others—like the time their mother went after their high school
for serving peanut butter when James was allergic (though he did not
actually eat any). As a result of actions like these, James kept to himself
at both home and school during most of his childhood. However, it was
not just because he was embarrassed by his family's legal shenanigans
that James kept a low profile. His reclusive behavior was also due to the
fact that he felt *different* from a very young age—he traces it as far back
as age five or six—due to his attraction to boys. He never told his
parents or his siblings about his burgeoning homosexuality, but as soon
as he had a chance, he left Alabama for New York City, where he hoped
to gain some freedom from his oppressive home environment. He
also yearned to be someplace where he could live an openly gay lifestyle. Today, James is the relative "success" story of the four children,
working on Wall Street as a trader while his three siblings remain at
home—well into their thirties—working a series of dead-end jobs in
the ever-expanding service economy.

In many circumstances, homosexuality, bisexuality, or other nonnor-
mative sexual identities trigger a process of self-discovery, often accompanied by geographic mobility to one of the more sexually diverse
neighborhoods in a major American city.[16] Often that move is also associated with career mobility; so, for someone coming from an impoverished or high-risk community, the journey often has the side benefit of
upward economic mobility vis-à-vis one's siblings. Of course, if someone is coming from a wealthy or otherwise privileged background, it
can trigger downward mobility. That said, such a contingent effect
must also be viewed in light of evidence that gays—specifically men—
still experience job discrimination that has real income costs in the
range of 11 to 27 percent.[17]

A similar contingent result of outsiderness can be found with respect
to extreme religiosity. When a child is extremely religious and this
stands in contrast to his or her family's ecclesiastical orientation, it
often makes that kid an outsider in—ironically—much the same way

homosexuality does (often without the attendant geographic mobility, however). Barry grew up in a family where nobody had gone on to college. But when Barry turned sixteen, instead of going wild with his newly issued driver's license, like a lot of his counterparts in high school did (including his sister), he commuted to a Bible study group and eventually became born again—much to the shock of his family, who had been mildly religious but not fervent in any respect. Thus, he kept his nose to the grindstone throughout high school and his grades did not suffer from late night partying, constant phone chattering, and time devoted to dating—as did his sister's. He was inspired to attend a Lutheran, religiously oriented college on full scholarship and excelled there as well, both academically and extracurricularly. By the time Barry had reached his twenties and decided that he did not believe in his religious principles after all, he had finished college, landed a good job as a manager in an insurance company, and had aged out of the self-destructive behaviors for which most teenagers are at risk. His sister was not so lucky and is still trying to finish college at a local commuter school (in her seventh year).

Barry stands in sharp contrast to Aaron, who was one of three sons born to a well-known author (his mother) and a politically active attorney (his father) in Burlington, Vermont. Both parents were children of the sixties who had traded in their beads for Beamers and now formed part of the liberal elite in upper New England (what David Brooks called Bobos—bourgeois bohemians).[18] There was always a heavy emphasis on cultural and intellectual achievement in the family. The kids were sent abroad during their junior years of high school—whether they liked it or not. They made regular trips with their parents to the theater, museums, and fund-raisers in Boston and New York. However, Aaron, the oldest, began to suffer from anxiety and depression in college, and has since failed to "meet the family's standards" by getting— and even liking—a job doing data entry. He has further created a rift with his family by becoming a Seventh-Day Adventist, thus repudiating his family's Jewish background (though they define themselves as neither practicing nor observant). He has very much embraced his new religious identity, and has even married a fellow Seventh-Day Adventist. Meanwhile, his family, frustrated, mystified, and feeling left out, does not understand why he would want to be religious at all.

Of course, while I have talked about homosexuality and religiosity in the same vein, there are important differences between these two forms of outsiderness. Specifically, as far as I know, nobody has discovered the gene for religiosity; and most scholars would agree that piousness is an achieved rather than ascribed status. If someone becomes religious, it may be cause or effect of other dynamics in her life. Sexual orientation, by contrast, may be largely a matter of ascribed biology. The newest school of thought is that sexual orientation is fairly innate and may have genetic roots. Thus, as in the comparison between obesity and skin color in the last chapter, we can be fairly certain that sexual orientation plays a causal role here while we should be less sure with respect to religiosity.

Conclusion

So what is the ultimate role of "luck"—i.e., outside influences? Though Christopher Jencks does cite luck as important in explaining the non-family portion of socioeconomic differences, he also admits that

> those who are lucky tend, of course, to impute their success to skill, while those who are inept believe that they are merely unlucky. If one man makes money while speculating on real estate while another loses it, the former will credit his success to good judgment, while the latter will blame his failure on bad luck. So, too, if a worker's firm expands rapidly and promotes him, he will assume this is a tribute to his foresight in picking the right firm and his talent on the job. If his firm goes broke and leaves him with an unmarketable set of specialized skills, he will seldom blame himself. In general, we [Jencks and his colleagues] think luck has far more influence on income than successful people admit.[19]

F. Scott Fitzgerald once wrote that "there are no second acts in American lives." But there are no counterfactual lives, either. We cannot know for sure whether Lincoln would not have turned to a life of crime without the disadvantages that befell him in childhood. We cannot know whether Esther would have scraped by without a sugar daddy or whether Esosa would have gotten a Ph.D. without having attended a magnet school. There is simply no way to know for sure. (Though evidence from a voucher program in New York City—the closest thing to a random assignment experiment that we have—shows that there are evidently few gains from attending a private school [not unlike a magnet school]. Apparently what matters is wanting to go and being good enough to get in.)[20]

But while there is no alternative universe that can answer these questions, there is some evidence on the role of elite colleges on life chances. Everyone who went through the process of applying to selective colleges remembers those anxious days of spring semester senior year when the daily trip to the mailbox brought cheer or gloom and one's entire future seemed completely out of one's hands. You'd already taken the SATs, written your essays, and mailed in your grades. If there at all exists a ritualized, random period of outside influence (or divine providence) in modern society, it is the time between mailing off your last college application and opening the mailbox a few months later to see to which college(s), if any, you were admitted. If you received a thin envelope (a rejection letter) from the school of your choice, gloom descended like a dark cloud, as you reconfigured your hopes, dreams, and sometimes your entire self-image. If you were lucky enough to receive a fat packet stuffed with an acceptance letter, catalogs, and other materials trying to convince *you* to attend, then you could ignore the warnings about maintaining your grades for the second semester of senior year and cultivate a full-blown case of senioritis. (If there is ever a time for "revenge of the nerds" it is the last portion of senior year.)

For borderline cases, the college admissions process is certainly random enough to approximate an experiment of sorts with respect to outside educational influences. Even admissions officers concede this.[21]

However, no one has data on the supersecretive decision-making processes of colleges. Ideally, we would follow a group of individuals who were arbitrarily rejected (though they could have just as easily gotten in) and a group that were arbitrarily admitted (though they could just have easily ended up in the "no" pile). As a substitute complementary experiment, economists Stacy Berg Dale and Alan Kreuger examined the outcomes of kids who were accepted to highly selective universities like Yale and Stanford but did not attend for some reason—instead opting for a less elite institution. In short, these are kids who were smart enough to get into Harvard but did not benefit from the cachet of a Harvard degree.[22] As it turns out, however, they may be even smarter than the rest of the kids who drop upward of a hundred grand to go to an Ivy League school, since they end up earning as much money as those who do go. In short, Dale and Kreuger's evidence suggests that— at least when it comes to the "upper end" of the educational ladder— outside influences (like fancy credentials) matter less than raw ability and drive.[23] Of course, we do not have the counterfactual to this counterfactual—individuals who did not "deserve" Princeton, but who got in anyway.

The closest we come to such a counterfactual are two groups that are admitted to elite institutions in greater numbers than they would be if acceptance was based solely on quantifiable assessments of academic records: minorities and athletes (added to this group could be legacies and those from geographically underrepresented communities). In *The Shape of the River,* authors William G. Bowen and Derek Bok demonstrate that minority students admitted with lower SAT scores than their nonminority counterparts go on to perform equally well as life marches on in a variety of contexts and measures in adulthood, ranging from professional achievement to community service, but not as well in others, such as income. By contrast, student athletes, James Shulman and William G. Bowen tell us in *The Game of Life: College Sports and Educational Values,* are admitted with the lowest average SAT scores of all groups and perform worse than their higher-scoring, nonathlete counterparts in terms of educational outcomes. Yet they end up earning more money anyway. So the evidence for the upper end of the class distribution is currently inconclusive.

As for the lower end of the status hierarchy: Lincoln was released from prison as I finished up this book. This is really his last chance to go straight, for if he is convicted of a felony again, he will likely be eligible for social security the next time he is released. If he commits his next crime in New York, he may be slightly luckier, as it is one of the few remaining states that has not adopted a "three strikes and you're out" law. But he better be mighty careful if he ever visits his sister and other relatives back in Georgia. Not to be outdone by California or Washington, which first started the trend in "three strikes" laws, Georgia has the most draconian policy of all: two strikes lead to a life sentence.

Though his incentives are strong for going straight, his chances of successfully making such a transition are slim. Though highly intelligent and verbally gifted, he now faces life with even more scarlet letters than he had before. He is African-American to begin with, a status against which employers tend to discriminate, all else being equal.[24] He has no formal education beyond the GED he earned during an earlier stint in prison. Meanwhile the importance of formal schooling has continued to rise in the economy around him. He is older than he was before, and while it is illegal to discriminate on the basis of age (as it is in the case of race) employers typically prefer either young people starting out or older individuals with experience. Lincoln is neither. And then, of course, he has two felony convictions, which research has shown is the next worse thing to having a swastika tattooed on your forehead. It is akin to a scarlet *F.* In Milwaukee, sociologist Devah Pager sent out "pretend" job seekers to apply for entry-level, low-wage jobs, with identical resumes except for the fact that some had "convictions" and others did not.[25] She found that whites with a conviction were 50 percent less likely to get a job than nonconvicted applicants in the audit study. For blacks, the results were even more striking: those with a conviction suffered a 64 percent reduction in employment opportunities. And these results were for a single, misdemeanor conviction—all else being equal. So while it is possible for Lincoln to "catch up" with his sister, it will certainly be a struggle. The odds are against him.

Lincoln embodies the tension between outside events (in his case being thrown from a bad school to a worse one) and internal attributes (like risk seeking). What his case illustrates is that the two go hand-in-hand. Just as Meredith's beauty and desire to perform made a chance encounter with an encouraging hairdresser count, Lincoln's particular personality, abilities, and liabilities combined with his disadvantaged social position to lead to a poor outcome. The same combination of internal and external forces can be seen when we view an individual not through the events that happen to him or her, but through their status as an outsider, such as a homosexual—the results depend on social position. In short, luck does matter. But *how* it matters depends on who that individual is and the family conditions that surround him or her.

EIGHT

FROM TRIBES TO MARKETS

Conclusions, Implications, and Insinuations

A Tale of Two Presidents

Bill Clinton had longed for political power in general and the presidency in particular all his life—at least since the moment that he shook President Kennedy's hand in the White House Rose Garden as a twelve-year-old boy.[1] However, the childhood biography of golden child Bill Clinton could not have been more different from that of the president whose hand he shook on that July morning in 1963. While Bill was born to an impoverished single mother who had dropped out of high school, Jack was the secondborn son of one of the richest and most powerful Democratic families in the country. But look at how their families were structured. Among the Clintons, Bill was always the chosen one, while in the Kennedy clan, Jack was the sickly son who lived in the shadow of his more successful older brother, Joe Jr. Both Kennedy and Clinton faced their own obstacles and forged their own paths through one of the most unequal societies in the world to reach the single most powerful position on the planet. However, if you view the two young presidents not as individual success stories, but as players within a web of family affiliations, they illustrate the class structure of American society better than any experiment a mad social scientist could have devised. How can we make sense of a society that fostered the very different paths that led both John F. Kennedy and Bill Clinton to the White House? The paradox that these national leaders represent is not one of political ideology, ethnic politics, or even regional power shifts. Rather, the larger contradiction embodied by the ascendance of these two figures on the national stage is one of social class and family background in America.

John Kennedy was born on May 29, 1917, the second child of Rose and Joseph Kennedy—who would go on to have seven more.[2] His was a political family. His maternal grandfather, known as Honey Fitz, had been a mayor of Boston, and his father—a self-made millionaire whose fortune was rumored to have been amassed by running liquor during Prohibition—was also involved in politics. Joseph became the chairman of the Securities and Exchange Commission under President Franklin D. Roosevelt, and later, in 1937, became U.S. ambassador to Great Britain.

Jack, as John soon became known, was a sickly, small child. He suffered through whooping cough, measles, chicken pox, and then, in the winter of 1920, scarlet fever. Even after he recovered, he never was very healthy; the family used to joke that mosquitoes better watch out, for they were taking a great risk in sucking his blood. Perhaps because of his childhood illnesses, or maybe merely due to birth order, Jack played second fiddle to his older brother, Joe Jr., who was two years his elder. This rivalry was exacerbated by the fact that Jack was the only sibling who posed any real competition to Joe Jr. (The immediate siblings after were girls in a family that prized only males.) Their rivalry was always apparent and perhaps best summarized by one bicycle race they had, suggested by Joe Jr. The race led to a head-on collision: Jack ended up with twenty-eight stitches, while his older brother walked away unscathed.

Jack clearly lived in the shadow of Joe Jr. For example, while he was popular at his elite boarding school, he did not excel academically. Overall, he rated a "fair" on his report card, the Choate headmaster writing, "He can do better than this" at the bottom of his grade sheet. His father once wrote him: "It is very difficult to make up fundamentals that you have neglected when you were very young, and that is why I am urging you to do the best you can. I am not expecting too much, and I will not be disappointed if you don't turn out to be a real genius, but I think you can be a really worthwhile citizen with good judgment and understanding."

With paternal letters like this, it is no surprise that Jack was a tad unambitious. Meanwhile, Joe Jr. always excelled academically and at a young age had announced to everyone that he would become the first Catholic president. World War II intervened. Both brothers, continuing their rivalry, entered the Navy as officers. Here the brothers' luck changed. Jack escaped the war with only minor injuries to his already weak back, but Joe Jr.'s plane was shot down, killing him in the process.

With Joe's death, Jack's career trajectory took off. He had been considering teaching or writing, but now the family mantle of politics fell upon him. He ran for the U.S. Congress in 1946 and won. Six years later, he was elected to the Senate. A mere eight years after that, he beat Richard Milhous Nixon in one of the closest elections in history.[3] After he was elected president, Kennedy rewarded his younger brother Bobby (child number seven, and the next oldest boy) for his hard work running his campaign by appointing him to the post of attorney general. When the nepotism issue was raised, Jack joked with the press that he could not "see that it's wrong to give him a little legal experience before he goes out to practice law."[4] After his brother's assassination, Bobby left his cabinet post to run for (and win) a seat in the U.S. Senate, representing New York. Four years later, he too ran for president, and just as the Democratic nomination seemed within his grasp, he too was assassinated.

Yet, Bobby was not the last Kennedy brother to enter the political fray. In 1962, Edward ("Ted") Moore Kennedy was also elected to the U.S. Senate, initially to finish his brother's term. Thus, Jack had—directly or indirectly—facilitated the entry of both his younger brothers into national politics. Like Bobby's, Ted's career benefited from his brother's presidency (and, of course, from his parents' resources). Like Jack and Bobby, he seemed destined to run for president. But then, on the night of July 18, 1969,[5] his political fortunes dimmed. Since Bobby's death the summer before, he had reportedly been drinking a lot. That day was no exception; he had attended a party on Martha's Vineyard. His pregnant wife, Joan, stayed home. After the party, Kennedy gave a ride to a young woman, a former secretary of his brother Robert. The car careened off a small bridge in Chappaquiddick. Kennedy claims that he did not recall how he got out of the sunken automobile; he also claims that he repeatedly dove down to the car in failed attempts to rescue the passenger, Mary Jo Kopechne. He made his way back to the party they had been attending and crawled into the backseat of a car parked there. It was not until the next morning that he contacted the police. Meanwhile, Kopechne had drowned. There are contested reports that Kennedy was fleeing a police officer when he lost control of the car. At the very least, it is confirmed that he was unlicensed at the time of the incident, having allowed his license to expire; his driving record before the incident was very spotty as well, dating at least back to his law school days in Virginia.

Yet it was not enough to derail his political career. He was a Kennedy. The privilege the family enjoyed even extended to convincing Richard McLaughlin, the Massachusetts Registrar of Motor Vehicles, to backdate Kennedy's license renewal, so he would technically not have been guilty of driving without a license. Decades later, he is still in the Senate, wielding enormous power—the second most senior member of that august institution.[6]

The case of the Kennedy brothers illustrates the counterfactual to the Clintons. Though the golden child of the Kennedy family did not live to make his father's dream come true, there were such forces of privilege at work that the Kennedy juggernaut rolled onward. Jack stepped in to fill the role that his older brother was meant to occupy, despite mediocre academic credentials and debilitating health problems that—according to recent reports—continued throughout his presidency. The Kennedy name has become so synonymous with political power that just to be a Kennedy (even three generations from Joseph and even by marriage) opens the door to elective office in states all across the Northeast. (And even for a Republican in the West—look at what Maria Shriver did for Arnold Schwarzenegger.)

Of course, the Kennedys are not the only presidential example of the magic halo. George W. Bush was a C-minus student at Yale and then a failed—but still rich—businessman. Meanwhile, his younger brother

Jeb was a star pupil (he graduated magna cum laude from the University of Texas at age twenty) and a policy scholar who worked his way up the political ladder (no doubt benefiting greatly from his pedigree). While Jeb was working as a successful real estate entrepreneur and positioning himself within the Florida Republican party, George W. was battling alcoholism. W.'s elite status protected him to such a degree that he made it almost all the way through the 2000 presidential campaign without his drunk-driving conviction coming to light. There are several other brothers who did not achieve nearly the political heights of Jeb or George W.; so the sibling story is more complicated. But the fact remains that by meritocratic standards and lacking the resources of his family and its connections, George W.'s life might not have turned out all that different from that of Roger Clinton. So, though someone of unusual ability and drive such as Bill Clinton can make it in American society, it also appears to be the case that those born of privilege enjoy a magic halo, a buffer around them that prevents them from falling too far, and that provides them each and every opportunity to succeed. In other words, the poor kid can make it, but the odds are much tougher for him. The rich kid has to really exert some effort in order to mess up his life for good. If Bill and Roger are two sides of the same coin, the Kennedy brothers are the sides of trick dice that always come up lucky sevens. How did we get to a point in history in which both these narratives are possible?

Sibling Class Differences: The View from History

At one time in history, there were no notable class differences in the outcomes of siblings simply because there were no significant class differences in society, period. That is, as common historical wisdom holds, we were all much more alike in earlier epochs than we are today, at least with respect to what we did for a living. Life in "premodern" society meant that humans subsisted using more or less the same set of skills. For instance, in a hunter-gatherer (or subsistence farming) society, though there might have been different functional roles for people based on age and gender, the range of occupational possibilities was more limited than it is in the contemporary world. Able-bodied men might have hunted game while adult women gathered food. The aged might have contributed other services like making clothing or providing childcare. Though there might have been skill differences between men and between women in their roles, the fundamental nature of the occupational roles remained the same. Deference, prestige, and respect were most likely based on dimensions other than what one did for a living or how much wealth she or he had amassed. Even today, in many tribal societies for example, age is the primary basis of status inequality.

In this semimythical past, everyone ground their own grain, cooked their own food, made their homes, and so on. There were many tasks to be done for survival, but they were more or less the same set that each family or village unit had to perform. There was no elaborate division of labor and specialization of skills, such as there is today. Of course, this is a gross (and politically incorrect) oversimplification of premodern cultures.[7] Historical and anthropological quibbles aside, however, the fact remains that there was not a range of *occupational* strata like there exists in contemporary American society; likewise, there was not a corresponding range of wealth inequities on the scale that exists today (or education differences, for that matter). So while it may be the case that my modern American eyes may be blind to the subtle sibling hierarchies among the Yanomami of the Amazon or similar such communities, it is safe to say that for the type of differences we are speaking of—education, occupation, and wealth—they are simply not of the same magnitude.[8]

The grand narrative of sibling class differences really gets started with the development of the division of labor, which also led to substantial increases in wealth. For this observation, we owe thanks to the grandfather of economics, Adam Smith, who wrote in 1751 that the average manual laborer in industrial England lived better than most African princes—all thanks to the division of labor. The premise is wonderfully simple, and in *The Wealth of Nations,* Smith illustrates it with the example of a pinmaker. An old fashioned pinmaker—that is, one who snips the metal, sharpens the point, forges and attaches a head, polishes it up, and packages it for sale—could probably produce a dozen pins a day, at best. The moment we break down the task—such that one person spends his whole day snipping pieces of wire the correct length, another only sharpens their points, another attaches the pinhead, and so on—productivity increases to the point that six men could produce on a daily basis not seventy-two pins, but rather something on the order of five hundred pins. This is partly because many tasks can be done more quickly if broken down into their constitutive parts, and it is also because specialization can lead to innovation. If you spent your whole life sharpening pins, you might come up with some pretty fast ways to get it done. (Mix in profits as an incentive and stir.) These might involve little manual tricks that you have come up with that you could pass on to other pin polishers from the next shift; or they might be machines that make your work easier (or at least more productive). Add in such technological advances and the sky's the limit with respect to productivity, or so the fairly tale of capitalism goes.[9]

However, the ironic consequence of increased abundance and its corresponding increase in wealth is that it produces inequality. The French Enlightenment philosopher Jean-Jacques Rousseau was perhaps the first to point out this paradox. In a state of nature (read: hunter-gatherer or similar societies), he argues, there is *natural* inequality but no *social* inequality. That is, you may be better off than I because you are faster, have better eyesight, better fine motor coordination, or for another similar reason, but this difference translates into an advantage only in the here and now. In other words, you may eat better than I, but you have no social power over me. The moment that there is enough abundance that private property emerges, this situation changes. Say that I learned how to cure meat and thus could save the amounts that I did not immediately consume. Now we have a situation of abundance and, perhaps, private property. If you are better than I at picking berries, that will not only result in your eating better than me in this moment, it might result also in your having jams that you can store up to consume when times are not so good, or to trade for other goods (with someone who is a better meat curer, for instance). In such a way, initial differences in "natural" ability can spiral out of control; through accumulation, the resulting social inequalities can be disproportionately large.

The arrival of surplus also means that you have to think about your "property"—i.e., your jellies stored back in your hut. In the time before the accumulation of goods was possible and/or socially acceptable, you might have given me the berries you could not eat (rather than have them go to waste). In fact, doing so would likely have been a wise choice, since I might return the favor if the situation were ever such that I had something that you needed. However, with the advent of assets, calculations became more complex.[10] New questions arose: Do I save things for myself or share them? How do I protect my wealth from thievery? Do I buy off a few people? The level of social organization and potential for politics thus became increasingly daunting. Some thinkers of the Scottish Enlightenment saw the advent of surplus in the form of private property as a positive development in the history of mankind: with increased ability to retain the fruits of one's own labor, now man had something for which to strive. The accumulation of goods in the form of private property was, for these Scots, the driving force in the development of society. But not everyone interpreted this turn of events positively. Our old friend Rousseau, for instance, bemoaned the advent of social inequality. He longed to return to a state of nature—that is, without the existence of private property—where natural inequality would again be the only form of inequality.

Such a return was, of course, impossible. With today's level of biotechnology, it even seems that social inequality has totally eclipsed so-called natural inequality. Take the case of myopia (nearsightedness). I was severely nearsighted as a child, a condition that has both genetic and environmental factors, but comes as close to what Rousseau called natural inequality as anything. Not being able to even read the big *E* at the top of the eye chart, I would have probably died off in the state of nature, as I would have been unable to see game or berries well enough to nab them. However, with the advent of optical technology, I was able to correct this disadvantage with glasses (and later contact lenses). I have even gone so far as to have laser eye surgery done to correct my myopia and astigmatism. Of course, who gets access to these technologies is a matter of social inequality. But the point here is that not only does social inequality exist in modern societies, it can often override natural differences.

The upshot is that with the arrival of modernity comes increasingly diverse roles in the economy and increased inequalities in wealth and property. So what determines who ends up doing which job and owning which size nest egg? The party line here is that with modernity and the division of labor inevitably comes a meritocracy of sorts. We could, theoretically, live in a caste-like society, in which there is a high degree of difference in occupations that are completely inherited. In such a society, the day laborer's son would himself become a day laborer, just as the stockbroker's son would similarly reproduce his father's occupational position. (This assumes no change in the types of jobs available over the course of generations, something I address below.) However, a caste society is somewhat inefficient, given that the inheritance of skills is probably not 100 percent; a barber's son, for instance, may or may not have the best ability for cutting hair himself. (If the degree of the division of labor in a society is low, of course, this would be less of a problem.)

Back in the old days, so to speak, technological advances were not so rapid as to make skills obsolete in a generation or two. In a traditional farming community, for example, the necessary skills could be transferred from parent to child fairly directly. People yoked oxen, planted corn, and milled wheat in the same way for generations. As changes in the way people produced goods became more rapid, kids could no longer learn at home what they needed to know in order to function in the economy. Hence, formal schooling began to be a necessity. In the modern world, school both makes up for what our parents cannot teach us and also acts as a sorting machine. Since we no longer do what our parents did (at least, not typically in the way that they did it), school "tells us" what we are good at doing. Sociologists call this historical change a shift from ascription (assignment to the pecking order based on birth) to achievement (assignment to the pecking order based on what we bring to the table ourselves, irrespective of things we cannot control [like which parents we happened to get, the color of our skin, and so on—with the notable exception of our genetic profile]). The idea behind this shift is that skill should trump all else in efficient free market capitalism. Put another way, money should level aristocracies and find talent, no matter where it lurks.

But of course, no society is a "true" meritocracy (a true free market). In the real world, race, class, and social connections all matter. So the real question becomes not whether it is social forces or genetics that determines who succeeds and who does not (within or between families); it is *What traits determine success?* Take the case of college admissions. What if we switched the "meritocratic" criterion for admission from SAT score to shooting percentage in a basketball tryout? After all, the rules are fair, simple, equally applied, and understood by all participants. Yet, aside from student athletes, most people would say it is absurd to admit people to, say, Yale based on such an "arbitrary" standard—even if everyone is starting from a socially level playing field (no pun intended). The argument that most people would use to reject this approach to admissions is that it is incongruent with the role that Yale should play as an educational institution. The underlying assumption to this critique is that students admitted on this basis would perform worse at Yale—and in life—than those admitted by the SAT standard. In other words, the legitimacy of the "meritocratic" criteria rests in how well they predict success in the downstream social institutions into which students are funneled (i.e., the labor market). So, engineering schools like MIT and Cal Tech, for example, rely to a greater extent on math scores since that is what their particular target labor market values. If the standard of success is skin color or height or foot size, for example, we may think of this as illegitimate. But if the criterion is something called ability—which is something very hard to define, of course—then we would allow that there can be a higher degree of inheritance (and sibling resemblance) while still being a meritocratic society.

Creating a truly meritocratic system is nearly impossible, even if we put aside this issue of what constitutes a "fair" measure of ability. To illustrate this point, it is worth thinking about what it would take to provide "true" equality of opportunity, which is the foundation of a fair, meritocratic competition. One way to start might entail forcing every child to go to equally funded public schools. But what takes place at home each evening would still make a big difference. Educated parents might tutor their kids, endowing them with advantageous knowledge. Rich parents might hire others to tutor for them. Children of individuals with wealth and power might develop the confidence to excel and achieve greater economic ends. Children from economically disadvantaged families might see their parents' struggles as reflecting something innately wrong with their family lineage and therefore with themselves. Thus, equal schooling would not be enough. Even if we added equal housing—à la some state socialist housing projects that everyone was forced to live in—and equal income and wealth, there would still remain family differences in power, success, and popularity that might unequally influence children.[11]

Despite the fact that the above suggestions would already be considered very draconian conditions by American political standards, we would nonetheless not have gone far enough in our quest to remedy inequality. In order to ensure a true meritocratic capitalist economy, children would have to be severed completely from their past lineage. Each generation would have to start from scratch to forge its own pecking order. One possibility might be to resort to a collective childrearing situation as seen on the kibbutzim of Israel or in some ashrams in the United States and Europe. However, even a collective childrearing arrangement would not be enough; as long as the identities of parents and children (and siblings) are known to one another, there is still the likelihood that family members will—even inadvertently—instill differential social advantages to their own. In order to provide true equality of opportunity, babies need to be snatched from their parents' arms before they bond at all. Better yet, since socially influenced prenatal and birth conditions—such as drinking, smoking, and so on—can have large effects on how kids turn out, children might need to be incubated in pods. Even so, such an outrageous situation would merely eliminate the transmission of *social* inequalities across situations. It would still allow for genetic differentiation. And, as we have seen, which genetic

characteristics are valued in a "meritocratic" society is a socially determined phenomenon.

The View from the Present

Today, America is the most unequal developed nation in the world. If
you make it here, the rewards are staggering and unparalleled in any
other democracy. The net worth of Bill Gates has been estimated to
peak at more than $85 billion—equal to the total net worth of the
poorest 45 percent of Americans. The average CEO of a Fortune 100
company earns $37.5 million per year—more than 1,000 times the pay
of typical workers.[12] At the same time, the United States also has the
highest poverty rate in the advanced world.[13] Children are particularly
hard hit; a full one in five American children live with incomes below
the poverty line.[14] There are a lot of different ways to measure economic
inequality, but they all come up with the same answer: Economic rewards are far more lopsided here than in European countries like social-
democratic Sweden and union-driven France. But the United States is
also much more unequal than even our closest cousins, Great Britain
and Canada. In fact, in terms of who gets what share, we fall somewhere
between Western European countries, on the one hand, and developing
countries like Pakistan, Mexico, and Nigeria, on the other. Of course,
we Americans like to brag that we have the highest incomes in the
world. And this is close to true. But, while these "developing" nations
do not come close to our overall standard of living, the way their
smaller pie is sliced is not that different from our own division of
resources. For example, in the United States, the richest 10 percent of
the population reaps incomes that are between 5 and 6 times larger
than the poorest 10 percent.[15] In Sweden the comparable figure is about
2.5; in the Netherlands it is about 3; and in Great Britain it is approximately 4.5. In Mexico, however, it is somewhere between 9 and 12,
depending on which year we are examining.[16] So while we have a way
to go to reach Third World levels, the United States does not quite fit
the model of most other industrialized nations either.[17]

Given the level of disparities, it becomes all the more striking that more than half of the inequality in American society is attributable to differences within families—i.e., between siblings. At first glance, this fact would seem to support the argument of those who defend the current American economic landscape. Even if we have a greater degree of inequality, they argue, we are more meritocratic than those stodgy old feudal societies: we have a higher degree of socioeconomic mobility than do European countries with their heavy-handed governments, unions, and protective industrial policies. Indeed, the Horatio Alger story of someone pulling himself up by his bootstraps is part of our cultural mythology. We love to read biographies of men like Harland Sanders—better known as the Colonel, of Kentucky Fried Chicken. Or Dale Carnegie. Or Bill Gates and Steve Jobs. The list of successful American entrepreneurs goes on and on and gets longer each generation. But the reality is that this story of economic mobility is only partly true. From some cross-national studies of occupational mobility, it seems that we do have more change from generation to generation. When we turn to studies of income, however, we find that there is more similarity in fathers' and sons' incomes in America than there is in other rich countries. In other words, there is less economic mobility in U.S. society, not more.[18]

How can we reconcile these two seemingly contradictory sets of findings? The answer lies in the difference between occupational mobility and income mobility. In short, the higher degree of occupational mobility comes not because America is an inherently level playing field that rewards the talented and/or hardworking and punishes the inept and/or lazy, regardless of their social origins. The appearance of mobility differences is really a result of the occupational tide rising for all. Over the course of fairly recent history, there has been an upward scaling of occupations. The twentieth century witnessed a great expansion in the number of professionals and managers. Since all of those new managers could not be children of managers themselves (assuming relatively constant managerial birth rates), they had to come from somewhere—hence, upward mobility. At the same time, occupations also die out. Take the nostalgic case of the farmer. We still have a cabinet-level agency for farmers and farming in the U.S. Department of Agriculture; farming takes up a lot of political airspace; and farm subsidies still cost a lot of money. Yet there are hardly any farmers to speak of left in the U.S. population. In 1900, one out of every two employed adults was a farmer. By 2000, one out of every two hundred Americans listed their occupations as farmer. Of course, farm families did not become an endangered species by not having children; they did not literally die out. Rather, this incredible transformation is a result of that old devil, technological change (and the division of labor). Today, factory farming relies on machines and conveyor belts, on pesticides and hormones; among the results is cheaper and more abundant food—and less need for human labor. Accordingly, farmers' children have become mobile by definition; increasingly, the jobs of their parents simply no longer exist.

This process is called structural mobility, which means mobility that is not zero-sum since it results from economic development (i.e., an expanding pie). Structural mobility stands in marked contrast to exchange mobility,[19] which is perhaps best (if most unrealistically) embodied in the popular imagination by Eddie Murphy and Dan Ackroyd in the movie *Trading Places,* in which Murphy goes from homelessness to chairmanship of the board of a large financial company and Ackroyd takes the exact opposite route.[20] It is structural mobility, however, that has historically made up the bulk of U.S. socioeconomic mobility. In other words, when an American parent tells his child that she can grow up to be anything she wants to be, it is largely because of opportunities that keep opening up with economic development that he can say this with a reasonable amount of confidence. The story of structural mobility is largely one of industrialization—of the children of small-town farmers (and African-American sharecroppers) moving to the cities to earn better wages doing more skilled work. (Unfortunately, since the 1970s the dominant story has been deindustrialization and increased polarization in the service sector, so whether inevitable upward structural mobility continues to prevail is an open question.) It is this dynamic of upgrading (for as long as it continues) that allows the seeming imbalance we see in the cases of the Kennedy and Clinton families. That is, some siblings from poor families can be upwardly mobile, without requiring concomitant downward mobility on the part of a rich kid. In other words, Clinton can make it despite the odds, and so can Jack, Bobby, and Ted—as the odds-on favorites.[21]

If the days of net upward mobility are truly over, then the amount of mobility we want to encourage becomes an open question. If family background currently explains less than half of where we end up, how much lower are we willing to push that figure (assuming we could lower it)?[22] Though equality of opportunity is seen almost universally across societies as a good thing, and though most observers agree that social position (i.e., family background) still matters more than it should, there exist real costs to generating a more level playing field. Those costs are exacted on the integrity of the family unit, particularly for adult sibling and parent-child relations.

The U.S. population is already one of the most geographically mobile groups of people in the world. In an average year, 18 percent of American children under the age of eighteen move homes.[23] Over a five-year interval 46 percent of Americans move at least once (though this rate has been declining over the last century).[24] These figures are greater than the corresponding statistics for European countries, and dwarf those of traditional, premodern societies (except nomadic peoples or war refugees). That means the average distance between an adult child and his or her parents and siblings is likely to be significant—making the maintenance of strong family ties more difficult.

This geographic distance is not unrelated to growth-induced socio-economic mobility in America. The labor market of the United States has long been viewed as less "sticky" than that of Europe due to the fact that individuals (or entire populations) are willing to move to work.[25] When geographic mobility is combined with socioeconomic differences, the challenges to the successful development of adult sibling relationships, parent-child ties, and grandparent-grandchild connections are even greater. To top it off, social norms that "enforce" sibling contact are very weak in the United States and other industrialized countries.[26] This fact makes sibling relations what psychologists and anthropologists call "volitional." This voluntary nature of adult sibling relations stands in contrast to sibling relations in premodern societies, which are institutionalized into particular roles and where siblings play an important part in one another's lives for most of their life course, often living in the same household even into adulthood. (For example, in some tribal societies, siblings marry in pairs—i.e., a brother and a sister marry the brother and sister from another family.) In modern American society, ties between pairs of sisters are the strongest, while ties between brothers are the weakest, and ties between opposite sex siblings tend to fall somewhere in between.[27] There is also ethnic and religious variation, with white Protestants of northern European descent demonstrating the weakest adult sibling ties in terms of levels of contact and emotional closeness. Our findings confirm these gender and ethnicity patterns.

When we compared siblings with one another as to how often they see their family (parents and siblings) and whether they socialize more often with friends than with siblings, we found that those siblings with higher education levels were more likely to see their siblings (and parents) than those with lower ones. However, factoring out education differences, those brothers or sisters with more prestigious occupations are less likely to socialize with their siblings and parents (overall and relative to their friends). It seems that more "serious" careers orient siblings away from their families and more toward other social worlds. Or such jobs could be more time-demanding.

However, while class mobility means that family ties to siblings and parents may be breaking asunder, new ties may also be forming along the way. One pattern that emerged from the interviews was that families stayed in closer contact with the set of parents and siblings that more closely resembled their class position as adults. For example, if Keith came from a working-class background but experienced such significant upward mobility that he became a white-collar professional, and along the way he married someone who had a similar adult class status (as is more often the case than not in the American marriage market) but who, unlike Keith, came from an upper-middle-class family, then Keith and his wife are more likely to socialize with her family than his.

Stories of estrangement resulting from class differences between siblings (or between siblings' in-laws) were littered across the interviews. However, when we examined the question of whether siblings' disparities in education or occupational prestige were associated with knowing fewer people in common (as measured by our network survey), we did not find any such pattern. Nor did we find that the *average* class status of the siblings—or of their parents—affected the similarity of the siblings' social networks.

Another common pattern that emerged from the life stories relates to the division of family labor—particularly elder care. Perhaps unsurprisingly, the burden of caring for ailing or aging parents most often fell upon women (i.e., sisters) in the families that we interviewed. However, within gender groups, it was often the least economically successful sibling that bore the largest burden of responsibility. Economists would tell us that this is rational: the cost in lost time (i.e., wages) is lowest for the least successful sibling, and therefore she or he *should* draw the short straw. While this may be true, it carries with it the consequence that resentments between siblings—already there from socioeconomic jealousies—can fester or even boil over when parental care disproportionately falls upon one child. As a result of declining fertility and longer life expectancies, the U.S. population is getting older, so this problem of unequal elder care will only get worse. In 2000, the median age in America was 35.3 years (up 2.4 years since 1990).[28] By 2020, it is projected to be 38.1.[29] People's careers are lasting longer, too, so the conflict between working and taking care of ailing parents will only intensify.

Conclusion: Lies My Mother Told Me

By now I hope that readers have a new lens through which to look at their own families of origin (that is, where they grew up) and their families of destination (those that they create through marriage and childbearing). I know that in writing this book, I have had lots of time to reflect on my own experiences growing up with a younger sister (younger by three years minus one week) and my own biases and worries as a parent of two children (and stepdad to a third). Thus, I conclude by telling you a little bit about my two families in the cause of full disclosure (others might call it confession). My sister and I are now the best of friends—mostly. Even today, tensions and scars run deep from the time we were kids. We were ruthless: I once wielded a kitchen knife against her. She has beaten me with our dog Knuckles' metal leash. I think I still have scars on my back. Despite our three-year gap—which my mother carefully planned out according to the latest research of the time—and despite the gender difference, it was dog-eat-dog (or dog-whip-dog, as the case may be).

In trying to resolve the intense sibling rivalry between my sister and me, my mother relied on three stock stories—all of which I have since learned were wrong. The first was that we should be nice to each other because someday we might need each other for a kidney. She would claim that, as siblings, we were closer to each other genetically—and hence better donors—than we were to anybody else in the world, even than to either of our parents. Once I learned a little about genetics, I found out that she was wrong: my sister and I share approximately 50 percent of our genes, about the same amount that we share with each of our parents. (The argument would have worked better if we had been identical twins.) Second, she used to say that her love was not a pie—that she loved us equally, and loving one does not take away from loving the other. But this, too, is not entirely as it seemed. In chapter 3 we saw that while love itself may not be a pie (though sometimes I still have my suspicions), everything else that parents provide their children can be thought of to some degree as a fixed pie. My sister and I, of course, differ on who got the smaller slice. Finally, my mother tried to teach us not to be obsessed with who got more or less. (After all, we did not really care whether love was a pie but, rather, who got more actual dessert.) Admittedly, it was usually me who did the complaining, and this often caused my mother to launch into her standard cautionary tale about my accountant-like tendencies.

"Maybe Alexandra did get more potato chips than you. . . ," she would begin. (One day it was potato chips, another it was cookies. It did not really matter. I could manage to count, to complain, and to angle for more of anything.) "Is it really worth caring about? Does it make it any better or make you any happier to be counting and complaining all the time?"

I would stand, unmoved—arms crossed, pout on my face.

She would continue: "When you die and get to the pearly gates of heaven, Saint Peter will be waiting there for you with his big book of life. He'll look down the pages of your life and scratch his chin. Then he'll nod his head and say, 'You know what, Dalton; you were right. You did get cheated. So here are your two potato chips. . . . *Now go to hell.*'" Of course, I cannot be absolutely sure that this is an apocryphal tale, but I certainly hope it is (as does my mother, who asked me not to include it in the book, for fear of the light in which it would cast her parenting).

However, to give my mother some credit (and to make up for the fact that I decided to include the above story over her protests), there was one piece of advice related to both fairness and the pie metaphor that did work for my sister and me. That was her introduction of the "you divide, I pick" system to guarantee fairness in our latchkey-kid world. My sister and I had a system of rules and regulations in our little after-school, unsupervised society. There were two main ones. The first was the "you divide, I pick" rule; the second one was "calling it"—the urban equivalent to yelling "shotgun" for car rides. When we arrived home, I might "call" the couch, and then Alexandra would have to lie on the floor to watch television. She might be quicker to the draw to call the TV on one particular afternoon so that I had to endure *Little House on the Prairie* rather than enjoy *Batman*. (Once, when my sister was quite young, I called the orange juice, the couch, the television, the floor, the air, the water in the pipes, the toilet, all the food in the cabinets and in the refrigerator, and everything else I could think of in my thirty-second rant. She broke down crying on the green shag carpet, and with no pity or remorse, I scolded her for wetting my floor with her tears.

Our mother—like the Supreme Court—interceded when she arrived home and declared that things could only be called for set periods of time and that—as at the library—we could only lay claim to a couple of things at a time. Other than setting this limit, however, our parents did not interfere with the rules and in fact got co-opted into the system.)

"Ma! Dalton took the whole table to do his puzzle, and now I can't do my homework."

Maybe it would have been better for our mother to order me to share the table space with my sister, but she did not. Instead, she asked us, "Who called the table?"

At which point my sister hung her head, her light brown bangs obscuring her eyes, confessing that I, indeed, had.

"Well, you go into the bedroom and work then," she would instruct.

What this method did was create a system of household property rights that could be traded and sold during each afternoon. So, for instance, I might strategically call the television for the 3:00 to 4:00 p.m. slot, even if I cared little about the shows during that time period. Then I could use that claim in order to get her to trade the cookie she had brought home from school that day.

Neither Alexandra nor I can remember exactly how our little system of family laws developed or even when it waned in importance. What we remember most are the bitter fights that ensued when the legitimacy of the system broke down. Since I was often the one who thought to call everything, it was usually Alexandra who found it in her interest to break the law, so to speak. If I pushed my luck and called the TV at a time that she absolutely *had* to watch a show, she might ignore me and switch the set to her channel all the same. Violence would usually ensue.

Though three years younger than me, she could nonetheless put up quite a fight when sufficiently provoked. When I got mad at her for some reason—such as her switching the television channel—I would shove or punch her and then bolt down the hall to the bathroom—the only room in the house with a lock on the door. That mildewed box of a room was our equivalent to the safe haven provided by a church or embassy. At that point the fight would shift to taunting, negotiating, pleading, or simply crying.

"I'll give you my dessert if you don't hit me," I might offer. "I'm sorry I hit you. . . ."

This story of rules and violence may sound familiar to anyone who grew up with other kids in the house, be they brothers and sisters, step-siblings, cousins, or unrelated kin. Families—and kids in particular—develop a pecking order that is completely indigenous to the household (yet, as we know by now, related to larger, societal forces). There is no simple hierarchy, but a complex tension of battling wills and relationships that may realign again and again over time, or break down completely. This book, of course, is about these local orders. Further, it is about how—in combination with the decisions of parents, the family's resources, class background, racial identity, and so on—household hierarchies forge our place in the larger pecking order called society.

When Alexandra and I get together and reflect on our respective childhoods, our perceptions could not be more different. While I talk about how miserable I was, she waxes nostalgic about the good old days. Birth order may be part of the story. Gender probably also plays a role. Even genetically based aspects of our personality structures may come into play. And, of course, our relationship to each other factors into the picture.

But our family's trajectory also plays a part. In many ways, Alexandra and I did live very different childhoods despite the fact that we both came home to the same house each night. For instance, while I hated the neighborhood where we lived because of how poor and run-down it was, my sister spent the majority of her childhood in the wealthier, more well-kept neighborhood where we eventually moved. Similarly, I hated the local public school I attended, where the teachers struck the students and violent crime lurked around each corner. But after witnessing my experience there, my parents learned their lesson and sent Alexandra to a magnet school she very much enjoyed. In short, because parents are learning as they go along and since a family is in constant motion—economically, geographically, even in its very makeup—siblings may experience very different realities growing up. These variations affect the household pecking order, and they affect the life chances of the siblings.

Gender and race also played a role. Though we grew up in the same neighborhoods—even if for differing amounts of time in each—the communities impacted us very differently by virtue of our sex. As a male in a rough and tumble neighborhood, I was expected to be tough myself. When I turned out to be a bit nerdy and shy—not to mention white—my local stock failed to accrue much value. (Of course, I don't know if my personality was cause or effect here.) The expectations put upon my sister in such an environment, however, were quite different. Girls often put the fear of God into the boys (and one another), but you *could* be a popular girl without being a badass. That was less common for boys. My sister, furthermore, had the advantage of being a light-haired white chick. Whereas for me, whiteness might have signaled wimpiness in our common cultural lexicon, for her it signified the dominant form of beauty in mass culture. So our social positions were very different by virtue of the intersection of race and gender.

But, to be completely thorough, I cannot really talk about these societal forces without taking into consideration our individual genetic endowments. Had I been tall and muscle-bound—instead of medium-height and wiry—then everything I have just said would have been moot. My social position vis-à-vis race, class, and gender would not have mattered much, because I might have been the baddest dude around, occupying a very central social position in the youth community. Alas.

Conversely, my sister might have been ostracized and shy had she been markedly ugly (of course, that is something that is socially defined by the wider culture as well). Luckily for her she fit the bill of cute white girl.

Today, my sister and I both still live in New York. Both of us have reproduced our parents' class status, albeit in different ways. The children of artists, we both sought careers in the world of "ideas" or "creativity," though both of us have forged a foundation of economic stability that would not have been possible as full-time artists. My sister manages a small, nonprofit theater company. She has committed herself to the business side of the arts. I, meanwhile, have gone into academia, which provides a level of job stability that rivals the civil service but which also offers a degree of tolerance for personal, creative expression.

For all these basic similarities, however, there are also major differences between Alexandra and myself. Even though she spent fewer years growing up in the impoverished, minority neighborhood than I did (because she was younger when we moved), she wears the mark of the community much more prominently than I do. She uses more of the local hip-hop slang, she moves in much more ethnically and class diverse circles than I generally do (partially on account of whom our respective careers put us in contact with). Our values also diverge. She is much less career focused than I am. She is happy to do a good job behind the scenes and let others take credit for her theater's successes. And, ultimately, what matters most to Alexandra is a comfortable home, a rich family life, financial security, and community service. I, on the other hand, hate working for other people and want to have total control over what I do or do not accomplish and put my name to—even community service. Our financial trajectories are also beginning to diverge substantially, as I work my way up the academic job ladder with complete job security (tenure) while she remains committed to a struggling arts organization where new crises crop up daily.

However, whereas I may be more stable financially, she has flourished in her personal life, while I have struggled for contentment. She is a relatively new mother, her son, Dante, having been born just over a year before this writing. Her marriage to her husband, Dan Leonardi, brings her love and happiness. Though they live in a cramped, railroad-style apartment, stress does not get the best of them; they fill their days with cute rituals like ADDs (all day dates) and kisses before all meals, and they call each other by cutesy pet names. Meanwhile, though I love my two children—ages four and five—fiercely, my marriage has been a tumultuous one that is ending as it began, with a struggle for control between my spouse and me. (The first time we ever danced, we both insisted on leading—tripping each other up in the process.) We are now muddling through the divorce process, not doing a very good job of containing our sadness and frustration in front of the kids. We both admit to having the emotional intelligence of teenagers—or perhaps two-year-olds. And of course, I worry about the impact of our tumultuous family life on our two children—especially in light of what I have written in chapter 4. It was not easy writing that particular chapter while going through a divorce myself.

How much of these differences between my sister's and my life are due to our family's trajectory, to the local pecking order among our peer groups, and to the way our parents socialized each of us? And, alternatively, which differences are due to other factors like gender differences, birth order, and random events? And what about innate genetic predispositions, what kind of role do they play? The answer to all these questions is, of course: "Yes."

ABOUT THE PECKING ORDER

A Technical Appendix

The Panel Study of Income Dynamics

To gain a textured portrait of inequality in American families I analyzed three national datasets and conducted in-depth interviews with another sample of respondents. First, to model the resemblance of siblings on education, occupational prestige, income, and wealth, I used sibling data from the Panel Study of Income Dynamics (PSID). The PSID is considered the preeminent survey of family economics in the world. Its comparative advantage lies in the data structure of the panel. The PSID began with five thousand households thought to be nationally representative at the time (with an oversample of low-income households). Those interested in the details of the sampling and survey methods should consult Martha Hill's *The Panel Study of Income Dynamics: A User's Guide.*[1]

Since the desire was to contrast siblings who were linked through having been sample members, this entailed using those respondents who had been children in PSID households but had now set up on their own. Since net worth and earnings data is more reliable as respondents enter middle age, I used the latest wave possible. Correlations were calculated between pairs of siblings who had valid responses on the various outcomes that I studied: educational attainment (measured in two ways—as years of schooling, capped at seventeen for "any graduate work" whether or not it led to a degree; and as whether or not a sibling completed college [yes or no]); occupational prestige (calculated as a Hodge-Siegel-Rossi score based on the 1970 U.S. Census coding that the PSID used); income (the natural logarithm of a multi-year average of total household income, with negative and zero values set to zero); and net worth (natural logarithm [with negative and zero values set to zero], excluding home equity).

Utilizing the latest survey years available for income entailed constructing an average of 2000 earnings (reported in the 2001 survey wave), 1998 earnings (reported in 1999—the PSID was cut back to being conducted on a biennial basis in 1999), 1997 earnings, and 1996 earnings. Occupational prestige is calculated from the census occupational code for the respondent's latest year in the survey in which she or he worked. Education level was taken from the 2001 survey (or the most recent earlier wave, if the data were missing for 2001).

Questions about the net worth of families were asked initially during the 1984 wave and then repeated every five years up through 1999. At each five-year wealth supplement, retrospective questions were asked of the householders about their intervening receipt of inheritance and gifts, their management (i.e., buying and selling) of assets, and changes in the values of assets. When the survey cut back to being conducted on a biennial basis, the decision was made to ask the wealth questions each time the survey was in the field. So the latest year for which wealth data were available was the 2001 wave. For the reasons mentioned previously, it was this latest wave that I used in order to maximize the age of the siblings under investigation. In order to qualify for inclusion in the sibling sample, respondents had to be the head or "wife" of their own household during the survey years in question (2001 for most variables; 1996–2001 for the multi-year income measure).

I examined correlations for the overall PSID sibling population as well as for various subgroups. The reports of sibling difference and sibling similarity presented in chapter 1 come from simple calculations of the R^2 of sibling regressions. Sibling similarity is the R^2; sibling difference is $1 - R^2$. The subsample comparisons I made included those along the following axes: race (blacks and non-blacks); parental class status (measured by maternal education in the latest year it was available; mother's education, cut at three points—completed college, completed high school [but no additional schooling], and less than high school); and sibship size (number of children ever born to the mother).

I compared subgroup correlations as well as unstandardized regression coefficients; I also ran pooled models with interaction terms between sibling values on the variable of interest (say, education or occupational prestige) and the race and class status of the family (as measured by maternal education at various cut points). Results from this exercise can be found in an accompanying working paper and are described in the notes to chapter 1.[2]

The Study of American Families and the 1994 General Social Survey

The second dataset that I examined is called the Study of American Families,[3] conducted in 1994 by the University of Wisconsin, in conjunction with the General Social Survey of that same year (the GSS has been fielded on an annual basis by the University of Chicago since 1972).[4] An overview of the GSS can be found in James Davis and Tom Smith's *The NORC General Social Survey: A User's Guide.*[5] The best description of the SAF comes from its own online documentation:

> The 1994 GSS topical module obtained identifying information for one randomly selected sibling for each of the 2,992 GSS respondents who had at least one living sibling above the age of 25. Using this information about siblings' addresses and telephone numbers, the *Study of American Families* (SAF) then conducted a telephone interview with 1,155 of those siblings, asking essentially the same questions that were asked of 1994 GSS respondents in person. The SAF went beyond the GSS interview, however, by collecting information about a second selected sibling (in addition to the GSS respondent) and by asking about the educational and occupational attainments of a much larger number of relatives.[6]

Module six of the Study of American Families asks respondents to identify their *least* and *most* economically successful living relatives. It is from these variables that I report in chapter 1 that "siblings" are most likely to fall into both the "most" and "least" successful categories. This module also asks for explanations as to why the most and least economically successful living relative occupies that distinction. It is from these responses that I culled the social-structural explanations and the individual-personality accounts. The SAF-GSS data also provided the evidence of how differently respondents remember (or experienced) their childhoods—on dimensions ranging from parental ages to education levels.

The Study of American Families was also used to analyze the impact of maternal employment on gender equity within families. In this case, sibling fixed effects models were used to examine three outcomes: the chances of having graduated from high school, the likelihood of having completed a four-year college degree, and the respondent's income (not the total household income). In the first two education models, the control variables were only age and sex (relative birth position is controlled by age). All other relevant (that is, competing) characteristics are assumed to drop out of a within-family model. Other individual-specific factors like occupation and income are assumed to be causally downstream from education, and thus are not included. For the analysis of sibling differences in income by gender, I controlled for age, sex, education level, and occupational prestige. For all three of these outcomes—high school, college, and income—I ran models for the entire sample and then separately for those families where the mother worked "for pay for as long as a year" while the GSS child was growing up ("MAWRKGRW").

The SAF asked respondents how often they socialized with friends, neighbors, and relatives (relatives were further broken down into siblings and parents). I analyzed whether selected siblings saw their parents and siblings "often," which I defined as more than once per month (on average). For sensitivity analysis, I also modeled the probability that siblings spend more time with their siblings than with their friends. These were sibling fixed effects models; in other words, the outcome measure was the difference between the siblings on their likelihood of socializing more or less, and the predictors were sibling differences in selected characteristics—namely, age, sex, education level, and occupational prestige. Traits common to the siblings, such as their family background, race, and so on, are automatically factored out since I am comparing within families. These results are discussed in chapter 8.

The U.S. Census and the Impact of Family Size and Birth Order

Finally, in order to address the issue of educational investment in children and academic achievement, I used data from the 1990 U.S. Census (the 5 percent sample). Before I address how I constructed my variables and dataset, I describe below the backdrop against which this analysis was performed: the debate over the importance of family size (number of siblings) on educational attainment.

Traditionally, the detrimental impact of large family size (better known as sibship size) has been considered one of the most robust (consistently powerful) effects in inequality research. Since 1967, when Peter Blau and Otis Dudley Duncan wrote their classic on the American stratification system, *The American Occupational Structure,* scholars have found that individuals who come from larger families—that is, who have more brothers or sisters—do worse in school. For example, in *Opportunity and Change,* David Featherman and Robert Hauser find that each additional sibling costs someone about one-fifth of a year of schooling, holding other background variables constant.[7] In explaining why sibling constellation matters in determining educational success, researchers have generated a number of competing hypotheses. These explanations have alternatively relied on economic, genetic, and social-psychological arguments to address the mechanisms by which sibship size has its effects on children. Some scholars hypothesize that the observed associations are due to the fact that additional children put a strain on the monetary and nonmonetary resources of the family. This "resource dilution" hypothesis (and its counterpart in economics: the trade-off between quality and quantity of children)[8] has been lent support by studies of the allocation of educational and financial resources within the family and by the fact that sibship size seems to matter more for poorer families where monetary resources are already scarce.[9] The major alternative theory to the resource dilution model has been the "confluence model." This competing paradigm attributes the negative effect of sibship size primarily to the psychological climate of the family.[10] This theory suggests that a family with a lot of children or one with many spaced close together in age results in a relatively inferior intellectual climate since children dominate the environment as opposed to adults, who have a greater influence on the intellectual milieu of a small family. In essence, this theory suggests that it is not the number of siblings that matters per se, but rather the age distribution in the household environment. Finally, some researchers in the "no effect" paradigm suggest that the effect is entirely artifactual—a result of the fact that parents with lower cognitive abilities may tend to have large families.[11] This skeptical "no effect" hypothesis had long received token lip service as researchers moved ahead in specifying which types of parental resources mattered, when, and how—assuming a true causal relationship along the way.[12]

Then in 1999, along came Guang Guo and Leah VanWey, who (rightly) questioned the causal interpretation of these traditional estimates.[13] It would seem likely that part of the observed effect of sibship size is spurious (biased upward) due to the fact that small families and large families vary in important ways that would affect children's success—independent of the fact of whether there are actually more children or not. Earlier strategies to account for this possibility relied on estimations with controls for potentially biasing factors such as parental IQ. The problem with adding additional controls is that there always remains the possibility of an association between family size, educational achievement, and something immeasurable—ranging from household environment, neighborhood conditions, ambition, ability, genetic makeup, health status, and so on—that also affects children's outcomes.

Rather than examining more and more variables that are difficult to assess, Guo and VanWey use fixed-effects models to address these possibilities. That is, they exploited the longitudinal design of the National Longitudinal Survey of Youth (NLSY) to assess the impact of *changes* in family size on *changes* in test scores between siblings and for individuals over time. Fixed-effects models adequately cancel out unobserved factors that might be associated with both the predictor of interest (sibship size) and the dependent variable (educational or cognitive attainment). However, they do so only under certain conditions. The first condition is that the unobserved (or lurking) variables must be stable across the unit within which we are differencing. So, taking the case of sibship size, if it is the underlying, immeasurable genetic profile of parents (i.e., *innate* ability) that determines both how many kids the parents tend to have and the educational performance of those kids, then we can be fairly sure that the genetic makeup of the parents is constant over time and across births as long as the composition of the family remains the same. However, if the lurking variable that is biasing traditional estimates happens to be something like "family intellectual climate," then it is not at all clear that such an unobserved factor is constant over time within families.

For example, what if parents adjusted their fertility patterns in response to the "quality" of earlier children produced in a Markov chain–like fashion (as has been shown to be the case by Mark Rosenzweig and Kenneth Wolpin)?[14] In other words, it could be the case that parents who have developmentally challenged children do not go on to have many additional offspring—thus biasing the effect of family size down to zero. Or, it could be the case that intellectually thriving children lead parents to have more than they had originally planned (again, biasing the effect to zero). Or perhaps the parents compensate for additional children by augmenting the intellectual climate in other ways, as the Majeskis did in chapter 3 with piano lessons and formal schooling.

The second condition has to do with the issue of parents adjusting their behavior in advance to reflect their intended or ultimate family size. Take the case of schooling. If a family knows that they intend to have more kids, they might be much less likely to send their first child to private school, given the anticipated cost of raising three children as opposed to one. To the extent that parents know their ultimate family size and plan accordingly, they undermine the logic of sibling (or individual) differences over time, which relies on the assumption that each change represents an independent source of variation.

A third, and perhaps most important, issue is related to what economist Arthur Goldberger calls the problem of "micronumerosity," more commonly known as multicolinearity.[15] The sample sizes that Guo and VanWey use range from 431 to 534 for the sibling analysis—depending on which cognitive test is the dependent measure—and decline for models that isolate races. (It is not clear whether this is individuals or pairs; if it is individuals then the actual degrees of freedom for difference scores are about half those figures.) For the individual fixed-effects (repeated measure) models, the sample sizes ranged from 694 to 1,048 (again, which might represent double the number of "difference scores" that are being analyzed). This does not leave a lot of degrees of freedom when they are controlling for gender, birth order, and age. It is not clear if Guo and VanWey controlled for other time-varying covariants such as family structure, income, and maternal education, which are controlled in the conventional regression models they estimate.[16] Particularly troubling is the probable colinearity between sibship size, age, and birth order in their models.

The seriousness of the problem lies in the fact that all of these vary in the same direction. So, for example, in *all* cases in the sibling difference models, the earlier born is the sibling with the smaller sibship. This leads to a catch-22. If, in a fixed-effects framework, we include birth order, then we run into problems of multicolinearity. If we leave it out, then the model is underspecified. Likewise, the age at test varies almost perfectly with sibship size (particularly since they limited their sample to those siblings who were at least six years apart in age).[17] The same problem comes to the fore with respect to the individual-change models as well. (Other commentators have leveled different critiques at these models, revolving around the generalizability of their select sample, the anomalous finding that sibship size is positively related to math scores, and the possibility that there may be spacing-size sibship interactions.)[18] However, even if Guo and VanWey's estimates stand up to methodological criticism, the fact remains that sibship size may still be detrimental to educational attainment, without affecting scores on their test measures—for example, through financial pressures. Given these lingering questions and the intuitive theoretical appeal of the arguments why sibship size *should* matter, the debate seems far from settled. In the analysis presented in chapter 3 (and below) I took a very different strategy to estimating "causal" effects that have grown increasingly popular in economics but have yet to make a significant mark in the sociological literature.

Another econometric approach to estimating "causal" effects that is distinguished from fixed-effects or difference models is what are called instrumental variable (IV) models. The general strategy in the IV framework is the following: find an exogenous, random source of variation in the independent variable of interest, which should not be associated with the dependent variable except indirectly through that measured independent variable. So, for example, economist Joshua Angrist used the Vietnam draft lottery (a seemingly random assignment to draft eligibility status based on a chance draw of Ping-Pong balls with birth dates on them) as a natural experiment to estimate the effects on wages of serving in Vietnam—purified of observable and unobservable factors that affect selection into actual service.[19] Essentially, the approach entails comparing the 1980s wages of men with draft-eligible birthdays with the wages of those who had draft-ineligible birthdays. Draft eligibility affects the likelihood of serving in Vietnam (though it does not explain all the variance) but is unrelated to all other characteristics since it was randomly assigned.[20] The IV approach, then, essentially uses a small but pure portion of the variance in the causal variable of interest in order to estimate variance in the outcome variable.[21] In the case of a binary instrument, such as Vietnam draft eligibility, the estimated parameter can be expressed simply as a difference in means in the dependent variable between the "treatment" group (i.e., draft eligible) and the "control" group (i.e., draft ineligible) over the means on the independent variable (likelihood of going to Vietnam).[22]

In the case of sibship size, the sex composition of the first two children can be seen as this random assignment to two groups: "same sex" and "mixed sex." Thus, in this instance, the denominator is the difference in probability of having at least one more child (among those who have at least two) between those who have same-sex children and those whose first two children are of mixed sex. The numerator is the difference in the educational attainment of the children for these two groups. It turns out that 42 percent of those families (in my subsample, described below) who have opposite-sex children for their first two go on to have three or more children while 49 percent of families who have same-sex children make the transition to three or more offspring. Since this difference in propensity to have more than two children is essentially randomly assigned (by God, fate, or destiny), we can exploit it to estimate the impact of additional children on the outcomes of offspring.[23] This particular sex-mix instrument has been used by other researchers to estimate the labor elasticity of parents' child-rearing behavior.[24] The resulting estimates are much smaller than traditional estimates.[25]

There are a number of assumptions that go into interpreting this approach that should be made explicit at this point. First of all, this approach can be interpreted as a local average treatment effect (LATE). This means that it is the effect of sibship size for "compliers" only. That is, the parameter estimate applies to those families who do go on to have an additional child after having same-sex children in their first two. In this strict interpretation, it does not apply to families that have one child, or stick to two, or even for those who have three children but have mixed-sex children for their first two. Nor does it tell us anything, necessarily, about the effect of having ten children as opposed to nine. Even to interpret this estimate as unbiased locally (that is, for the treated compliers), we must make a couple of assumptions. First, we must assume that assignment to the treatment group (same-sex) or the control group (mixed-sex) is truly random. Given that there is no reason to expect systematic differences in the likelihood of having two boys, two girls, or a mixed-sex pair across the population, this seems reasonable.[26] Further, there appears to be no association between sex mix and any measurable variables in the present study. We must also assume monotonicity; that is, we must assume that for no subgroup does having same-sex children make them less likely—on average—to have additional children. Finally, we must assume that the sex mix of children does not affect their educational outcomes in any other way than by virtue of affecting their parents' likelihood of going on to have more children.

But this is akin to saying that sibship sex composition has no effects on educational success. If, for example, there were significant returns to scale for same-sex children—i.e., parents saved significant amounts of money by being able to use hand-me-down clothes or were more able to have same-sex children share a bedroom, freeing up funds for education—then our estimates might be biased.[27] The evidence on this question is mixed.[28] I tested for this possibility in the current context by examining the sex composition of sibships greater than two and found no effect of this variable (coded in several ways) on the educational outcomes under study.[29] Thus, we can be reasonably confident that the effects of sex composition are due to their association with additional fertility, not returns to scale or any other sex-composition-related effect.[30]

In order to generalize this estimate beyond a local average treatment effect (the effect for those with two same-sex children who do go on to have a third), we must make additional assumptions; namely, we must assume homogenous treatment effects. That is, we must assume that each subgroup in the population has the same strength of relationship between having mixed-sex children for their first two births and the propensity to go on to having a third. Also, to generalize beyond the difference between two and three children, we must assume that there is a linear relationship between sibship size and educational attainment. By contrast, it may be the case that the transition from one to two children (or from four to five, for instance) is different in its educational effects than the transition from two to three. In fact, this is likely to be the case. However, that fact does not take away from the importance of properly estimating the effect for the two- versus three-child leap, especially since this is one of the most common transitions.

Assessing the degree to which the IV estimate differs from other estimation techniques provides purchase on how biased (and in what direction) estimates for other sibship size differences are inconsistent.

Since the IV method typically uses only a small portion of the variance in the independent variable, it is data-demanding; in other words, this approach requires very large sample sizes that most social surveys do not provide. The U.S. Census, by contrast, does have the kind of power necessary for the analysis. For this study, I used the 1990 Five Percent Public Use Microdata Sample (long-form respondents). The frame is the following: We include married men and women with at least two children residing at home, the eldest of whom is no older than nineteen years of age. Ideally, we would have adult respondents who have completed their education and could tell us about their family composition growing up (with a minimum degree of measurement error). However, using the census, we have educational attainment data only on those individuals still co-residing. Some adult children still reside with their parents, but this is a selective subsample of the population. The solution to this problem is to focus on children younger than age nineteen who are still living at home and who thus have outcomes on two educational measures (to be discussed in detail below): attending private school or having been held back a grade. The constraint of the child having to live at home excludes institutionalized and runaway adolescents, but this should bias any results toward zero rather than inflate them.

Another constraint of using the census is the fact that I must make assumptions that the children in the household are all the children of the householders (and that they do not have other offspring elsewhere). To make this assumption more reasonable, I limited the sample not only to those who had at least two children in the household, but also to units where there are no children residing who are not the biological children of the head of household, where there were the same number of children currently residing in the home as the primary female adult has ever had, where there were no subfamilies residing in the unit, and where there were no twins or triplets in the family. While these decisions limit the generalizability of these findings to nonnuclear family forms, they were necessary to make sure I was dealing with a clean measure of family size.

Since I only had information about children still residing in the household, I needed to exclude cases where the total number of children born to the adult female (householder or wife) differed from the number living there. For example, if she had grown children who had moved out of the house, we would not know the sexes of these children and would not be able to properly compute the sex-mix instrument. Likewise, if the total number she had was fewer than those currently residing in the home, then we would not know how to treat the extra children that may be the offspring of a male householder—but not of the "wife"—and who live in the unit now (since we would not know when they moved in and what their relationship to sibship size is).

Still, it could be the case that a woman has had four children from a previous marriage, they have grown up and moved out, and now she is residing with four children of her new husband. I would have no way of distinguishing this (albeit rare) possibility from the case where they were her own children. The problem is not so much that they are her stepchildren, but that the male householder, their father, may have had six children and the two oldest are also grown up. I could not know if these were all the children he has ever had, since men are not asked about total fertility. I am fairly certain that the number of cases where the number of stepchildren a woman happens to be living with matches exactly the number of her own previous children who do not live with her is relatively low. (If any of her own children from a previous mate lived with them, the household would be removed from my sample since I was only interested in those households where all the children are the biological children of the householder [her children would be stepchildren of the householder and thus eliminated]). Additionally, the presence of other relatives, nonrelatives, or subfamilies complicates the issues around family size, since family size and household size become noncoterminous and the exact relationships of the various children residing in the unit become unclear. Thus, I eliminated these units as well. Finally, I eliminated units where there are twin or triplet children residing since the presence of twins complicates both the assumptions about childbearing decisions and those about the impact of additional children on educational outcomes.

The first educational outcome I examined is whether or not a school-aged child in the household has been held back a grade (or more). This is ascertained by comparing a child's age to the highest grade he or she has completed—for children currently enrolled in school. Since birthday cutoffs may result in children starting late, I used a conservative estimate, which underestimates the total number of children held back in school. For example, a seven-year-old child must not have completed kindergarten in order to be classified as "age inappropriate." While a child could have completed kindergarten by age seven and still have been held back, it is not possible for a child to be seven years old and not have completed kindergarten unless they have been held back or out of school for some reason. However, it is possible—though un-likely—for a six-year-old to have not completed kindergarten, yet be "on track" with his or her schooling. This could occur if a child was born early in the year, such that she or he enrolled in kindergarten when they were 5.75 years old (in September of their fifth year of life), and his or her parent filled out the census long form after their sixth birthday, but before the end of the school year. A further complication to this measure stems from the fact that the census collapses grades seven through ten into one category; so seventh, eighth, and ninth graders may be held back unbeknownst to researchers such as myself. This, too, results in an underestimation of the proportion "age inappropriate" for their level of schooling. So, it comes as no surprise to find that the percentage of census children that receive this classification is much smaller (0.7 percent) than the figures from the National Center for Educational Statistics. In 1992 the National Center for Education Statistics reports that 11.1 percent of the U.S. adult population had been retained a grade or more.[31] Though this is more than an order of magnitude greater than the figure I find in the census, keep in mind several mitigating factors (besides the overly strict definition of dropping out that I use). First, the larger figure includes dropouts as well as those who completed school; meanwhile 25 percent of those held back dropped out (compared to about 10 percent for those who had never been held back). By contrast, my measure includes only those who are still enrolled in school (which is necessary for me to identify those who are behind in their level of schooling as distinct from those who have simply dropped out). Second, their figure is for all cohorts of adults, not for children, and, furthermore, it is retrospective. That said, clearly my measure vastly undercounts those who have been held back. Even so, my results are similar when a weaker standard for age appropriateness is used.

I also wanted a measure of parental investment in the education of offspring. So for children ages six through eighteen who are currently enrolled in school, I used two-stage least squares regression to predict the likelihood of that child's school being private as opposed to public elementary or secondary school. (Private refers to both secular and religious institutions.) This measure represents an attempt to isolate the particular "financial" impact of additional siblings on educational choices. This measure is also used in other analyses as an indicator of differential parental financial investment in siblings. Of course, paying private school tuition is just one way among many that parents can invest in their children, but it is nonetheless an important financial measure. Also, while it certainly may be the case that a particular private school may represent a worse educational alternative than a particular public school, statistics suggest that children in private schools typically receive more resources. For example, in 1990 (the year I studied), the average pupil-to-teacher ratio in U.S. elementary and secondary public schools was 17.2, while it was 14.7 in private schools.[32] The best evidence that we have about the impact of private schooling on test scores (which is immune to selection bias problems) comes from voucher experiments where some children who would not have otherwise been able to afford to attend a private school were able to do so as a result of a voucher lottery. When Alan Krueger and Pei Zhu compared the test scores of those who "won" the voucher lottery with those who entered but did not win one, they found no remarkable differences between the test scores of the two groups three years out from baseline.[33] Of course, test scores in elementary school are not everything, and attending private school may be more about gaining social and cultural capital—i.e., useful connections and class confidence—that translates into occupational and earnings success in later life. That said, as the importance of "human capital" (i.e., formal education) has increased over the years, the proportion of children attending private (high) school has also remained relatively stable, fluctuating in the 7- to 10-percent range for most of the twentieth century.[34] The real change has been in the total proportion of students attending any high school, which has increased steadily over time.[35]

One final note with respect to the educational outcome measures: the 1995 wave of the PSID actually asked whether the respondents attended private school during their elementary and secondary schooling experience. That same wave also asked whether they had ever been held back a grade. So I linked these responses to the sibling responses on other variables—hoping to see how my census-based measures of educational investment and performance related to other outcomes, such as ultimate educational attainment or earnings. However, the number of sibling sets who had valid responses on these variables and, further, who displayed discordancy on them (in order to contrast the difference with differences in outcome) was too few to conclude anything about the impact of private schooling or of being held back on later outcomes. Even if these measures turn out not to be critical ones downstream, so to speak, they still should be of importance to parents who are concerned with investing in their children's education and getting maximal academic performance out of their children.

In-Depth Interviews

Numbers tell us a certain amount, but they never go the distance. In order to write this book (rather than just a couple of academic papers for obscure journals), it was necessary to talk to actual siblings about their childhoods, their family relationships, and their socioeconomic trajectories. Together two research assistants and I interviewed 175 individuals from 68 families. (Names and other identifying details were changed in the text for purposes of confidentiality.) Of course, often the accounts of siblings from the same family differed (even on basic questions of fact in terms of family history, which raises important questions about the validity of standard, retrospective surveys where only one family member is interviewed). But often it was those differing accounts that made the grist for the dramatic unfolding of their family's history.

Not only were the in-depth interviews needed in order to get a sense of the mechanisms that undergirded the large-scale quantitative results, they also shed light on issues that cannot be adequately addressed in impersonal surveys such as the census. For example, though some survey researchers try and succeed to differing extents, most people do not feel comfortable talking about their sexual orientation unless they get to know their interlocutor (especially if the respondent is not heterosexual).[36] The issues of outside influences were also not ascertainable through readily available, large-scale datasets. This is partly due to the fact that I did not know what I was looking for at the time I was looking for it. That is, the range of outside influences—both negative and positive—were so particular to each case that there would be no single question or battery of questions that would preempt the myriad of possibilities. We would have needed to have found a survey that asked about service in the Vietnam War, legal trouble, rape, mentors, busing, and so on.

So, in chapters 1 through 3, the in-depth interviews are meant to be the meat—the muscle that attaches to the bones—of the survey results. But in chapters 4 through 7, they largely stand alone (with notable exceptions), supported primarily by other prior research. In these cases, I was building on studies that may not have followed a sibling design, but which the sibling interviews could speak to. For example, with respect to the importance of health status, I used respondent accounts to describe the causal mechanisms that underlie research on health and socioeconomic status that others and I have published elsewhere. Sometimes, there was a dearth of prior information upon which to guide the interpretation of the interview data. For example, there was little information about how the effects of parental death or divorce varied by birth order or by whether or not the child had left the family home. In these cases, the interviews provide a first pass at understanding complex social dynamics within the family and should be followed up by future researchers with large-scale statistical analysis to confirm (or reject) the theories generated from this sibling study.

The interviews were conducted with what social scientists call a "snowball" convenience sample of respondents. My research assistants and I canvassed our own social networks to obtain starting points. We asked acquaintances if they knew cases of siblings who turned out differently in terms of socioeconomic success and who might consent to being interviewed for the study. (So, in our initial recruiting, we explicitly sampled on the "dependent" variable; in subsequent referrals we did not ask for siblings who specifically turned out differently, but often referees inferred this regardless.) We also asked for specific subsamples we wished to overrepresent—such as twins, or sibling sets where one or more were homosexual. We began with these references—who were one step removed from us personally—and then branched out from there through the "snowball" method, asking each interviewee if she or he could recommend other sibling sets that might consent to be interviewed. In our initial contacts and in our subsequent snowballing, we attempted to maintain age, class, nativity, race, and geographic comprehensiveness. In other words, if, for example, we had too few sibling sets that had grown up in the western United States, we asked for references to additional potential interviewees who had grown up in that region. Likewise for age, race, and so on. In this manner, we tried to maintain a convenience sample that was spread across social and geographic boundaries. (Thus, in the follow-up referrals, we selected on the independent variables, so to speak.) Ultimately, however, we cannot know the sample's representativeness, and it cannot serve, on its own, to draw inferences about the population distribution of the varied conditions and processes we observe in the sample. We can, however, speculate that the processes we gleaned from the interviews might play important roles in the patterns we find in the large-scale data analysis, but the interview data cannot be interpreted as evidence that the speculation is correct. That is a job for future researchers.

We can take some solace by comparing the demographic profile of the respondents we interviewed to the national population. For example, the respondents that we interviewed are all adults, but represent a wide range of ages. The median age of respondents was 36. This figure is slightly higher than the median age of the entire U.S. population in 2000 (35.3); however, it is by definition younger than the median *adult* population (which is the relevant comparison since I was sampling only adults).[37] A good argument could be made that I should have focused on older individuals, people whose careers and lives have already etched deep grooves. After all, a thirty-five-year-old may still strike it rich, but—with notable historical exceptions—a seventy-year-old is not likely to go back to school, change fields, start a brand-new business, or reinvent him- or herself in any highly dramatic way. So, in many ways the lives of many of the younger respondents presented here are still unwritten (or written in pencil as opposed to pen). However, had I focused exclusively on siblings ages 45 or 50 and over, I would have missed a lot of the dynamics that are particular to the current economy and social landscape. For example, my generation (those born in the late 1960s) is the first to grow up with parental divorce being normal and very common. We are also the children of the postindustrial, service, and information economy. Also, family background and dynamics seem to matter more in the earlier portions of adulthood (like for landing one's first job), which then sets the stage for one's career and life path. So, it is among this group where parents' choices and other family-related influences seem to play out most strongly; in this way, interviewing people still finding their way in life is sort of like catching them in the middle of a dance, adding insight to those processes that may not be as easily gleaned once they are long past.

The sample does not appear drastically different from the U.S. population on other demographic dimensions. Seventy-eight percent of the respondents identified as white, 11.5 percent as black, and 7.4 percent as Asian. We did have an underrepresentation of Latinos—at 3.3 percent.

This may be partly a result of conducting interviews only in English, which excluded a sizable portion of the Latino population from the "snowball." Geographically, 39 percent of respondents grew up in the Northeast, 28 percent in the South, 16 percent in the West, and only 6 percent in the Midwest. ("Other locations"—meaning overseas mostly, as well as a few individuals who moved around continuously during childhood—represented 11 percent of the sample.) So, it appears that we have undersampled Midwesterners and oversampled Northeasterners through our snowball approach, but have got about the right amount of non–native born respondents.[38]

The family sizes of our respondents were also fairly representative. Keeping in mind that we excluded only children, 24 percent came from families with two children; 41 percent from families with three children; 14 percent from families of four kids; 6 percent from families of five; 7 percent from families of six; and 8 percent from families of ten children. (Of course, there are fewer very large families, but we generally interviewed more siblings [though not all] from large families.) The sex distribution was biased moderately toward females: 58 to 42 percent. This is due to the fact that more male siblings refused requests to be interviewed for the study. (Overall, despite more males being born than females, the U.S. population contains more females than males due to higher mortality rates for males. The figures for 2000 were 50.9 percent to 49.1 percent, for females and males, respectively. The bias toward women grows as we move up the age ladder.)[39]

In our sample, 54 percent of mothers did not work regularly while the children were at home. In the General Social Survey data (years 1994, 1996, and 1998), 38 percent of the respondents report that their mothers did not work regularly outside the home (variable: MAWRKGRW)—however, they use a looser standard of "ever work for pay for as long as a year, while you were growing up." Though we may have included more families with nonworking mothers, the class status of the parents in our sample was higher than average for the U.S. population. Nationally, about 34 percent of Americans held managerial or professional occupations in 2000.[40] However, in our sample, 44 percent of the fathers and 26 percent of the mothers who worked regularly held these sorts of jobs.

Likewise, the respondent population was also employed in more prestigious occupations than the national average. Among the sibling respondents, 53 percent held managerial or professional jobs—45 percent of the female respondents and 65 percent of the male siblings.

Interviews lasted approximately two to three hours each and covered a wide variety of topics, most of which are touched upon in this text, but some of which are not—such as the political views of siblings. Interviews were semistructured in nature. There was a set range of topics that needed to be covered, but enough freedom was allowed so that respondents could follow tangents and new topics could emerge.

Sibling Social Circles

Finally, I was interested in the relationship between socioeconomic achievement and sibling social circles. Specifically, I wanted to know whether siblings who knew more people tended to be more successful (regardless of whether the wider social circle was cause or effect of that success). Interest in this question arose halfway through the study when I read Malcolm Gladwell's book, *The Tipping Point: How Little Things Can Make a Big Difference.* As I mention in chapter 7, Gladwell claims that more highly educated, successful individuals generally tend to know more people. However, because there were a number of problems with the way he did his "research" (described below), I wanted to do what he did, in the context of sibling comparisons. I was also interested in how much the social worlds of siblings overlapped or remained separate. In particular, I wanted to know if larger class disparities led to smaller overlaps in the sibling social worlds.

There is no good way to measure the size of someone's social network. There are, however, a lot of mediocre ways. Thus, I chose the mediocre way that best fit my two purposes. (And which matched up to some extent with Gladwell's approach.) That method is called the Reverse Small World (RSW) experiment. In an effort to better understand social networks, in 1978, Ithiel de Sola Pool and Manfred Kochen proposed the RSW experiment—in which a given sample of people were presented with a list of surnames and asked to check which ones they knew personally.[41] This exercise could be done with a specifically chosen list for a target population, or it could be a more randomly selected list from a wider population. It is this general approach that I used to map the overlap of the social networks of the siblings in the study.

I mailed a list of 250 surnames to each of the interviewees. (I would have given them the "test" at the time of interview, but this was a part of the study that was added on after most of the interviews were already completed.) I asked the respondent to put the first initial of someone next to each family name for whom she or he knew an individual personally. If they knew more than one person with that particular last name—and those people were not of the same family—I asked them to put one initial for each person they knew.[42] The requirement was that they know each person independently. So if I knew a Kevin Acosta, for instance, and through him met his cousin Jim Acosta, I should put either *K* or *J* next to Acosta, but not both. But if I knew Kevin from work and Jim from high school and met them completely independently, and they are of no relation, then I would list both initials next to the name Acosta on the survey.

The reason I did not have people just put a check mark was twofold. First, I thought that with certain ethnic groups there might be higher ratios of unrelated people who share last names, and I did not want to penalize these groups' measured network size. For example, a Korean-American independently knowing many Kims is more likely than an Anglo-American knowing multiple independent Johnsons. If the distribution of names had the same flavor (shape) across ethnic groups, the chances of this happening would be randomly distributed, but since certain ethnic groups display greater or lesser concentrations of popular last names, I decided to allow multiple checks. Second, since we wanted to record only those people whom the respondent knew fairly well, I thought that adding the burden of coming up with the first initial raised the bar slightly higher. Thus, respondents could not reason to themselves, "Yes, I think I know a Gonzalez; I'm sure of it." They had to come up with the exact name, first and last, for it to qualify. The exact wording of the instructions was the following—largely taken from Gladwell's text:

> The definition of "know personally" is fairly broad. You do not have to know the person extremely well. Simply, it means that if you ended up sitting next to this person in a public place, you would probably recognize the person and they would know your name, if prompted. So, you have to be able to remember them by face and name, and they have to know you as well. This eliminates people who you know but do not really know you (like celebrities) or know through other people but have never met personally (like friends of friends). This also eliminates people you know quite well but have never met in person—say, for example, someone you have been instant messaging or having a relationship with in an online chat room or other such venue.

In order to test whether or not our respondents were using the right standard, I performed a little trick. In addition to 248 names that were selected using a particular method (to be described below), I snuck in two extra names: "Giuliani" and "Schwarzenegger." These were meant to test whether the respondents were filling in names of celebrities they knew well, but not personally. I chose Rudolph Giuliani and Arnold Schwarzenegger since—at the time of the survey—these were celebrity names that were well known across America. More important, however, they were celebrity last names that are among the most uncommon in the news, media, sports, and so on. I could have picked, for instance, Britney Spears, Bill Clinton, or Michael Jordan. However, each of these last names appears fairly regularly in the general population and thus would not provide the test we were after. Giuliani, on the other hand, only generated 1,048 hits on the public records database at the time we searched it. Schwarzenegger yielded only 26 names. So, while it is still possible that someone knows a Giuliani or "the" Giuliani, it is exponentially less likely that she or he would know a Giuliani *and* a Schwarzenegger. It is still less probable that someone would know personally an R. Giuliani and an A. Schwarzenegger. No one recorded knowing any Schwarzenegger, but two respondents did list an R. Giuliani. Though I can't help but be suspicious, it is possible that they do know the former New York City mayor. Maybe he would recognize the sibling respondents, if, perchance, they sat down next to each other on a commuter train. Maybe.

In any case, while the requirement of first initials may have helped tighten respondents' tendencies to want to inflate their network size by listing vaguely recollected acquaintances, it did not serve to address the possibility of multiple, independently known respondents. This is because it was clear upon entering the results that many people did not read the instructions properly.[43] Some people put only one initial per line; others put many on multiple lines. Almost no one put an extra on just a couple of names. Since it was highly suspicious that someone would know, for example, six "Englishes" completely independently, I followed up by phone with some of the respondents. Indeed, some respondents did not read the instructions carefully and put multiple initials for people from the same family. Another issue that I followed up on by phone was the converse case: when siblings put only one initial for a last name, but they did not match. For example, was "J Bond" listed by one respondent a completely distinct person from the "S Bond" listed by her sibling? Follow-ups showed that this was likely to be two individuals who were known to both respondents. A brother may have listed John Bond, because that was who he was closest with while growing up, while his sister listed Sarah Bond, since she was her best friend. For the spirit of our investigation, I chose to treat these as an overlap, since if asked, "Do you know Sarah Bond?" the brother would respond, "Yes"—likewise for the sister with respect to John Bond. Ultimately, however, there is a trade-off between false overlaps and false independents. Hence, I chose to recode all the first initials into check marks. This errs on the side of false overlaps, minimizing false independents. From follow-up phone debriefings, I found that this would reduce the total misclassified responses.

Aside from Giuliani and Schwarzenegger, the other 248 names were taken from the list of last names in the 1990 U.S. Census. Here is where pilot-testing comes into the picture. Originally, I was modeling this study after the survey that Malcolm Gladwell reports and reproduces in *The Tipping Point*. Gladwell (and his predecessors Pool and Kochen) were interested in a quick, rough way of gauging how "connected" an individual is. In short, he found that older, better-educated, more successful people tended to have higher scores *on average*. But the relevant point was that there were huge ranges. His list came, he claims, from a random selection of names from the New York City telephone book.[44]

Not wanting to bias my results by region or place of residence, I shifted my sampling universe to the entire United States. I began by trying to develop a random list of 248 names that would represent the U.S. population. To do this, I used reverse look-up phone directories online—that is, phone directories where you can type in a number and get a name. So through a process of generating random ten-digit numbers (three for the area code and seven for the main number), I slowly started to compile a list. (Prefixes that yielded non-U.S. numbers were eliminated.) However, this was a slow and tedious process, since the vast majority of ten-digit numbers were misses instead of hits (given that a ten-digit number yields 9,999,999,999 [one shy of 10 billion] possibilities and there are only 325 million people in the United States and many fewer households). For this reason—and because I soon realized that it was biased instead of truly random—I eventually abandoned this approach. (The bias comes in the fact that certain groups are more likely not to have a phone [poor people], or to have an unlisted number [rich or famous people and people who want to stay hidden, such as aliens, deadbeat dads, and so on], or to have multiple phone numbers [rich people or people with home businesses].) Instead, I turned to the 1990 census.

The census bureau provides a list of last names in order of commonality from first to almost last.[45] I say "almost last" since the list ends with 89.9 percent of the population's last name listed and drops off the last 10 percent or so. This is done, I imagine, since the 10 percent of rarest names probably only appear once or so, each. Adding them, therefore, would make the list unmanageably long. The list also provides the relative frequency of each last name. For example, Smith was the most common last name; in fact, 1.1 percent of the population was named Smith. My first stab was to take a weighted random sample of the top 90 percent of names in the United States in 1990.[46] In an ideal world, I would have been able to use the 2000 census results since the ethnic composition—and therefore last name composition—of the population has changed over the intervening decade. Unfortunately, this list is not available and will be some time in coming.

However, the resulting list of names did not have the flavor I was looking for. It did include some common surnames, but relatively rare ones dominated the list. This is a generalizability problem in sampling a relatively small number of cases from a vastly large pool. When I pilot-tested the survey on a few people (who were not part of the sibling study), they knew hardly anyone. (And given the distribution one would expect from such a weighted random selection, I have come to the belief that Gladwell's list cannot be such a random sample from the New York City population [especially since it just "happens" to include Gladwell as one of the names].)

As a solution, I tried the 248 most common names in 1990. This did not work either, since now people knew too many names. Survey fatigue grew and the new pool of trial respondents failed to complete the survey. Eventually, I settled on the 502nd and 504th to 750th most common names in the United States and got reasonable distributions of results. (Name 503 is Conley, and I did not want to give the impression that I was testing a remembrance of or connection to the person conducting the study.)

This is but one of many flawed ways to assess a person's network size. But these flaws should be less troubling for my purposes than they have been for other researchers who are interested in comparing across random individuals, rather than across siblings. For example, ethnic minorities may be disadvantaged by the fact that they know lots of people with say, Persian-sounding last names, but those names are not on this list. They might have large networks concentrated in a few names. If siblings ostensibly belong to the same ethnic group (with the notable exceptions of the multiethnic stepfamilies, half families, and adoptee families I write about), there is reason to expect that their over-all number of "hits" will be biased upward or downward in the same direction. Of course, one sibling may travel in a particular ethnic community more than another through business, marriage, or some other social affiliation. However, since I am principally interested not just in whose network is bigger, but how much overlap there is between siblings, the disjuncture between brothers and sisters on this regard would be very real and legitimate.

Yet another problem is the fact that this may be more of a test of memory than an actual, accurate network appraisal. There is really nothing I can do about this issue. The only real solution to this problem is to deploy a very invasive method of study, such as following a person around for quite some time and recording each person with whom she or he interacts or examining every phone bill, address book, e-mail log, and so on to generate a fairly complete list of social contacts. This, of course, is an unrealistic possibility. Results should be interpreted with this limitation in mind. In other words, what I am actually testing, as it turns out, is not how many people one knows, but how good one is at remembering the names of the people one knows. However, this is not unimportant in its own right. After all, how useful is a social connection if you cannot remember his or her name?

I received surveys back from 71.4 percent (125 out of 175) of the interviewees; the mean number of respondents per family unit was 2.7. Nonrespondents tended to be more male than the responding pool, but did not differ systematically in other ways. I first analyzed whether or not sibling differences in total number of known individuals were associated with sibling differences in socioeconomic success as measured by education level and occupational prestige (using sibling fixed-effects models). They were not related (nor were they related in cross-family models). I then checked whether the extent to which the names that siblings in a given family knew overlapped was associated with the overall spread (standard deviation) in their socioeconomic status. It was not. Thus, the sibling network survey did not validate any hypotheses; however, given the small sample size and the nonrandom sample, I would also be cautious in throwing out these potential associations. Future researchers may want to adopt a sibling comparison approach to examine the relationship between socioeconomic success and network characteristics. In the meantime, you and your friends and family can map your own overlap by filling out the survey yourselves (pages 219–221).

SIBLING SOCIAL NETWORK
OVERLAP SURVEY

_____ Acosta	_____ Bradford	_____ Conway
_____ Anthony	_____ Bradshaw	_____ Dalton
_____ Ashley	_____ Branch	_____ Davenport
_____ Atkinson	_____ Brennan	_____ Decker
_____ Avila	_____ Browning	_____ DeLeon
_____ Ayala	_____ Bruce	_____ Dickerson
_____ Ayers	_____ Buckley	_____ Dodson
_____ Barr	_____ Bullock	_____ Dominguez
_____ Barron	_____ Burnett	_____ Dorsey
_____ Bartlett	_____ Calhoun	_____ Dudley
_____ Bauer	_____ Callahan	_____ Duran
_____ Baxter	_____ Camacho	_____ Durham
_____ Bean	_____ Cameron	_____ Dyer
_____ Beard	_____ Campos	_____ Eaton
_____ Beasley	_____ Carey	_____ Ellison
_____ Benton	_____ Carrillo	_____ English
_____ Best	_____ Chang	_____ Espinoza
_____ Blackburn	_____ Charles	_____ Estes
_____ Blackwell	_____ Chase	_____ Everett
_____ Blanchard	_____ Chen	_____ Farrell
_____ Blankenship	_____ Christian	_____ Finley
_____ Blevins	_____ Clay	_____ Fischer
_____ Bond	_____ Cline	_____ Flynn
_____ Booker	_____ Cochran	_____ Foley
_____ Booth	_____ Combs	_____ Frost
_____ Boyer	_____ Contreras	_____ Gaines

_____ Gallagher   _____ Johns   _____ Mercado

_____ Gallegos   _____ Joyce   _____ Merritt

_____ Garrison   _____ Juarez   _____ Meyers

_____ Gates   _____ Kane   _____ Middleton

_____ Gentry   _____ Keith   _____ Miranda

_____ Giles   _____ Kemp   _____ Molina

_____ Gilmore   _____ Kent   _____ Monroe

_____ Giuliani   _____ Kerr   _____ Montoya

_____ Glass   _____ Kirby   _____ Morrow

_____ Glenn   _____ Kirk   _____ Morse

_____ Golden   _____ Knox   _____ Moses

_____ Grimes   _____ Koch   _____ Mosley

_____ Guerra   _____ Kramer   _____ Mueller

_____ Haley   _____ Landry   _____ Navarro

_____ Hancock   _____ Lang   _____ Nicholson

_____ Hardin   _____ Lara   _____ Nixon

_____ Harding   _____ Larsen   _____ Noble

_____ Harrell   _____ Leach   _____ Nolan

_____ Hartman   _____ LeBlanc   _____ O'Connor

_____ Hatfield   _____ Leon   _____ Olsen

_____ Heath   _____ Lester   _____ O'Neal

_____ Hensley   _____ Livingston   _____ Orr

_____ Henson   _____ Lowery   _____ Pace

_____ Herman   _____ Marks   _____ Pacheco

_____ Herring   _____ Marquez   _____ Parrish

_____ Hess   _____ Mathews   _____ Patel

_____ Hickman   _____ Maynard   _____ Pennington

_____ Hobbs   _____ McCall   _____ Petersen

_____ Hodge   _____ McClain   _____ Pitts

_____ Hood   _____ McClure   _____ Preston

_____ Hoover   _____ McConnell   _____ Prince

_____ Horn   _____ McCullough   _____ Pruitt

_____ House   _____ McDowell   _____ Pugh

_____ Huffman   _____ McIntosh   _____ Randall

_____ Hull   _____ McKee   _____ Randolph

_____ Humphrey   _____ McLean   _____ Rich

_____ Hurst   _____ Mejia   _____ Richard

_____ Hutchinson   _____ Melton   _____ Rivas

_____ Rivers

_____ Robles

_____ Rojas

_____ Roman

_____ Roth

_____ Rush

_____ Salinas

_____ Savage

_____ Sawyer

_____ Schroeder

_____ Schwarzenegger

_____ Sellers

_____ Serrano

_____ Sexton

_____ Shaffer

_____ Shannon

_____ Shepherd

_____ Sheppard

_____ Shields

_____ Short

_____ Skinner

_____ Sloan

_____ Small

_____ Snow

_____ Solis

_____ Solomon

_____ Spears

_____ Stafford

_____ Stephenson

_____ Strong

_____ Sweeney

_____ Tanner

_____ Trevino

_____ Trujillo

_____ Vance

_____ Vazquez

_____ Velasquez

_____ Velez

_____ Villarreal

_____ Vincent

_____ Wall

_____ Walls

_____ Walter

_____ Ware

_____ Weeks

_____ Weiss

_____ Whitaker

_____ Whitehead

_____ Wiggins

_____ Wiley

_____ Wilkinson

_____ William

_____ Winters

_____ Wolf

_____ Woodard

_____ Woodward

_____ Wyatt

_____ York

NOTES

ONE *Inequality Starts at Home*

1. David Maraniss, *First in His Class: The Biography of Bill Clinton* (New York: Simon and Schuster, 1995), p. 424.

2. Ibid.

3. This is represented by $1 - R^2_S$ (where R^2 is the square of the sibling correlation coefficient in log-income). Mary Corcoran, Roger Gordon, Deborah Laren, and Gary Solon estimate a brother-brother correlation in *permanent* income of .45 using data from the Panel Study of Income Dynamics. See page 364 of their "Effects of Family and Community Background on Economic Status," *American Economic Review* 80 (1990): 362–66. Their estimates for women's sibling correlations in family income is .276 and .534 for men's log-earnings. (Gary Solon, Mary Corcoran, Roger Gordon, and Deborah Laren, "A Longitudinal Analysis of Sibling Correlation in Economic Status," *Journal of Human Resources* 26 [1992]: 509–34.) Sibling resemblance for other outcomes like welfare usage, education, and occupation follow similar patterns and are sensitive to the specification deployed—particularly for nonlinear measures. For example, if a woman's sister has received welfare, she is over three times more likely to use it herself (.66 versus .20 probability in their PSID sample). Differences for "persistent participation" in welfare programs by sibling welfare status are even greater. When I reanalyze more recent waves of PSID data—in which the siblings are on average older and more stable economically—I find that the sibling correlation has not changed much overall, but notably for sisters (see Dalton Conley, "Sibling Correlations in Socio-Economic Status: Results on Education, Occupation, Income and Wealth," working paper, Center for Advanced Social Science Research, New York University, 2003). The

sibling correlation is .449 for the natural logarithm of brothers' income-to-needs ratio (slightly lower for log-income); for sisters the correlation in log-income-to-needs is .555. (It is .517 for all siblings). For sisters the total (logged) family income correlation (as contrasted to the logged income-to-needs ratio) is .508, significantly higher than the figure of .276 reported by Solon, Corcoran, Gordon, and Laren in their "A Longitudinal Analysis."

4. For the natural logarithm of total net worth (i.e., accumulated wealth minus debts), sibling correlations are .224 for all siblings, .239 for brothers, and .271 for sisters (Conley, "Sibling Correlations"). In this analysis, those with negative or zero net worth are set to zero on the log scale. This approach yields the *highest* sibling correlation between randomly selected adult siblings in the 2001 wave of the PSID. Correlations are not much different for other recent waves.

5. These probabilities come from table 4 in Solon, Corcoran, Gordon, and Laren, "A Longitudinal Analysis," 526.

6. The actual figure is a .48 probability that a randomly selected sibling of an individual who graduated from a four-year college will not have graduated. This result comes from analysis of the 2001 wave of the Panel of Income Dynamics (see Conley, "Sibling Correlations"). Daphne Kuo and Robert Hauser analyze the Occupational Changes in a Generation (OCG) survey data and find that for education, sibling differences (within-family variance components) for various age groups of black and white brothers range between 38 percent and 52 percent. (See Kuo and Hauser, "Trends in the Family Effects on the Education of Black and White Brothers," *Sociology of Education* 68 [1995]: 136–60.) In the PSID, I find a lower degree of sibling resemblance in education level (measured as a continuous variable from 1 to 17 years of schooling). The correlation coefficient for siblings in the 2001 wave is .429. For brothers it is .529, and for sisters it is .400. These correlations, when squared, imply a less robust within-family component than found by Kuo and Hauser. Likewise, one-quarter of sibling pairs in the Study of American Families diverge substantially in terms of the prestige of their jobs. ("Substantial" means the difference between a professional such as a lawyer or businessman, on the one hand, and a salesclerk or blue-collar worker on the other.) In the PSID, the sibling correlation in 2001 occupational prestige is only .225 for sisters, .302 for brothers, and .233 for all siblings (Conley, "Sibling Correlations").

7. These results come from analysis of the Study of American Families.

8. These data come from the GSS-SAF survey. People may be more likely to explain others' relative success with outside social factors than individual attributes in order to lessen the taste of the sour grapes.

9. It is generally said that siblings (other than identical twins) share 50 percent of their genes (the same degree of similarity as with their respective parents); however, this is only true if parents were randomly assigned to mate with each other. The reality is that there is a process called assortative mating where reproductive mates select each other based on traits that have some sort of genetic basis. This assortative mating can result in a lower than 50 percent genetic similarity among siblings if "opposites attract." More likely, however, it results in a greater than 50 percent similarity since parents are positively matched on attributes and thus are contributing some of the "same" genes to their offspring, reducing the variability and increasing the similarity between their children (and themselves). These issues will be discussed in greater detail in the sections that follow.

10. The actual figures were 25 percent discrepancy for mother's year of birth and 26 percent for father's year of birth; these and preceding figures come from analysis of the Study of American Families data linked to the 1994 General Social Survey, which are described in this chapter and in the appendix. These discrepancies do not seem to be statistically related to discrepancies in how the siblings turn out class-wise, their respective sexes, or even their age differences. All siblings are full siblings.

11. This transition has been noted as early as 1971 by Alain Touraine in *The Post-Industrial Society; Tomorrow's Social History: Classes, Conflicts and Culture in the Programmed Society* (New York: Random House, 1971).

12. There is, of course, a certain degree of attrition. Families have also been added through relationships to the original households and through a new "corrective" sample of Latinos and other new immigrant populations.

13. Americans do not give much conscious thought to class in our public discourse—at least as compared to other developed nations. For example, there is no U.S. Labor Party advocating explicitly for the "working" man and woman. Class, class politics, and class warfare are dirty words in American politics, though sometimes race acts as a stand-in for class. Yet, for all our conscious disregard of the notion, class informs our every social interaction. Every time we meet someone new, we are engaged in a semiconscious evaluation of class standing. Is this person a snob? Are they tacky? Most importantly, class impacts our family life in invisible ways—generating sibling differences along the way. How we feel about class with respect to our own siblings is particularly important, since they represent us to the world, and they are the people with whom we spend our entire childhood in competition; they are our reference group, so to speak. Never does this become as explicit as when we are

bringing a new romantic interest home to dinner: suddenly small class differences may seem like enormously unbridgeable chasms.

14. See Conley, "Sibling Correlations"—these results are based on coefficients from sibling regressions of likelihood of having graduated from a four-year college from the 2001 wave of the PSID. The difference in the coefficients is significant at $P < .05$ (one-tailed test). (Results are similar for other maternal educational splits, like "some college" or "high school graduate.") In other words, if a kid from a lower-class family makes it, it usually implies that she or he is "leaving his family behind."

15. If a 2001 PSID non-black sibling graduated from college, the probability that his/her randomly selected brother/sister also graduated was .574. If a 2001 PSID black sibling finished a four-year college, the chances that his/her randomly selected brother/sister also did was only .210. This difference is significant at $P < .05$. This is only partially due to the lower overall odds that African-Americans complete a four-year college degree (see Conley, "Sibling Correlations").

16. The regression coefficient for a sibling's occupational prestige on one's own occupational prestige in the 2001 wave of the PSID was .195 for non-blacks; for blacks it was .081; for college completion the parameter estimates from linear probability models were .327 and .151, for non-blacks and blacks, respectively. See Conley, "Sibling Correlations." At least as far back as 1967, researchers have observed that the strength of family background was weaker for African-Americans compared with whites. Peter Blau and Otis Dudley Duncan described a dynamic of "perverse equality" where—no matter what the class background of a black respondent—he was most likely to end up in the bottom of the occupational distribution. Those who did make it up the ranks seemed to do so through "tokenism" at that time, since predictor variables that had stronger influences for whites did not seem to make as much of a difference for blacks. In other words, who succeeded and who did not seemed fairly random—at least with respect to family background. Such a phenomenon would generate sibling differences. See Peter Blau and Otis Dudley Duncan, *The American Occupational Structure* (New York: Wiley, 1967).

17. The codebook of the General Social Survey (appendix G) reports:

The prestige scores assigned to occupations in this study were taken from rating systems developed at NORC in 1963–1965 in a project on occupation prestige directed by Robert W. Hodge, Paul S. Siegel, and Peter H. Rossi and updated on the 1989 GSS. The 1989 update scale was prepared by Robert W. Hodge, Judith Treas, and Keiko Nakao. This concept of prestige is defined as the respondents' estimation of the social standing of occupations. The prestige scores in the Hodge-Siegel-Rossi and GSS studies were generated by asking respondents to estimate the social standing of occupations via a nine-step ladder, printed on cardboard and presented to the respondent. The boxes on the ladder were numbered 1–9 from bottom to top. In addition, the first, fifth, and ninth boxes were labeled "bottom," "middle," and "top," respectively. The occupational titles were printed on small cards and the occupational prestige ratings were collected by requesting respondents to sort the cards into boxes formed by the rungs of the ladder.

Paul S. Siegel, "Prestige in the American Occupational Structure" (Ph.D. dissertation, Department of Sociology, University of Chicago, March 1971), available from Photoduplication Department, University of Chicago Libraries, Chicago, 60637. Other occupational scales have been recommended, such as the Duncan SEI index (Socioeconomic Index of Occupations); see Keiko Nakao, Robert W. Hodge, and Judith Treas, "On Revising Prestige Scores for All Occupations," *GSS Methodological Report* 69 (Chicago: NORC, 1990), and Keiko Nakao and Judith Treas, "Computing 1989 Occupational Prestige Scores," *GSS Methodological Report* 70 (Chicago: NORC, 1990). Most recently, Robert Hauser and John Robert Warren suggest an approach that uses the educational distribution across occupations to construct prestige indices. (See, e.g., Robert M. Hauser and John Robert Warren, "Socioeconomic Indexes for Occupations: A Review, Update and Critique," *Sociological Methodology* 27 [1997]: 177–298.)

18. For the cross-society correlation between prestige rankings, see Donald J. Trieman, *Occupational Prestige in Comparative Perspective* (New York: Academic Press, 1977), and Donald J. Trieman, "Problems of Concept and Measurement in the Comparative Study of Occupational Mobility," *Social Science Research* 4 (1975): 183–230.

19. We must also keep in mind that Harris is talking about personality and speech patterns; we are talking about socioeconomic success.

20. Despite the organizational complexity and ever-changing nature of the family, there are some recognizable patterns. Let us take the question of which siblings resemble one another the most. One hypothesis is that younger siblings most resemble their eldest brother or sister. Let us call this the "leader" theory of sibling relations: the eldest as role model. The countervailing theory

would posit that those who are proximate to each other resemble each other most strongly. This might be because they socialize with each other more than they do with siblings more distant in age; or it may be a result of experiencing a more similar family environment overall and experiencing demographic and economic transitions at more similar moments in the course of their development. Whatever the ultimate reason, it turns out that siblings who are more proximate in their birth positions experience more equal investments by their parents and more similar educational outcomes (not controlling for age, gender, or other attributes).

For example, my analysis of the census shows that in a three-sibling family, if the eldest goes to private school, the last born is 29 times more likely to go to private school than in families where the eldest did not. That is a large difference. But if the middle child goes to private school, the third is 77 times more likely to go also, as compared to a family where the middle child did not attend private school. The same pattern holds true in four-sibling families. The last born is 26 times more likely to go to private school if the firstborn went. But she or he is 55 times more likely if the secondborn went and 113 times more likely if the thirdborn went. In looking at other combinations of siblings the same pattern bears out: the most proximate siblings are the most similar in terms of parental investment.

The same is true for educational performance. If the eldest was held back in school, then the thirdborn is 8 times more likely to lag behind his peers. However, if the middle child is held back, the chances increase 41-fold for the thirdborn. Results are no different for dropping out of school. When the firstborn drops out, the thirdborn is 7 times more likely to quit school as well; when the secondborn drops out, the thirdborn is 36 times as likely to drop out. This same pattern holds for four-sibling families. (I specifically said educational "outcomes" since parental investment in private schooling displays a slightly larger similarity between the first and second siblings of four-sibling families than among the second and third—only when I do not hold constant the private schooling status of the other siblings [i.e., siblings three and four in the first instance and siblings one and four in the latter case].)

Thus, the "leader" theory goes down in flames. But, as always, how we read these results is another story. The interpretation that siblings close together experience changing family conditions, transitions, and so on more similarly is certainly plausible and probably explains a part of these observed differences. However, the enormous magnitude of the difference in similarities between the various siblings on all three outcomes suggests that this is probably only a small part of the story. Most families simply do not change that dramatically to generate such large differences in such a systematic manner (i.e., always in the same direction). Rather, it would appear that siblings' cross-socialization explains most of this story. This interpretation is supported by the fact that sibling effects on educational outcomes get stronger in the middle of the sibling packs—the more siblings are surrounded by one another and less influenced directly by parents. For example, in three-sibling families, the strongest similarities are between the second and third siblings. The effect of the second being held back on the third also suffering this fate is at least three times as large as the effect of the first on the second. For dropping out, the difference in sibling resemblance is at least twofold. Likewise, in four-sibling families the most powerful similarities in educational outcomes are between the second and third siblings. The effects of parents get weaker (and the effects of siblings increase) when kids are surrounded by kids on either side. Firstborns (and last borns in large families) get to experience some of their childhoods as only children. Those stuck in the middle are influenced by siblings coming and going. This is something we will return to in chapter 3.

21. The figure rises to four in five births being out of wedlock for teen mothers. See *Childtrends: Facts at a Glance,* http://www.childtrends.org/PDF/FAAG2002.pdf (July 6, 2003).

22. S. C. Clark, "Advance Report of Final Divorce Statistics, 1989 and 1990," *Monthly Vital Statistics Report,* vol. 43, no. 8, suppl. (Hyattsville, MD: National Center for Health Statistics, 1995). National Center for Health Statistics, "Advance Report of Final Divorce Statistics, 1985," *Monthly Vital Statistics Report,* vol. 36, no. 8, suppl. DHHS Pub. No. (PHS) 88-1120 (Hyattsville, MD: Public Health Service, 1987).

23. Kathy Stilley, "Statistics in Adoption in the United States," *The Future of Children,* 1993. (Keep in mind that average family size has been decreasing during this period but that the overall size of the U.S. population has increased.)

24. See Dalton Conley and Neil G. Bennett, "Is Biology Destiny? Birth Weight and Life Chances," *American Sociological Review* 65 (2000): 458–67.

25. Fashion provides an apt metaphor. If a female friend asked you in 1970 what she needed to do to be in fashion, to look like a winner, you might have told her to get herself a pair of bell-bottom jeans, tall boots, and a pair of round, Janis Joplin–style sunglasses. Of course, if she wrote this down as gospel and used it as her guide, it might have the exact opposite effect in, say, 1982. If she realized this and came back to you for help, you might tell her to

get herself a headband and a pair of leggings. A few years later the advice might be to buy a sports jacket with big puffy shoulder pads. (I shudder whenever I look at my own high school yearbook picture—think Miami Vice.) You get the picture; there is no simple set of fashion instructions that will be durable for longer than a year or so. So if you were not going to see this person for twenty years and wanted to impart fashion wisdom, what would it be? It would probably not be anything specific to wear or not wear. It might consist of a set of strategies for figuring out what is in fashion: Look at particular magazines (though they, too, may go in and out of style); watch television; look at what the stars are wearing (though you could not name particular stars since they come and go, too); try to mimic the rich (though often fashion innovations come from the "bottom" up). You would probably do okay copying what the socioeconomic elite wear; but you would hardly be on the cutting edge.

Fashion follows its own logic and the hippest of the hip can come from all walks of life; what makes them hip is their position in the "cool" hierarchy (which has some—but by no means a complete—relation to other status dimensions). One year it might be the surfer subculture that defines what's in. Another year it might be rappers. In short, you could help your friend out by telling her to wear what successful people in her field wear, but that will only get her so far. You cannot tell her how to be cutting edge, since not only do the answers to the questions change over time, the very rules of the game (and the contestants) change, too. This metaphor can be extended to academic and economic success. Telling someone to read to his or her kids is probably a pretty good bet, but which books to read may change over the years (some classic children's stories are now considered racist, for example, or scientifically misleading). (I recently learned this lesson when I insisted to my son that a particular dinosaur in a kids' book was a brontosaurus. "No, apatosaurus," he countered. "See, it says brontosaurus right here," I insisted, pointing to a word in the book. Of course, I could have been pointing to anything since he could not read yet. It turns out that he was right; the book and I were wrong.) It may even be the case that time they spend on an interactive, educational computer game might be better spent than time you spend teaching your young child to read.

Today we speak of a digital divide. Some congressmen want to put a computer in every classroom and every home. The access to information that connectivity provides is seen as critical to the education of children in a high-tech era. But anyone who watches how a teenager actually uses a computer might become a bit suspicious of this view. Sure the family encyclopedia (once the symbol of parental investment in a child's education among working-class families) may have become obsolete with the arrival of the Internet. However, the Internet also makes it easier to plagiarize or to get bad information. Kids who are online are also probably spending a lot more time instant messenging their friends or downloading music (or more naughty stuff) from the World Wide Web. The kid with the beat-up copy of *Encyclopedia Britannica* may be better off than the kid with Google at her fingertips. In fact, getting kids *offline* may be a major educational challenge of the coming years. As access to an advantageous technology broadens out, its nature and uses also change.

We all now take for granted that television is not generally good for kids in anything more than very small doses. This was not always the prevailing view, however. In fact, back in the 1960s many left-leaning academics and analysts were arguing that there was a digital divide of sorts with respect to television. They made arguments that television could provide the intellectual stimulation that was lacking in many households where the parents were less educated themselves. This was the social welfare argument for the creation and funding of public television in general and children's educational television in particular.

When we read this analysis thirty-odd years later, the instinct is to chuckle to ourselves: how naïve we must have been back then! It would seem that researchers of past decades were woefully misinformed about what is good for kids. Decades of research ranging from long-term follow-up surveys to brain-imaging studies of kids watching cartoons have shown that, in fact, television is *detrimental* to children's intellectual development. Though researchers acknowledge that some television is better than other television (for instance, the public television that researchers were arguing for is superior to commercial television), most developmental psychologists, sociologists, and the like would concur that time spent watching television is better spent doing another activity—whether reading, structured learning, or even free play. However, it may be the case that while television *is* bad today it *was not* bad then. It is not that television has deteriorated in quality—though that may be true too (alas, where has *Schoolhouse Rock* gone?)—rather that we know better and the options have changed as the social landscape has changed.

Another example is the consumption of red meat. During the 1960s, poor people ate better than rich people, by today's standards. They ate more legumes and starches and vegetables and less fatty meat (due to the prohibitive price of meat). However, today the class-diet gradient has been turned completely upside down. Is it that meat has become more accessible to everyone by virtue of a drop in prices? Or is it simply that when it started to become known that red meat is bad for you, more highly educated people were able to take advantage of this new information to a greater degree than less educated people? Another case is that of smoking. Before 1956, the dangers of smoking may have been suspected in some quarters, but they had not been established as "fact." With the issuance of the first Surgeon General's warning of cigarettes' ill effects in 1956, suddenly a strong gradient emerged in smoking patterns. Smoking rates went down more drastically among the highly educated than they did among the less well educated. Suddenly, smoking displayed a class gradient as a result of this new information. It seems all improvements in knowledge result in a gradient of some sort. For a discussion of this "fundamental cause" phenomenon as it relates to health status in particular, see B. Link, M. Northridge, J. Phelna, and M. Ganz, "Social Epidemiology and the Fundamental Causes Concept: On the Structuring of Effective Cancer Screens by Socioeconomic Status," *Milbank Quarterly* 76 (1998): 375–402.

TWO   *Butterflies in Bialystok, Meteors in Manila*

1. Their father remained in Poland, but the twins insist that nothing is wrong in their parents' marriage and that they are still close to their father. So far, however, only Jacek has returned to their homeland to visit their dad.

2. The separation of family from politics and economics is not particularly American or particularly new. Liberal philosophers concerned with issues of redistribution and justice have taken the family as a given—having its own innate, separate rules of fairness and equality (see, e.g., John Rawls, *A Theory of Justice* [Cambridge, MA: Harvard University Press, 1972], and Michael Walzer, *Spheres of Justice* [New York: Basic Books, 1984]). Even the radical political economy of Karl Marx has been critiqued for taking the family as prepolitical (see Jacqueline Stevens, *Reproducing the State* [Princeton, NJ: Princeton University Press, 1999]).

3. Genetically identical, or monozygotic, twins occur in about 3.5 per 1,000 births (or 1 in 285 births). This rate is generally assumed to be universal and random since it holds constant across race, ethnicity, and geography ("Odds of Multiples," HTML document available at http://www.childbirthsolutions. com/articles/pregnancy/oddmulti/index.php [August 7, 2003]). Also see http:// mypage.direct.ca/c/csamson/multiples/twinbasics2.html and R. Bortolus, F. Pa-

razzini, L. Chatenoud, G. Benzi, M. Bianchi, and A. Marini, "The Epidemiology of Multiple Births," *Human Reproduction Update* 5(2) (1999): 179–87. However, one's chances of having identical twins does increase at younger and older ages, so some have hypothesized that the likelihood of identical twins may be dependent on hormonal imbalances seen at these ages (although the factors affecting identical twinning are generally very poorly understood—National Organization of Mothers of Twins Clubs, "Twinning Facts," HTML document available at http://www.nomotc.org/library/twinning_facts.html [July 8, 2003]).

The occurrence of fraternal, or dizygotic, twins, on the other hand, is not so universal or random and varies systematically by several factors. For instance, there is sizable variation in rates of twins across nations. Japan has a very low rate of twins with only about 6 per 1,000 births being fraternal twins (or 1 in 166). Meanwhile, Nigeria has a strikingly high rate of twins with 45 per 1,000 births being fraternal twins (or 1 in 22). The United States lies in between these two countries with about 11 of 1,000 births being fraternal twins (or 1 in 90) ("Odds of Multiples"). Further, as we might expect based on such variations, twin rates also vary significantly by race and ethnicity. White rates of twin births are often significantly lower (1 in 69 births) than black rates of twin births (as high as 1 in 40 births) (although this difference is becoming increasingly small in the United States with the increased use of infertility treatments among whites). However, rates of twin births among Asian groups tend to be even lower than those for white groups. For individuals of Japanese descent about 1 in 150 births are twins, while for individuals of Chinese descent about 1 in 250 births are twins ("Odds of Multiples").

The likelihood that a woman will give birth to fraternal twins varies by several additional factors as well. For instance, one's chances of having fraternal twins increase with maternal height and weight, with younger ages at first menstruation, and with shorter menstrual cycles (National Organization of Mothers of Twins Clubs, "Twinning Facts"). One of the most important recent factors affecting the chances of twin births, however, is a marked increase in the use of infertility treatments, particularly among older, middle-class, and white women. Largely as a result of infertility treatments, we are witnessing sizable shifts in the epidemiology of multiple births. Overall, the number of twins in the United States has increased from 90,118 to 104,137 in the short time from 1989 to 1997 (J. Martin and M. Park, "Trends in Twin and Triplet Births: 1980–97," *National Vital Statistics Report* 47[24] [National Center for Health Statistics, U.S. Department of Health and Human Services, 1999]). The majority of this increase appears to result from an increase in the rates of twin births among older women—that is, those women who are more likely to use infertility treatments. Between 1980 and 1997, the twin birthrate rose 63 percent for women forty to forty-four years of age, and 1,000 percent for women forty-five to forty-nine years of age. Indeed, there were more twins born to women ages forty-five to forty-nine in the single year of 1997 than during the entire decade of the 1980s ("Multiple Birth Rate for Older Women Is Sky Rocketing," news release, September 14, 1999, HTML document available at http://www.cdc.gov/nchs/releases/99facts/multiple.htm [July 6, 2003]). These changes in rates of twin births have further almost eliminated the traditional difference in twin rates between whites and blacks in the United States. Because white women are more likely than black women to delay childbearing and to seek fertility treatments, whites' rates of twins are quickly approaching blacks' rates. In 1997, 28.8 of 1,000 births to white women were twins, while 30.0 of 1,000 births to black women were twins (Martin and Park, "Trends").

4. Even if this were not true, we would still have to assume that the families into which these split twins were placed were not atypical in any way—that is, that they might as well have been randomly selected. Such an assumption is not likely to be true. In order for a real twin experiment to work, each sibling would need to be randomly assigned to a family. Furthermore, the receiving families could not choose whether to accept them or not. They must be randomly assigned, too. That is because it could be the case that families that tend to take in adoptees are special in some way—say more compassionate, loving, and altruistic, or just infertile—and it is these characteristics that make twins reared apart actually experience similar environments. To add another layer of complexity to this experiment, the twins themselves would have to not know that they were special in any way. In other words, they should not be told that they are one-half of a twin set, that they are adopted, that they are participating in an experiment, and so forth. They cannot be allowed to figure this out themselves—by say, placing a blue-eyed, red-haired baby with an African-American family (or vice versa). Furthermore, the parents cannot know that they are raising an adopted child either. This is because parent-adoptee relationships might be systematically different from biological family ties in a way that generates environmental similarities between the separated siblings. In short, such a twin experiment would be impossible.

5. Elisa Gootman, "Separated at Birth in Mexico, Reunited at Campuses on L.I.," *New York Times,* March 3, 2003: A1.

6. Judith Harris, *The Nurture Assumption* (New York: Free Press, 1998), pp. 33–34.

7. In fact, those who *do* get reunited must have more direct or indirect social connections to each other than those who never find their other "half" and than those who never even know they have a twin out there somewhere. After all, how did the twins from Trinidad and Germany get together if the family did not have some contact all along?

8. A better strategy might be to make a list of one hundred traits (before we meet our twin) and then see how we match up. The traits could be anything: body tattoos, having a pet bird, cigarette brand, and so on. You get the picture. Essentially, researchers need to play a game of twenty questions.

9. Lawrence F. Katz and David H. Autor, "Changes in the Wage Structure and Earnings Inequality," in O. Ashenfelter and D. Card, eds., *Handbook of Labor Economics,* vol. 3A (New York: Elsevier Science, North-Holland, 1999), pp. 1463–555. Philip Trostel, Ian Walker, and Paul Woolley, "Estimates of the Economic Return to Schooling for 28 Countries," *Labour Economics* 9 (2002): 1–16.

10. See Phillip Cook and Robert Frank, *The Winner-Take-All Society* (New York: Free Press, 1995).

11. The "about" 50 percent shared genes comes from the fact that there is most likely positive assortative mating going on with respect to most characteristics with which we might be concerned. There may be cases in which there is negative assortative mating occurring in our population, and these would actually lower the genetic correlation between nonidentical twin siblings below 50 percent for a given trait. For example, it could be the case that aggressive personalities are attracted to passive ones. Assuming that aggressiveness was a genetically related trait, we would then observe a less than 50 percent genetic similarity between nonidentical twin siblings.

12. Expressed mathematically the heritability is estimated as $H^2 = 2 * (r_{mz} - r_{dz})$ where r_{mz} is the correlation between monozygotic twins and r_{dz} is the correlation between dizygotic twins.

13. Behavioral geneticists are aware of this problem of special "twinness" and try to take into account how similarly twins are treated. This is called the problem of genetic-environmental (GE) covariance. How much do genetic similarity and environmental similarity go hand in hand? And how do they affect each other (additively, multiplicatively, et cetera)? The truth is, no one knows, and thus the structural models estimating heritability are under-identified. Behavioral geneticists have also tried to deal with the issue of assor-

tative mating raised in earlier notes. The mating problem is much more straightforward, since you can more likely measure the degree to which parents match on the relevant characteristics (though how much of that match is due to environmental similarity and how much is due to their genetic similarity is a trickier question). At least one study tries to avoid the entire issue of twin "specialness"—that is, by not comparing identical and fraternal twins but instead focusing on the children of twin brothers (i.e., cousins). Some of these cousins are sons of brothers who were identical twins and therefore share 25 percent of their genes. Others are children of fraternal twin brothers and thus share approximately 12.5 percent of their genes. They find that the children of identical twin brothers have much more similar incomes than the children of fraternal twin brothers. This approach attempts to sidestep the special status of the identical twins themselves, but it does not take into account the spillover effects of twin status on childrearing. For example, identical twins are more likely to live in close proximity, to see each other (and each other's children) more often, and, therefore, these cousins are more likely to share key environmental characteristics.

For example, a future researcher comparing the children of Amy and Abby might attribute their similarities to the fact that they share 12.5 percentage points more genes than typical cousins; but we cannot really know whether that extra few percentage points of genetic similarity is what matters. By contrast, what really counts might be having been raised by these two sisters who endured such a unique experience together—an experience that has shaped their views of family, parenting, and so on—plus the fact that they still see each other a few times a week.

A possibly stronger case for genetic effects on socioeconomic success is made by studies that exploit natural experiments of a sort. For example, with the advent of DNA identification, we can now—with maximal certainty—distinguish identical twins from fraternal ones. Some parents, it turns out, misclassify their fraternal twins as identical, and thus rear them as such. Others, more remarkably, mistake their identical twins for fraternal ones. It is these cases of misclassification that are the interesting ones. If those who are mistakenly thought to be identical are more different than those who are wrongly thought to be fraternal, then genetics matters more than environment for that given trait. Likewise, if kids raised as identical turn out more similar than those raised as fraternal when the genetic truth is the opposite, then this might imply that the label is more important than the genes.

As it turns out, however, parental classification and misclassification of twins is not a black-and-white issue. I interviewed one set of parents who had a bet with each other as to whether their boys were monozygotic or dizygotic. They could not tell from the architecture of the placenta. (In some cases, fraternal twins have very distinct placentas, making it obvious that they are fraternal. In other cases, they share a placental mass and cannot be distinguished from identical twins on this basis.)

"I think they are fraternal since they act so differently and since one is really skinny and the other is chubby."

(Even birth size can vary substantially among identical twins based on who enjoyed a better position with respect to the placenta.)

Her husband disagreed. "They are exactly the same, I think," he explained. "These differences are how they carve out their own niche."

They had DNA testing performed to satisfy their curiosity and resolve their bet. It turned out that he was right. They were identical, despite the fact that at age six, one weighed forty-five pounds and the other a whopping sixty-eight. The question of whether these kids were misclassified or correctly classified depends on which parent you survey. The kids illustrate another point, which is that in some cases twinness leads to deliberate sibling difference in an effort to shed the stigmatizing label of twin. So we may find that the misclassified identical twins end up more similar than the misclassified fraternal twins only because the "identically" reared fraternal twins reacted to their labeling as identical by differentiating themselves.

14. A brief exchange with one set of twin sisters illustrates this point:

"Are you the San Francisco singing twins?" I asked two elegant silver-haired women seated in front of me on a red-eye flight from California late one evening.

"Oh, no, we're the United Airlines twins."

"Oh, I see," I responded, nodding slowly, in the way that I usually did when people dropped the name of books I was expected to have read but had not.

"Yes," one answered. "We do like to dress the same, and we do work the same flights, but we are both married to men who are not brothers. We live in Monterey, California."

I had noticed their matching black velvet hair bows, their identical dresses, and the fact that each wore the same watch, albeit on opposite wrists. Their answers were clearly scripted; they obviously got questioned a lot. They seemed to relish their unique (albeit shared) identity as the United Airlines twins. Their respective experiences of the social world were quite similar due to the very fact of their twinness. In fact, they volunteered that they were not married to brothers. In other words, we should not draw definite conclusions about the impact of nature and nurture on the rest of us from their rather atypical lives.

15. In some societies the special role of twins is made even more explicit. Among the Yoruba people of West Africa, for example, twins are more common than in many other societies (45 births out of each 1,000, about four times the U.S. rate). They worship a twin god of twins, Ibeji, and greet the birth of twins with celebration since they are said to portend good fortune if cared for properly. Some other African societies view twins (and other atypical births) as having a special connection to deceased ancestors. For a review of how anthropologists have viewed the roles of twins in various African societies, see Susan Diduk, "Twins, Ancestors and Socio-Economic Change in Kedjom Society," *Man, New Series* 28, no. 3 (Sept. 1993): 551–71.

16. Since I did not perform DNA blood assays on any of the subjects, I call them identical because they appear identical and refer to themselves as such. None of the cases I discuss as identical had any doubts about their zygosity if asked.

17. Skin color, hair color, and eye color all vary within families, and so would be "detected" by the methods used by behavioral geneticists. But if race, for example, followed a more caste-like logic—as some argue that it does here in the United States—and did not vary within families, then it would yield no genetic heritability component using the methods of MZ and DZ twin comparisons yet would be completely hereditary.

18. We could try to measure ability, parental resources, and anything else that might affect both schooling and wages, and then compare individuals who were the same on all these characteristics. Ultimately, though, this would be futile, since we could never capture all of the possible traits that might influence both education and income, and the ones we do capture, we tend to measure with a lot of error. (For instance, how do you quantify "knowing how to work the system"?) Just as in the case of understanding the influence of genes through twins separated at birth, what we would ideally want is an experiment where we could randomly assign kids to different levels of schooling and see how they turned out. We could secretly admit fifty kids with poor scores to Harvard and reject fifty who would have gotten in (and then follow both groups). Too bad Soviet-style education systems have gone out of fashion lately and too bad for research ethics.

19. As far back as the 1930s, economists began attempting to address this

issue by comparing siblings as a sort of natural experiment (see Joshua D. Angrist and Alan B. Krueger, "Instrumental Variables and the Search for Identification: From Supply and Demand to Natural Experiment," *Journal of Economic Perspectives* 15 [2001]: 69–85). Since siblings should be more similar on factors such as intelligence or motivation (which are usually notoriously difficult to pinpoint and measure) than unrelated individuals, relating differences in siblings' earnings to differences in their education levels has frequently been assumed to factor out unobserved differences that would artificially inflate estimates of how much additional schooling raises earnings. However, environmental and genetic differences between siblings can still be sizable. As a result, more than a few researchers have proposed stricter models of twin—particularly identical twin—comparisons.

20. The "special" social status of twins—which was a thorn in the side of the genetic psychologists—plays right into the economists' strategy, since it makes unmeasured environmental influences on the twins likely to be more similar. However, despite the apparent strictness of such comparisons, estimates based on twins have been controversial. Early estimates from Ashenfelter and Krueger, for instance, found that twin estimates yielded *larger* returns from education than OLS estimates, challenging the assumption that earlier estimates were upwardly biased. (O. Ashenfelter and A. Krueger, "Estimates of the Economic Returns to Schooling from a New Sample of Twins," *American Economic Review* 84 [1994]: 1157–73.) This surprising initial result, however, began a debate about the possibility of upward bias resulting from endogenous heterogeneity in twin comparisons. This finding was later revised (once further data became available) and these early results are now generally assumed to be at least partially the result of an odd sample (for a review of this work, see J. Bound and G. Solon, "Double Trouble: On the Value of Twins-Based Estimates of the Returns to Schooling," working paper 6721, National Bureau of Economic Research, Cambridge, MA, 1998). Since this earlier work, most estimates based on twin comparisons have been lower than corresponding traditional ordinary least squares regression estimates, and such twin-based estimates are now generally assumed to reflect an upper bound of the returns to education (ibid.).

21. Some authors, such as Ashenfelter and Rouse, have largely dismissed such possibilities of bias—at least in the case of genetically identical twins—assuming that differences in the educational attainment of identical twins in the same family "result from either measurement error or random deviations from the optimum schooling level" (O. Ashenfelter and C. Rouse, "Income,

Schooling and Ability: Evidence from a New Sample of Identical Twins," working paper 6106, National Bureau of Economic Research, Cambridge, MA, 1997). In other words, variation in the level of schooling between twins should be exogenous and random (or at least unrelated to the outcomes that schooling is said to predict) and therefore should not affect estimates of educational returns. Other authors, such as Bound and Solon, in their "Double Trouble," have not been so optimistic and suggest to the contrary that such unobserved heterogeneity does exist, causing significant problems for twin comparisons. According to Bound and Solon, even though the unobserved differences between twins may be very small, they still may be strongly associated with both education and wages and, therefore, may still bias (likely in an upward direction) twin-based estimates of the returns to education. Because of such endogenous heterogeneity, these authors conclude that "it is unclear whether the covariance estimator based on between-twins variation is subject to less inconsistency than the conventional OLS estimator" (Bound and Solon, "Double Trouble," 14). This inconsistency in twin comparisons can become compounded if measurement error is taken to be regressive to the mean, as opposed to randomly distributed as in the classic errors-in-variables case (ibid.).

22. Army personnel were much more likely to see combat during America's involvement in Southeast Asia than were airmen. Two-thirds of U.S. troops in Vietnam were Army, while only 13 percent were Air Force. Also, the two-year gap between the brothers' periods of service made a great deal of difference. In 1965, the year Rich's stint in the Air Force ended, 184,300 U.S. servicemen were stationed in Indochina. By 1967, the year that Bill left for Vietnam, the United States had committed almost half a million troops to supporting the government of South Vietnam. The actual figure is estimated at 485,600; source: http://members.aol.com/warlibrary/vwc18.htm (July 6, 2003).

23. See, e.g., E. H. Lennenberg, *Biological Foundations of Language* (New York: Wiley, 1967), or W. Penfield and L. Roberts, *Speech and Brain Mechanisms* (Princeton, NJ: Princeton University Press, 1959), or for a more recent review, see Kenji Hakuta, Ellen Bialystock, and Edward Wiley, "Critical Evidence: A Test of the Critical Period Hypothesis for Second Language Acquisition," working paper, School of Education, Stanford University, 2002.

24. Kissinger was born on May 27, 1923. "On August 20, 1938, . . . the Kissingers set sail for London, to spend two weeks with relatives, and then on to America." Walter Isaacson, *Kissinger: A Biography* (New York: Simon and Schuster, 1992), p. 28.

25. But it is also worth noting that twins are more than just a curiosity.

They are also a real public policy issue, since the number of twins in the United States is rapidly rising as a proportion of the total population. Between the years 1980 and 1997, the number of twin births rose 52 percent (from 68,339 to 104,137) and triplet and other higher order multiple births increased by a staggering 404 percent (from 1,337 to 6,737 births). Almost this entire rise took place among white women. The reason is that as white, professional women increasingly delay childbearing, they are more likely to give birth to twins. This trend is compounded by the fact that the use of fertility treatments also increases the likelihood of a multiple birth. It used to be thought that this increase was concentrated only on fraternal twins, but as it turns out, the number of identical twins has been rising as well. So the relationships between biology and social forces are getting further enmeshed. (National Vital Statistics Reports, vol. 47, no. 24, 1999.)

26. There are *some* systematic twin differences that we can be fairly confident in discussing, however. Twins vary in their birth order and in their birth weight. I find that twins who are heavier and/or born first are more likely to thrive. (See Dalton Conley, Kate Strully, and Neil Bennett, *The Starting Gate: Birth Weight and Life Chances* [Berkeley and Los Angeles: University of California Press, 2003].) The problem of endogenous heterogeneity among twins, however, is likely not a concern in analysis of birth weight and infant mortality. Because we are dealing with infants, particular tastes or motivation are not likely to be salient issues. While systematic variation in social environments may emerge as twins age—entering different schools or classrooms, or making different friends—environmental variation during infancy will likely be quite minimal, provided that twins reside in the same household (which will most likely be the case). In an industrialized nation with a low infant-mortality rate like the United States, it is also rather unlikely that parents' behavior will significantly bias twin comparisons of infant mortality. In a nation with considerably fewer resources and a higher incidence of infant mortality it may be more likely that we would witness systematic bias in the allocation of resources toward the larger or stronger twin within a pair, which could lead to spurious birth weight effects. If such factors were at work, it could be the case that the smaller twin is neglected and left to "make it or not" on his or her own through a process of natural selection. Behind such a tendency could be psychological mechanisms. As an example, smaller size could signal mortality risk to a parent, causing the parent not to bond with the child for fear of losing him/her (see, e.g., Nancy Scheper-Hughes, *Death Without Weeping: The Violence of Everyday Life in Brazil* [Berkeley and Los Angeles: University of California Press,

1992]). Where such selective or protective strategies are at play, it might be the case that the source of birth-weight-related differences in mortality rates between twins is an endogenous artifact of parental (or societal) behavior. But in the United States such bias will likely not take place on a wide enough scale to create spurious (or even inflated) associations between birth weight and infant mortality. In fact, it may be reasonable to assume that in the context of an industrialized nation with a relatively low infant-mortality rate—like the United States—*more* resources and attention would be given to the high risk (i.e., lower weight) twin, and thus our estimates of the impact of birth weight on survival would be biased downward (as compared with those that would be associated with equal treatment of the two twins).

Among identical twins, if one weighs a pound less than the other (which is quite common), he is 13 percent more likely to die in the first year of life. The corresponding figure for fraternals is higher (22 percent), suggesting that underlying genetic differences explain part of the association between birth weight on infant mortality in the general population. The effect of birth order—net of weight—is smaller. (That said, the firstborn twin is more often than not the heavier twin.) While which twin makes varsity may not be random, which enjoys the better position in the womb is—by definition—a matter of chance. Birth weight, it appears, may have long-term effects as well. For example, comparing identical twins, Jere Behrman and Mark Rosenzweig find that each additional pound of flesh is worth 7 percent higher earnings over a lifetime. They and other researchers (including myself) find birth weight to be related to schooling. Behrman and Rosenzweig use the relationship between twin differences in birth weight, in schooling, and in wages to estimate the returns to schooling; however, this runs into the same problems as other twin-based estimates. Namely, are the lower earnings of lower birth weight twins related to the fact that they completed less school or something else (like cognitive, social, or health problems that may predict both lower schooling and lower wages)? (See J. Behrman and M. Rosenzweig, "The Returns to Increasing Body Weight," working paper no. 01-052, Penn Institute for Economic Research, University of Pennsylvania, 2001. HTML document available at http://www.econ.upenn.edu/Centers/pier/Archive/01-052.pdf.)

So while we can be fairly confident of a causal relationship between conditions at the time of birth and later outcomes (at least for identical twins), anything after that is still a crap shoot. Paradoxically, the further back in time we look, the more clarity we gain. Our understanding of "causal" relationships between more recent events like education and job choices is fuzzier, always clouded by counterfactuals. It is as if the only tool we have to understand twin differences (and those of all siblings, by extension) is the social science equivalent of the Hubble Space Telescope—a lens that peers into the earliest moments of the universe in order to better understand how we got where we are today.

As for the cases presented here, Bill—more athletic and aggressive than Rich—muscled his way out into the world first (by ten minutes). Abby not only tried gymnastics first, had a nervous breakdown first, and got married first; she was also born nine minutes before Amy. The more outgoing, adventurous Jan also left the womb first, starting his life five minutes earlier than his brother. Finally, April arrived to the world prior to Liwayway. While in four out of four cases here, birth order predicts dominance in the twin pair, in general there is no single magic variable (such as birth order) that predicts which sibling will thrive and which won't. This chapter was intended to show how even for the seemingly straightforward case of identical twins, what you see is not always what you get. While there is no single factor that explains perfectly well who gets ahead and who doesn't, there are a host of discernible patterns that we *can* speak of—including family size and birth order, gender, race, sexuality, and so on. All present their own complications and complexities. Even something as seemingly straightforward as birth order matters sometimes and not others, and for a whole host of reasons.

27. One final note with respect to twins concerns the case of clones. While no scientist could ethically clone a human being—except perhaps to harvest fetal stem cells for medical purposes—surely some less ethical individual, company, or even cult (like the Raelians) will (or has already) cloned a human being. While clones might be a bioethicist's nightmare, they are a sociologist's dream come true. Envision a society where clones had become normalized. In such a society we could answer all sorts of questions about *nurture* by having held nature constant and documenting the systematic differences between clones born at different times. For example, while the economists can never be 100 percent sure why some twins differ in their levels of schooling, if we track clones and their identical twin relatives born thirty or more years before, we might be able to figure out how society-wide changes in schooling, in the labor market, and in social policy affect the opportunities of individuals. The irony of cloning is that it tells us more about the environmental influences than about genetic ones. But until we are besieged by armies of doppelgangers, we will have to be content to let the Gordian knot of nature and nurture rest in peace.

THREE   *Love* Is *a Pie*

1. Doctors' occupational prestige is topped only by that of judges. For a discussion of the historical development of doctors' prestige in America, see Paul Starr, *The Social Transformation of American Medicine* (New York: Basic Books, 1982). (With the latest transformation of health care into a managed care scenario, in combination with the widespread availability of technical medical information thanks to the Internet, doctors are losing some of their status, authority, and autonomy.)

2. You can do this same experiment for other folk categories, like birth sign.

3. What does birth order matter for? In the recent book *Born to Rebel,* author Frank Sulloway argues that it is the dark horse variable that explains much of scientific history (F. Sulloway, *Born to Rebel: Birth Order, Family Dynamics and Creative Lives* [New York: Pantheon Books, 1996]). He starts from the premise, drawn from evolutionary psychology, that there is no competition fiercer than that within the nest—that is, than sibling rivalry. From this premise, he concludes that since younger siblings are generally weaker and developmentally behind their older siblings (by definition), they lose out in the battle for parental attention and family resources. An alternative strategy developed by these children is to strike out on their own paths, creating unique niches within the family unit. In other words, they rebel. Thus, he sees an important link between birth order and (scientific) creativity. Sulloway's evidence for this claim is that over the course of history, scientific revolutions have been much more often initiated and accepted by secondborns. He has extended the argument to claim that firstborns are *generally* more conservative and cautious.

Sulloway, however, defines birth order rather conveniently by including older siblings who may have died off, for example, when convenient to his thesis, and discarding them when they pose problems. Methodological issues aside, let us return to Sulloway's central theoretical claim about birth order: secondborns carve out their own paths since the firstborns have already laid claim to parental inheritance. It is true that for much of European history, primogeniture was the rule of thumb. The firstborn male got the family farm; the rest worked for their brother or struck out on their own path (often moving to cities, which, in turn, contributed to the industrial revolution). But we must keep in mind that for most of European history, nobody had any property. The history we read about is the history of the elite, not of the multitude of peasants who were trapped in serfdom or subsistence farming. In other words, the importance of the rules of primogeniture is overstated since it applied largely in Europe (and select other places in the world), and even there was relevant only to a small slice of society.

But is he right about this? I have found, for example, that later borns will often appeal to authority when faced with a competitor who is bigger, stronger, and more developed than they are. My own younger sister often did this. Indeed, according to political science theories of conflict, this is what we should expect. The paradigm of "conflict contagion" suggests that it is almost always in the interests of the losing party to expand the theater of war. In other words, if Germany and France are fighting, and it appears as though Germany's chances of victory are slipping away, there is an incentive for German leaders to try to drag in others on their side (this is exactly what Germany did, according to a new history of World War I—see Hew Strachan, *The First World War: To Arms* [Oxford: Oxford University Press, 2001]). Of course, this could lead to innovation, too, as Sulloway would predict. The losing party may resort to desperate measures—i.e., creatively change the rules of combat, say through the use of guerrilla tactics. My point is that there are multiple responses and the path depends on the resources and strategies available to the litigants (i.e., what role the parents play).

Meanwhile, the incentive for France is to keep the battle just the way it is. So assuming parents care about all of their children (something that evolutionary psychologists might dispute, but that most parents in modern society would take as a given), it was in my interest to keep my conflicts with my sister between us when we were growing up, and it was in her interest to appeal to the fairness of higher authority. In other words, how birth order matters to our personality development depends on who we are in other dimensions—gender, ability, and so on—as well as what our environment is like, how responsive our parents are, how strong a norm of fairness they have, and so on.

4. Let us consider the research on personality and birth order. In the most careful assessment of birth order research, Cécile Ernst and Jules Angst reviewed every study that included birth order between 1949 and 1980. What they found can be summarized by the following quote: "Birth order and sibship size do not have a strong impact on personality." (C. Ernst and J. Angst, *Birth Order: Facts and Fiction* [Berlin: Springer-Verlag, 1983], p. 284). Sulloway selectively reinterpreted their results and found more support for the claim that birth order matters. Then Judith Harris came along and reanalyzed Sulloway's reanalysis of Ernst and Angst (such are the ways of academia). In an appendix to her book *The Nurture Assumption,* which directly addresses Sul-

loway's claims, she finds that he selectively interpreted the studies and did not properly weight them for how large or small they were. (It turns out that large-scale studies, which are more reliable, disconfirm birth order effects, while the small-scale studies, which are more prone to bias or error, find significant birth order effects.) Sulloway also counted as multiple studies multiple results by the same author(s) in the same study. That is hardly ideal, since the results are based on the same sample of subjects, so if it is biased for one outcome (say anxiety) it is likely to be biased for others (e.g., depression or goal orientation).

More important than the work of Ernst and Angst, or even than Sulloway's own analysis, is recent research that has attempted to confirm or repudiate the claims made in *Born to Rebel.* As it turns out so often in social research, the results are mixed at best. Psychologists Richard Zweigenhaft and Jessica Von Ammon studied students who participated in civil disobedience and were arrested for it, and compared them with two control groups (one randomly selected from the college and one made up of the friends of those arrested). They found that later borns were, indeed, overrepresented in the group of rabble-rousers. This study is better than most in that it is measuring an actual behavior rather than just what someone tells a survey taker. However, it suffers from a major flaw since the researchers did not take into account the sizes of the families of their subjects. So the higher prevalence of later borns in the "rebel" group might merely mean that kids from large families tend to be more rebellious. Indeed, as we shall see below, family size matters a lot.

However, other work casts doubt on Sulloway's claims. Sociologists Jeremy Freese, Brian Powell, and Lala Carr Steelman examined 202 types of attitudes in a nationally representative large-scale survey of the U.S. population. (In fact, it was *the* survey of American attitudes: the General Social Survey.) They found no relationship between birth order and social attitudes on dimensions such as political preference, respect for authority, or "tough-mindedness." (Jeremy Freese, Brian Powell, and Lala Carr Steelman, "Rebel Without a Cause or Effect: Birth Order and Social Attitudes," *American Sociological Review* 64 [1999]: 207–31.) Much more predictive were factors such as gender, race, social class, and—key to making sense of all birth order research—family size.

5. Even within occupational positions there seems to be room for a lot of different personality styles. The most successful professional football coaches have been both the quiet, orderly types like Tom Landry and Bill Walsh, and the hotheaded "lunch pail" guys like Bill Parcells and Vince Lombardi. We have had gregarious presidents like Bill Clinton and George W. Bush, and we have elected more socially cautious ones like Richard Nixon and George Bush (Sr.).

6. The technical term for the number of brothers and sisters an individual has is "sibship size"; however, in this chapter I will mostly use the more colloquial term "family size."

7. Ernst and Angst in *Birth Order* declared that neither birth order *nor* sibship size made any difference to personality, but while they may be right for sibship size and *personality,* they are not right in terms of socioeconomic success.

8. Careful analysis by sociologist Douglas Downey shows that economic resources get spread thin the fastest, but interpersonal resources, like parental time and energy, also begin to get drained—albeit more gradually—as the number of children in a family rises. What's more, not only does Downey find that the resources per child dwindle, he also provides evidence that they benefit children less. Even something as intangible as parental expectations—as in the hopes and pressure to go to college—matter less in larger families. (Douglas B. Downey, "When Bigger Is Not Better: Family Size, Parental Resources, and Children's Educational Performance," *American Sociological Review* 60 [1995]: 746-61.)

9. Psychologists who are devotees of this paradigm extend it to the nation as a whole, going so far as to argue that cohorts that are large in size (like the baby boomers) do worse on the SATs than those from smaller cohorts. Of course, if this is true, this stylized fact could also be a result of the "resource dilution" theory: they might suffer in more crowded classrooms and get fewer financial resources per capita. It is also the case that those from larger birth cohorts tend to have higher rates of unemployment and lower wages due to increased competition for jobs. (Robert Zajonc and Patricia R. Mullally, "Birth Order: Reconciling Conflicting Effects," *American Psychologist* 52 [1997]: 685-99.)

10. See Peter Blau and Otis Dudley Duncan, *The American Occupational Structure* (New York: Wiley, 1967), pp. 298-307.

11. See Guang Guo and Leah K. VanWey, "Sibship Size and Intellectual Development: Is the Relationship Causal?" *American Sociological Review* 64 (1999): 169-87.

12. That said, natural experiment alternatives exist. For instance, we can compare a family with, say, five children and two miscarriages with a family of six kids. In this comparison, we would be positing that the family with five children and multiple miscarriages really shares "six child" family characteristics and that it was just chance that prevented them from actually having six children. The problem with this approach is that it rests on the assumption that families that have miscarriages are the same as families that do not (or, at

least, that those differences do not matter for the outcomes of the children). That seems like a stretch, since miscarriages, especially repeated ones, may indicate larger health problems, or may generate a sense of frustration and stress that may adversely affect already-existing children. Besides, accurately tracking miscarriages is a tough job, especially since about one-fourth of all pregnancies spontaneously abort, often so early that the women do not even know they are pregnant. (S. J. Ventura, W. D. Mosher, S. C. Curtin, J. C. Amba, and S. Henshaw, "Trends in Pregnancy Rates for the United States, 1976–97: An Update," *National Vital Statistics Reports* 49 [Hyattsville, Maryland: National Center for Health Statistics, 2001].)

Another possibility for a natural experiment lies in the fact that no one plans for twins. If two families each have one kid during the first pregnancy but then, on the second try, one has a single baby and the other has a set of twins, we might reasonably argue that the second twin is an "extra" child, more or less randomly assigned—as in our government-controlled experiment. (See, e.g., J. D. Angrist and W. N. Evans, "Children and Their Parents' Labor Supply: Evidence from Exogenous Variation in Family Size," *American Economic Review* 88 [1998]: 450–77.) But there are several problems with this approach, too. First, we cannot know for sure whether the family that finds itself with three kids was not going to go on and have three kids anyway; it may have just happened a little faster than they expected. However, this potential problem is not insurmountable since we know from overall figures in the population how many families have three children and how many have two, and we can adjust the chances based on those figures. A larger problem is that families with twins are different from families without twins in several important respects. First, some things about the parents may be different. Traditionally, for some reason, African-American women are more likely to give birth to twins than are white women: "In 1980, the black twin birth ratio of 23.8 per 1000 live black births was more than 31% higher than the white twin birth ratio of 18.1 (P < .001). By 1999, the black twin birth ratio of 32.0 per 1000 live black births was 11% higher than the white twin ratio of 28.8 because of increasing rates of white twin births (P < .001)." See page 130 of Rebecca B. Russell, Joann R. Petrini, Karla Damus, Donald R. Mattison, and Richard H. Schwarz, "The Changing Epidemiology of Multiple Births in the United States," *Obstetrics & Gynecology* 101 (2003): 129–135. This is changing, however, even as you read the words on this page. The growing popularity of fertility treatments, in combination with delays in childbearing, has greatly increased the number of twins and triplets born in the United States in recent years. Most of this boom in twins has occurred among older, wealthy, white moms. So, if you are a twin baby these days, you are more likely to either be African-American or to have a middle-aged, white, well-off mother. Not only are the mothers who have twins decidedly different (on average) from those who have singleton births, important distinctions emerge after the kids are born. First of all, spacing matters; paying for clothes, cars, and college is difficult enough when kids are separated by a few years. When children hit parents all at once, as with twins, the financial implications can be overwhelming. To top it off, twins often need more medical attention early in life, since they often do not go the full term of pregnancy. Further, the presence of twins in a household not only affects their own success, it can have spillover effects onto the other children, thanks to the unique demands that they place on the family. So comparing families with twins with those without does not provide us with a perfect natural experiment, either.

13. Unlike miscarriages and twins; in other words, we need something that is quite normal in the everyday course of family life.

14. With the exception of selective abortion after determination of the sex of the child, a phenomena that is extremely rare here in the United States, but which may be more common in China—particularly under the one-child policy. See Neil Bennett, ed., *Sex Selection of Children* (New York: Academic Press, 1983).

15. There is less genetic material on a "male" sperm, so its lighter weight confers an advantage in speeding to the egg.

16. The reason I say "at least for the first few children" is that when a family has had four or more children of the same sex, the likelihood of the next child being that same sex rises—much to the chagrin of those searching for the missing girl/boy to complete the set. For example, in his book *Sex Selection of Children,* Neil Bennett (1983) writes in the introduction:

Ben-Porath and Welch (1976), using the public use sample of the 1970 United States census, have shown that there is a slight trend effect in actual births. If the first three children are boys, then the probability of a boy on the fourth birth rises from .513 (the probability of a boy on the first birth) to .534. However, even this small change in the probability does not occur unless all the previous children are of the same sex. For example, if the family consists of three boys and one girl the likelihood of a boy on the fifth birth is only .515, which is essentially the same as the probability of a boy on the first birth. Thus, it is reasonable to conclude that couples should assume that without sex selection the probability of a boy is always approximately equal to the probability of a girl.

See Neil Bennett, ed., *Sex Selection of Children* (New York: Academic Press, 1983), p. 19. Also see Y. Ben-Porath and F. Welch, "Do Sex Preferences Really Matter? *Quarterly Journal of Economics* 90 (1976): 285–307.

17. Indeed, the genders of the first two kids are unrelated to any other measurable characteristic. That is, the six-percentage-point difference on the likelihood of having a larger family is constant across race, class, and so on (see Angrist and Evans, "Children and Their Parents' Labor Supply"). That said, I included only white intact families in one-family households with no other kin or non-kin residing, for methodological reasons explicated in the appendix.

18. Of course, I must exclude families with only one child. The actual method is a version two-stage least squares (2SLS). It involves generating a prediction of the likelihood of having more than two children, using the sex mix as an instrumental variable (IV), and then using this predicted value (along with other variables) to predict the outcomes of the children. For the full treatment of this "natural experiment" see Dalton Conley, "What Is the 'True' Effect of Sibship Size on Attainment? IV Estimates from Exogenous Variation in Fertility," working paper, Center for Advanced Social Science Research, New York University, 2003. There is one slight complication to our approach and that is the following: what if the sex mixture of the kids matters to their future success? It could be the case that those with all boys or all girls are better off (or worse off) than those with a mix, aside from the issues of how many kids there are altogether. For example, it could be the case that there exists what economists call "returns to scale" within genders. That means that each additional kid of the same gender costs less than another kid of a different gender. This might be the case if kids of the same sex can more easily share rooms, wear the same clothes, and so on. On the other hand, it could be the case that having same- or opposite-sex siblings is good or bad for a child's future success for psychological reasons relating to peer relationships. Same-sex children may experience more competitive sibling relationships, which, in turn, may spur them to do better in school (or bring them down). At the same time, those children with an opposite-sex sibling may learn how to relate to peers across genders better than those without an opposite-sex sibling. All sorts of possibilities arise. In examining data, however, it does not appear that the sex mixture of children affects their success (though it probably affects their personalities greatly).

19. See Conley, "'True' Effect of Sibship Size?"

20. Ibid. I am not alone in finding this pattern. Economist Eric Hanushek studied sixth-grade reading scores and found that while there were no birth order effects for small families, for large families there was a U-shaped effect. In other words, the children in the earliest and latest birth positions significantly outperformed those in the middle. Hanushek's results are consistent with the interpretation that the kids in the middle experience a large family for their entire childhood and get caught between the eldest and the babies of the family. (Eric A. Hanushek, "The Trade-Off Between Child Quantity and Quality," *Journal of Political Economy* 100 [1992]: 84–117.) However, neither my comparison of birth positions nor Hanushek's addresses the issue of the endogeneity of child quality (though the experiment with respect to the transition from two to three or more children does address this issue). That is, parents may alter their behavior—fertility and investment patterns—based on the quality of earlier children in a way that, alternatively, accentuates or compensates for these differences. In other words, a parental decision as to *when* or even *whether* to have a third child may be based on how the first two turned out (though I do control for the spacing along with parity-spacing interactions).

21. The authors do note some benefits to the birth of an additional sibling, however. For example, family stability increases with the birth of the new baby; that is, the parents are less likely to split up. The mother also withdraws more from the labor force. This can be a mixed blessing, however; she may be more available to her children but, on the other hand, financial hardship increases at the same time that additional resources are usually sorely needed. (Nazli Baydar, April Greek, and Jeanne Brooks-Gunn, "A Longitudinal Study of the Effects of the Birth of a Sibling During the First Six Years of Life," *Journal of Marriage and the Family* 59 [1997]: 939–56.)

22. Other researchers find that birth spacing matters greatly for other parental resources as well—such as college tuition. (See, e.g., L. C. Steelman and B. Powell, "Acquiring Capital for College: The Constraints of Family Configuration," *American Sociological Journal* 54 [1989]: 844–55.) Of course, we do not know for certain whether or not the birth of the additional child per se causes these family changes, but given that these changes are noted within the same families over time, these results are much more persuasive than studies that merely contrast the parenting styles and outcomes of children in larger families with those from smaller ones.

23. See Centers for Disease Control, "Achievements in Public Health, 1900–1999: Family Planning," *Morbidity and Mortality Weekly Report* 48

(1999): 1073–80, Atlanta, Georgia. The 2000 figures come from J. A. Martin, B. E. Hamilton, S. J. Ventura, F. Menacker, and M. M. Park, "Births: Final Data for 2000," *National Vital Statistics Reports* 50 (5) (Hyattsville, MD: National Center for Health Statistics, 2002).

24. These figures come from a comparison of parameter estimates for sibling regressions of PSID data. The coefficients are .515 and .414 for the natural logarithm of five-year average income, for small and large families, respectively. The net worth sibling coefficients are .281 and .177, for small and large families, respectively. The differences in the strength of coefficients are just shy of statistical significance at the p = .05 level (one-tailed) with t-values of 1.60 and 1.61 for income and net worth, respectively. Education and occupational prestige sibling coefficients demonstrate similar differences but do not approach statistical significance. See Conley, "Sibling Correlations."

25. While maternal education is generally associated with delayed (and perhaps lower overall) fertility (see, e.g., Ronald R. Rindfuss, S. Philip Morgan, and Kate Offutt, "Education and the Changing Age Pattern of American Fertility: 1963–1989," *Demography* 33 [1996]: 277–90), the relationship between income and fertility is not so straightforward in the United States. Frank Bean and Charles Wood analyze the 1960 and 1970 U.S. Census and find that "the effects on completed fertility of the income measures are positive for Anglos and negative for Blacks, while in the case of Mexican Americans the effect of potential income is negative and that of relative income is positive. Income effects on the parity progression probabilities are similar in pattern to those from the analyses using completed fertility, although somewhat different patterns tend to appear at different birth orders, especially among Anglos." Page 629 in Frank D. Bean and Charles H. Wood, "Ethnic Variations in the Relationship Between Income and Fertility," *Demography* 11 (1974): 629–40.

26. Jere R. Behrman, Robert A. Pollak, and Paul Taubman, "Family Resources, Family Size and Access to Financing for College Education," *Journal of Political Economy* 97 (1989): 398–419.

FOUR   *Death, Desertion, Divorce*

1. While there is disagreement as to how long-lasting the deleterious effects of parental divorce are on children's academic performance and emotional well-being, from my interviews it seems that the timing of parental conflict or divorce matters a lot in determining long-term academic and socioeconomic

outcomes. If divorce occurs, say, during a period when important life choices are being made—like the end of high school—then the turmoil it causes can affect a child's outcomes much more drastically than if it happens when an offspring's path is more or less stable.

2. Edwin remembers vividly one of the times he tried to involve his father in what he was interested in:

"Dad, guess what I did in school today?"

His father didn't respond from behind the curtain of his opened newspaper. "Dad, I learned this cool thing with sound waves! It's really neat. And my teacher said I'm really good at working with them!"

Still no response.

"Isn't it neat, Dad? Dad? I'm going to see if I can make music by myself soon and . . ."

"Don't you ever shut up? Can't you see that I need a break? Who cares about your stupid waves—it's just a waste of time!" His father exploded suddenly, startling Edwin. Without another word, he folded up his newspaper neatly and stomped off. Edwin, crushed, would never again bring up his interest in sound waves to his father—nor would he have much success bringing up much else with his father over the years.

3. This pattern is not uncommon, where formal social rules such as laws or fines serve to undermine informal norms and expectations. Dan Kahan writes about many examples of this in "Gentle Nudges vs. Hard Shoves: Solving the Sticking Norms Problem," *University of Chicago Law Review* 67 (2000). One parallel case he studies is that of a child care center that tried to curb the occasional lateness of parents in picking up their children by instituting a strict fine system. As it turned out, after this change was made, lateness *rose,* instead of falling. Once parents quantified the penalty for being late, making it commensurable with money, they felt free from the informal social pressure of being on time, figuring they could just "pay the fine" if they found themselves held up for an important reason.

4. This took place before the New Deal, so there was not much of a welfare state to take care of destitute families.

5. These quotes all come from page 55 of *The Nurture Assumption;* see Judith Harris, *The Nurture Assumption* (New York: Free Press, 1998).

6. Usually, last borns get to experience part of their childhood as an only child, though in this case, since Samantha never moved out, George never enjoyed that particular benefit.

7. These are the women who reputedly come to the aid of single fathers,

casserole dishes of "home cooked" meals in hand. According to lore and to research accounts, single mothers get less of this type of mutual aid, though that may be changing as gender norms and parenting expectations change and equalize between men and women.

8. Between 1860 and 1864 the combined death and divorce rate was 33.2 dissolutions per year per 1,000 marriages. In 1970, the combined rate was 34.5, hardly different at all, but the percentage ending from divorce had risen steeply. Andrew Cherlin, *Marriage, Divorce, Remarriage* (Cambridge, MA: Harvard University Press, 1992), p. 25.

9. The divorce rate kept rising such that the total dissolution rate peaked at 41 per 1,000 marriages per year in the late 1970s and early 1980s. That is drastically different from the 1860 figures, in which almost nobody divorced (though, of course, there was desertion going on). To be fair, the divorce rate for marriages with children is lower—particularly those with sons, since having a male offspring seems to increase fathers' commitment to childrearing. (See, e.g., Philip S. Morgan, Diane N. Lye, and Gretchen A. Condran, "Sons, Daughters and the Risk of Marital Disruption," *American Journal of Sociology* 94 [1988]: 110–29.) This divorce-reducing effect of children has been the conventional wisdom among demographers. However, one study that tries to model fertility and divorce decisions simultaneously and as mutually causal, finds that the "childbearing pattern—number of children and age of youngest child at the beginning of the marital interval being studied and fertility during the interval—did not influence the likelihood of separation in simple or consistent ways over the marital life course, nor did marital strife (as indicated by separation) seem to affect childbearing throughout marriage." From page 129 of Helen P. Koo and Barbara K. Janowitz, "Interrelationships Between Fertility and Marital Dissolution: Results of a Simultaneous Logit Model," *Demography* 20 (1983): 129–45.

10. See Sally C. Clarke, "Advanced Report of Final Marriage Statistics, 1989 and 1990," *Monthly Vital Statistics Report* 43 (12) (1995), Supplement, Center for Disease Control and Prevention.

11. Keep in mind, however, that this is mostly a result of selection bias. People who find themselves in a second marriage obviously have much more liberal attitudes toward divorce (since they most likely have gotten one already) than does the total pool of people who are in first marriages (since that group also includes people who have very strong antidivorce attitudes and who will never divorce).

12. Continued debate about the impact of divorce is partly due to the fact

that divorce is not the kind of thing you can generate experimental data about. Someday, someone may come up with a nice natural experiment to measure the impact of divorce on children, but until then, we are stuck with increasingly political debates. Some researchers have thought of using state to state variation in divorce laws and child support enforcement as an instrument to generate a natural experiment with respect to divorce. See, e.g., Meta Brown and Chris Flynn, "Investment in Child Quality over Marital States," working paper presented to the Institute for Research on Poverty Summer Workshop, University of Wisconsin at Madison, 2002.

13. When a parent dies—even if the marriage was not an ideal one—the surviving family members tend to remember that person fondly. There is "respect for the dead." The same cannot usually be said for divorcees' accounts of their exes. Further, with the exception of some young children (and others in certain circumstances), kin who survive a death in the family do not generally blame themselves for the tragedy. By contrast, self-doubt among exes and children seems to linger after cases of divorce. Research shows that, although death may be the most tragic event we can imagine, most children adapt well enough to their new circumstances after the death of a parent, partly because of these differences. Of course, parental death also often has economic consequences for the family that are not so easily recovered from.

14. With a "control group" of another fifty from intact families.

15. Sociologist Linda Waite and columnist Maggie Gallagher echo this view in their book, *The Case for Marriage: Why Married People Are Happier, Healthier and Better Off Financially* (New York: Doubleday, 2000). (The title, in this case, says it all.) In this book, Waite and Gallagher claim that married parents provide better homes for their children than do divorced ones because—they argue—they have more money to spend on them, have more time to spend *with* them, enjoy stronger emotional bonds to their children, have more social capital (connections) that will be helpful to their children's chances for success, and are physically and mentally healthier. By contrast, divorced families are more likely to manifest more child abuse and neglect, more delinquency, and attain less education.

16. One study of 13,017 subjects who participated in the National Survey of Families and Households found that for whites and for black and Hispanic females, young adults who experienced a separation from one of their parents during childhood had lower average socioeconomic attainments in early adulthood when compared with those who had lived continuously with both parents. At the same time, there appeared to be no effect for black or Hispanic

males. The negative effects of parental marital dissolution appeared to be mediated through the education and marital status of the offspring. See Paul R. Amato and Bruce Keith, "Separation from a Parent During Childhood and Adult Socioeconomic Attainment," *Social Forces* 70 (1991): 187–206. In a meta-analysis (a summary of other research studies) dating back to 1991, Amato and Keith found "that adults who experienced parental divorce exhibited lower levels of well-being than did adults whose parents were continuously married. The strongest estimated effects occurred in the areas of one-parent family status, psychological adjustment, behavior/conduct, and educational attainment." See page 43 of Paul R. Amato and Bruce Keith, "Parental Divorce and Adult Well-Being: A Meta-Analysis," *Journal of Marriage and the Family* 53 (1991): 43–58.

17. Based on a sample of 2,500 kids from 1,500 families (including a control group of intact families).

18. Six years after their parents have split up, one-quarter of children see their noncustodial parent once a year or less. (Of course, this may be a good thing if, say, that parent was hostile or abusive.)

19. Christy Buchanan, Eleanor Maccoby, and Sanford Dornbusch conducted a similar study called the Stanford Custody Study in which they followed children of divorced families for several years. Unlike the other researchers listed above, their intent was not to compare the children of divorce to the children of intact families; rather they wanted to examine differences within the divorced population. For example, they found that if parents recouple when the kids are still young (i.e., prepubescent) that is generally better than when they recouple during their adolescence. If parents do recouple, their kids adapt better, these researchers claim, when that recoupling results in actual remarriage rather than just dating or cohabitation. They also find that adolescents who make the transition from living with their mothers to living with their fathers tend to have the most problems; however, they speculate that this is largely a case of reverse causality—namely, the teenagers with behavior problems are more likely to be sent to live with their fathers than those who do not display such "acting out." (They support this hunch by showing that teenagers who *always* lived with their dads are no different in their behavior or affect than those who always lived with their moms.)

Finally, the evidence on whether or not parental presence matters or not is mixed. This debate has found its most strident tone with respect to the issue of single parenthood. Many pundits and researchers claim that unwed parenthood disadvantages children (and the adults who have the kids). Others claim that the observed differences between kids from married parents and those from unmarried ones are the result of the different socioeconomic backgrounds of the two groups. However, it appears that most of this effect is related to the lower economic circumstances in which these kids find themselves. See, e.g., Sara McLanahan and Gary Sanderfur, *Growing Up with a Single Parent: What Helps, What Hurts* (Cambridge, MA: Harvard University Press, 1990); also see Arline T. Geronimus, "On Teenage Childbearing and Neonatal Mortality in the United States," *Population and Development Review* 13 (1987): 245–79.

Issues of causality aside, from a purely descriptive point of view, those who have lived with only one parent for part or all of their childhood generally demonstrate lower average education levels and adult socioeconomic statuses. Donna Morrison and Andrew Cherlin followed 1,123 children from across the nation whose parents' marriages were intact in 1986. (See Donna Ruane Morrison and Andrew J. Cherlin, "The Divorce Process and Young Children's Well Being: A Prospective Analysis," *Journal of Marriage and the Family* 57 [1995]: 800–12.) By 1988, 10 percent of those children had divorced or separated parents. When Morrison and Cherlin compared the rate of behavioral problems for those whose parents were still together and those whose parents had separated, they found that for girls there was no effect from the marital dissolution, but boys in the divorced group experienced greater behavioral problems than those in the other nine-tenths of the sample. Keeping in mind that they are testing these (very young) kids when presumably the effects of divorce should be at their worst (within the first two years postbreakup), it is even stronger evidence that divorce itself may be just one event in a larger process of family jostling and is not so significant in its own right.

Another study of the same national sample of 870 children aged four to six compared those from intact families with those in disrupted families. (See Alan J. Hawkins and David J. Eggebeen, "Are Fathers Fungible? Patterns of Coresident Adult Men in Maritally Disrupted Families and Children's Well-Being," *Journal of Marriage and the Family* 53 [1991]: 958–72.) Hawkins and Eggebeen found essentially no differences in verbal-intellectual ability and psychosocial functioning (i.e., child mental health) between the two-thirds in disrupted families and the one-third in intact households. (I am using "household" and "family" conterminously here though they have a distinct meaning in the scientific literature.) Among the disrupted group, they broke the population down into several subcategories based on the presence or absence of an adult male in the household. Kids with no "dad" in the house were doing no better or worse than those with a stepfather, those with a "chaotic" household (meaning the entry and exit of one or more men), and even those with a reunited father (meaning their biological father moved back in). The only exception to this pattern was that those who lived with a grandfather tended to display more psychosocial problems. This finding was replicated more recently in a different sample of African-American children by Ariel Kalil, Mary Patillo, and Monique R. Payne, "Intergenerational Assets and the Black/White Test Score Gap," in *After the Bell: Family Background and Educational Success,* ed. Dalton Conley and Karen Albright (London: Routledge, 2004). (But, of course, there is the question of cause and effect here—it may be that single mothers with problem children tend to move into their parents' home for added disciplinary support.) The bottom line of Hawkins and Eggebeen's research seems to be that dads do not matter much. (They do not examine single-father families; it may be not that dads per se do not matter but rather that a second parent is not so necessary.)

Adding to the confusion, this rather provocative conclusion is called into question by research on child support payments. Obviously, if a father pays money to support his kids, they are better off financially (and developmentally, in turn). But paying child support acts as a signal that a dad is responsible and cares and maybe even that the parents are acting somewhat cooperatively as opposed to conflictually. That is, of course, if the child support is voluntary as opposed to court ordered. Laura Argys and her colleagues found (using the same sample of kids that Hawkins and Eggebeen did) that net of the added dollars that child support provided, the very fact of receiving it helped young children's cognitive achievement. There were, though, unexplainable variations in these effects depending on race and type of nonresident paternity (i.e., divorce, never married, and so on). See Laura M. Argys, H. Elizabeth Peters, Jeanne Brooks-Gunn, and Judith R. Smith, "The Impact of Child Support on Cognitive Outcomes of Young Children," *Demography* 35 (1998): 159–73. It appeared as though voluntary payments mattered more than court-ordered ones, but their evidence on this distinction was shaky, at best.

What is even more amazing is the fact that paying child support may actually draw dads into a more positive relationship with their children. When Argys and her colleagues ran a natural experiment of sorts—using state-to-state variation in child support policy and other factors—they found that when child support was more likely to occur due to favorable external circumstances (regardless of the fathers' dispositions), kids still thrived. This may mean that the act of financially investing in their children brings fathers into the fold in other beneficial ways (i.e., to see their biological *and* financial investments succeed); it could mean that when kids receive support, their mothers and children are less stressed out about their circumstances (again, regardless of their total income); it could mean that other aspects of pro-support states are good for children (for example, by providing more educational funding); or it could mean any combination of the above factors. (States with good economic circumstances, good child support enforcement, and high awards may also invest more in preschool and elementary school education. So, while better than a straight comparison, this natural experiment by no means closes the book on the matter.)

Paul Amato and Joan Gilbreth conducted a meta-analysis in 1999 of the research on paternal effects in disrupted families. After reviewing sixty-three studies, they come to more or less the same reading: "Analysis showed that fathers' payment of child support was positively associated with measures of children's well-being. The frequency of contact with nonresident fathers was not related to child outcomes in general. Feelings of closeness and authoritative parenting were positively associated with children's academic success and negatively associated with children's externalizing and internalizing problems." See Paul R. Amato and Joan G. Gilbreth, "Nonresident Fathers and Children's Well-Being: A Meta-Analysis," *Journal of Marriage and the Family* 61 (1999): 557–73.

20. Al Gore and Tipper Gore, *The Spirit of Family* (New York: Henry Holt, 2002) and *Joined at the Heart: The Transformation of the American Family* (New York: Henry Holt, 2002).

21. It is not good enough to just compare divorced families with a control group of households that stayed intact (as Hetherington and Wallerstein do), since the married group does not provide the right counterfactual. It is as Tolstoy has famously written at the start of *Anna Karenina*: "Happy families are all alike; every unhappy family is unhappy in its own way." Rather, true insight into the impact of divorce comes not from comparing unhappy with happy families, but rather from comparing unhappy ones that stay together with unhappy ones that break apart. This, of course, falls into the rather large category of social science experiments we cannot perform. However, changing American norms about divorce over the last few decades provides a natural experiment of sorts (though one that is itself complicated by myriad other changes that have taken place simultaneously). Fifty years ago, many unhappy families

that would have been divorced in today's world stuck it out for better and, mostly, for worse.

22. This may be why we find fewer detrimental effects for parental death than for parental divorce; it may be that parental death is more "random" (i.e., exogenous) and therefore not as associated with the problems of selection bias. Though, of course, parents who die young are not—on average—the same as parents who live through their children's childhoods. They are more likely to be poor, uneducated, racial minorities, and unwed parents, and to live in distressed communities. All of which makes parental death subject to some of the same selection bias issues as divorce, though perhaps less so for the reason that sometimes death is a truly exogenous event. By contrast, those who divorce may be fundamentally different from those who do not, and the "effect" of divorce may be more related to selection than to the act of parental separation itself.

23. The Hetherington-Kelly and Wallerstein studies include control groups to use for comparisons. So, for example, when Hetherington and Kelly report that 20 percent of adolescents in the divorced group are depressed, we can compare that figure to the percent depressed in the "intact" family group (though some of the families in the intact group eventually divorced and some in the divorced group reconciled or remarried other partners). This is a step forward, but it does not go far enough. (See E. Mavis Hetherington and John Kelly, *For Better or for Worse: Divorce Reconsidered* [New York: Norton, 2002].)

24. Furthermore, it is very difficult to separate out the effects of the divorce itself on kids, from the effect of the lousy marriage that led up to the divorce, from the events that follow a divorce. In other words, whether or not parents stay married may not matter as much as the quality of their parenting, their social circumstances, and trajectory, or the relationships between the parents themselves. Divorce may merely stand in as a somewhat arbitrary marker.

25. Others could have examined the variable impact of divorce by position within the family. For example, Hetherington and Kelly had some families with multiple siblings in their study (they had 1,500 families and 2,500 subject children). Likewise, the Stanford Custody Project also had multiple siblings for some households (with a sample of 522 adolescents from 365 families). Unfortunately, neither research study made use of this unique opportunity to study the variable impact of divorce. Instead, they treated the multiple observations from the same families as a statistical problem that needed to be overcome. The same is true for most research that uses the children of the

National Longitudinal Survey of Youth (NLSY), where there are multiple siblings in many families.

26. In fact, at least one study shows that kids from high-conflict marriages that stay together may do worse than kids from high-conflict marriages that break apart. (See Donna Ruane Morrison and Mary Jo Coiro, "Parental Conflict and Marital Disruption: Do Children Benefit When High-Conflict Marriages Are Dissolved?" *Journal of Marriage and the Family* 61 [1999]: 626–37.) Another study finds that when divorce is preceded by a high level of conflict, its impact on offspring is lessened. See Paul Amato, L. Loomis, and Alan Booth, "Parental Divorce, Marital Conflict and Offspring Well-Being During Early Adulthood," *Social Forces* 73 (1995): 895–915. Also see Cosandra McNeal and Paul R. Amato, "Parents' Marital Violence: Long-Term Consequences for Children," *Journal of Family Issues* 19 (1998): 123–39.

27. For the effects of marital dissolution on women (and children), see, e.g., Pamela J. Smock, Wendy D. Manning, and Sanjiv Gupta, "The Effect of Marriage and Divorce on the Economic Well-Being of Women," *American Sociological Review* 64 (1999): 794–812. For the effects on men, see, e.g., Patricia McManus and Tom DiPrete, "Losers and Winners: The Financial Consequences of Separation and Divorce for Men," *American Sociological Review* 66 (2001): 246–68.

FIVE   *Movin' On Up, Movin' On Out*

1. Like most of U.S. social policy, child care is means-tested. That is, there exist limited programs for families who meet the criterion of low income (among other requirements), but there are no government programs for the rest of families. This has the effect of setting up strange incentives for families and leaving those who are above the threshold—but not by much—in the biggest bind of all. Finally, means testing makes the public support of government programs tenuous. Since such programs target the neediest among us, they lead to a morality-tinged discourse of "handouts" for the "undeserving" poor. Compare, for example, the almost-holy sanctity of Social Security and Medicare (the closest we come to "universal" programs in the United States) to the debates over Temporary Assistance to Needy Families (TANF) and Medicaid (health insurance for poor families). For a discussion on the issue of universal versus means-tested government policies, see Gosta Esping-

Andersen, *The Three Worlds of Welfare Capitalism* (Princeton: Princeton University Press, 1990).

2. See Timothy M. Smeeding, Michael O'Higgins, and Lee Rainwater, *Poverty, Inequality and Income Distribution in Comparative Perspective: The Luxembourg Study* (Washington, DC: Urban Institute Press, 1990) and Sheldon Danziger and Peter Gottschalk, eds., *Uneven Tides: Rising Inequality in America* (New York: Russell Sage Foundation Press, 1993). Also see, by the same authors, *America Unequal* (Cambridge, MA: Harvard University Press, 1996).

3. Long-term trends in "real" (that is, inflation-adjusted) income are hard to pin down, since the way the inflation rate itself is calculated is a matter of some debate among economists. The Consumer Price Index (CPI) works for short-term (i.e., year-to-year) changes quite well, but when we are comparing the cost of living over a two-decade stretch, the task becomes much harder since the basket of goods upon which we should base our estimate of the standard and cost of living changes dramatically. Take, for example, the cost of information; arguably, with the advent of high-powered personal computers and the World Wide Web, the cost of information has plummeted; these kind of changes, however, are not figured into the Consumer Price Index. For a debate over how inflation is calculated, see Bart Hobjin, "On Both Sides of the Quality Bias in Price Indexes," staff report no. 157, Federal Reserve Bank of New York, 2002.

4. In other cases, family breadwinners may be stuck in dead-end jobs in what economists call the "secondary" labor market. The "primary" labor market is defined by the presence of career paths that potentially, at least, lead to upward mobility. Professionals, managers, civil servants, small business owners, and even skilled laborers all have the potential to see their earnings rise fairly steadily over their lifetimes if they play their cards right. People unlucky enough to be trapped in the secondary labor market often do not enjoy such opportunities for economic betterment or career advancement. These jobs include most service-sector employees such as waiters and waitresses (which is still the largest occupational category for women in the United States—see Allison Owings, *Hey Waitress! The USA from the Other Side of the Tray* [Berkeley and Los Angeles: University of California Press, 2002]).Unfortunately, these are the sectors that are growing most rapidly in the contemporary American economy. So the upward mobility that most families experienced (and came to expect) in the period between the end of World War II and the mid-1970s may be a relic of a particular historical moment.

5. Mathilde described the four sisters as like the sisters in Louisa May Alcott's *Little Women:* Eleanor, the oldest, was Meg; Anne, the sweetest and the most vulnerable, was Beth; Mathilde, the relatively scrappy one, was Jo; and Margaret, the more petulant and somewhat spoiled sister, was Amy.

6. That figure really understates the magnitude of change for the younger generations since they are where all the action is (in contrast to ninety-year-olds who are probably not increasing their rates of college completion, yet who make up part of the denominator). On the other hand, there is the countervailing trend of a long-term, steady decline in verbal test scores—which may explain within-family differences in verbal ability. See Duane Alwin, "Family of Origin and Cohort Differences in Verbal Ability," *American Sociological Review* 56 (1991): 625–38.

7. The similarity between fathers and firstborn sons in terms of occupational careers is greater than the similarity between fathers and secondborn sons. One interpretation is consistent with the first part of Sulloway's theory: firstborns are more closely identified with the parents and thus reproduce their career paths while secondborns are left to strike out on their own, more rebellious paths in life. However, there are alternative explanations that may be more consistent with these and other results. It could be the case, for example, that the difference between firstborns and later borns in how closely they reproduce their parents' status has to do with the overall trajectory of an ever-changing economy.

SIX   *Legacies and Role Models, Fat and Skin*

1. Home discussion of mathematics has been found to be critical for students who continue on to advanced mathematics courses during high school, and particularly so during grades ten and eleven. Parental involvement clearly has a significant effect on both children's learning and their willingness to continue on in advanced mathematics (Xin Ma, "Dropping out of Advanced Mathematics: The Effects of Parental Involvement," *Teachers College Record* 101 [1999]: 60–81).

2. Psychotherapist Nancy Atwood (Nancy C. Atwood, "Gender Bias in Families and Its Clinical Implications for Women," *Social Work* 46 [2001]: 23–36) argues that the experience of girlhood gender bias is associated with clinical depression and a number of destructive behaviors in adult women,

including involvement in demeaning intimate relationships, self-doubt about competence in comparison with males, an isolating distrust of relationships, and the sacrifice of personal and relational development to serve parents and/or compensate for problematic brothers. Atwood conceptualizes gender bias along three dimensions: devaluation, where the woman perceives that she was less valued by her parents than a brother; abuse without redress, where the woman reports that she was abused by a brother and perceived herself as unable to get redress from her parents; and deprivation, where the woman perceives herself to have been deprived of resources or privileges that a brother had.

3. It probably comes as no surprise to learn that over the past few decades there has been a substantial amount of psychological and sociological research documenting gender biases, which tend to favor males over females in many families. Sometimes these biases are explicit and hard to ignore, such as the fact that a majority of Americans have reported that they would prefer their first child to be a boy, and, if they plan to have more than two children, that they would like to have a predominant number of boys—even if their actual behavior belies these purported preferences, as we saw in chapter 3. (Roberta Steinbacher and R. Ericsson, "Should Parents be Prohibited from Choosing the Sex of Their Child?" *Health* 24 [1994].)

4. Susan M. McHale, Ann C. Crouter, and Corinna J. Tucker, "Family Context and Gender Role Socialization in Middle Childhood: Comparing Girls to Boys and Sisters to Brothers," *Child Development* 70 (1999): 990–1004.

5. Similarly, differential investment patterns between families with sons and families with daughters have been documented. Using data from the Consumer Expenditure Survey, economists Shelly Lundberg and Elaina Rose found that housing expenditures are significantly higher for families with a male child rather than a female child—in fact, such families spend almost $1,200 more per year on housing than do families without a son. According to Lundberg and Rose, families with boys also spend more on other "investment-type" costs, including things like health insurance, charity, and political contributions (cultivating social capital and demonstrating more concern about the "future"), and books and toys. Lundberg and Rose also note that at least part of this result "might be interpreted as a reflection of gender differences in activities, since spending on recreation services is also higher in boy families overall and the consumption aggregate 'Entertainment and Recreation' shows a strong positive boy effect." (Shelly Lundberg and Elaina Rose, "Investments in Sons and Daughters: Evidence from the Consumer Expenditure Survey," paper prepared for the Joint Center for Poverty Research Institute Conference, Family

Investments in Children's Potential: Resources and Behaviors That Promote Children's Success, Chicago, 2002.)

In fact, sociobiologists argue that different parental investment by gender makes a certain amount of sense. In 1973, Robert Trivers and Dan Willard came up with a theory that high-status parents typically invest more in their sons than in their daughters, while low-status parents invest more in their daughters than in their sons. The reasons Trivers and Willard gave for this have to do with evolutionary practicalities. They argue that parents are trying to maximize their resources and their socioeconomic position in the hierarchy. Because the reproductive success of males tends to be tied to their social rank, high-ranking males have a much better chance of mating with more than one female, while low-ranking males have less potential to produce many heirs than do their low-ranking sisters. Therefore, low-status parents of daughters will have more descendants—and, thus, a better chance of survival—than will low-status parents of sons, so they are better off if they invest more in their daughters. For high-status parents, on the other hand, it makes more sense to invest in their sons than in their daughters; because their sons are more likely to produce more descendants than will their daughters (women's reproductive potential being less variable than men's), investment in sons is a good way to secure their genetic continuation. (Robert L. Trivers and Dan E. Willard, "Natural Selection of the Parental Ability to Vary the Sex Ratio of Offspring," *Science* 179 [1973]: 90–91.)

As intriguing as this idea is, there are a number of problems with the Trivers-Willard hypothesis. One problem is that in many ways this hypothesis seems to be a better fit for less developed societies (or for nonhuman populations) than it does for people in today's Western industrialized societies, for whom high status does not have to be tied to reproductive success. (Indeed, evidence in support of the Trivers-Willard hypothesis has been documented in several nonhuman species. See J. P. W. Rivers and M. A. Crawford, "Maternal Nutrition and the Sex Ratio at Birth," *Nature* 252 [1974]: 297–98; M. McFarland Symington, "Sex Ratio and Maternal Rank in Wild Spider Monkeys: When Daughters Disperse," *Behavioral Ecology and Sociobiology* 94 [1987]: 110–29; T. H. Clutton-Brock, S. D. Albon, and F. E. Guinness, "Great Expectations: Dominance, Breeding Success, and Offspring Sex Ratios in Red Deer," *Animal Behaviour* 34 [1986]: 460–72.) In fact, as we have already seen in previous chapters, in modern industrialized societies too much reproductive success (too many children) can drain a family's resources, which often translates into less success for that family's offspring. However, the biggest trouble lies in the fact that, even though it became quite a popular idea in scientific circles, it went untested for a long time and thus had no real data to back it up. After actually testing the Trivers-Willard hypothesis with hard data, sociologists Jeremy Freese and Brian Powell found little evidence that it held up—at least in contemporary America. They argue that gender biases are due less to biology than they are to the particular social and cultural forces that we are surrounded with every day. The hypothesis does not, in fact, explain differential investment by gender; instead, it claims that other factors are a lot more critical to parental investment. These factors include the total amount of resources that parents have at their disposal, the number of other dependents competing for those resources, the level of parents' education, and contemporary cultural norms regarding childrearing. Many of these social and cultural forces, of course, still reflect the traditional sex-role expectations that have been with us for much of history, even if they do not make as much sense in the modern era, when women do not have to be tied down exclusively by domestic responsibilities. We can see this with regard to differential inheritance by gender, for instance; in many families, male children still get more than their fair share of property. (Jeremy Freese and Brian Powell, "Sociobiology, Status, and Parental Investment in Sons and Daughters: Testing the Trivers-Willard Hypothesis," *American Journal of Sociology* 104 [1999]: 1704–43; Jeremy Freese and Brian Powell, "Making Love out of Nothing at All? Null Findings and the Trivers-Willard Hypothesis," *American Journal of Sociology* 106 [2001]: 1776–88.)

6. Philip A. Cowan, C. P. Cowan, and P. K. Kerig, "Mothers, Fathers, Sons, and Daughters: Gender Differences in Family Formation and Parenting Style," in *Family, Self, and Society: Toward a New Agenda for Family Research,* eds. P. A. Cowan, D. Field, D. A. Hansen, A. Skolnick, and G. E. Swanson (Hillsdale, NJ: Erlbaum, 1993), pp. 165–91; Jacqueline J. Goodnow, "Children's Household Work: Its Nature and Functions," *Psychological Bulletin* 103 (1988): 5–26; Laurence D. Steinberg and Wendy Steinberg, *Crossing Paths: How Your Child's Adolescence Triggers Your Own Crisis* (New York: Simon and Schuster, 1994).

7. Michael E. Lamb, "The Changing Roles of Fathers," in *The Father's Role: Applied Perspectives,* ed. M. E. Lamb (New York: John Wiley, 1986), pp. 2–27; Reed Larson and Maryse H. Richards, *Divergent Realities: The Emotional Lives of Mothers, Fathers and Adolescents* (New York: Basic Books, 1994); W. Jean Yeung, John F. Sandberg, Pamela E. Davis-Kean, and Sandra L. Hofferth, "Children's Time with Fathers in Intact Families," *Journal of Marriage and the Family* 63, no. 1 (2001): 136–54.

8. Michael E. Lamb, Joseph H. Pleck, and J. A. Levine, "Effects of Increased

Paternal Involvement on Fathers and Mothers," in *Reassessing Fatherhood: New Observations on Fathers and the Modern Family,* ed. C. Lewis and M. O'Brien (Newbury Park, CA: Sage, 1987); Philip S. Morgan, Diane Lye, and Gretchen Condron, "Sons, Daughters and the Risk of Marital Disruption," *American Journal of Sociology* 94 (1988): 110–29.

9. However, there is some debate about this claim. Thomas examines the relationship between parental education and child height, a common indicator of health and nutrition status. He claims that differences in the allocation of household resources are dependent on both the gender of the child and the parent, finding that maternal education has a bigger effect on the height of daughters and paternal education has a bigger effect on the height of sons. (Duncan Thomas, "Like Father, Like Son; Like Mother, Like Daughter: Parental Resources and Child Height," *Journal of Human Resources* 29 [4] [1994]: 950–88.)

10. Unpublished research by economists Gordon Dahl and Enrico Moretti discussed by Steven Landsburg, "Oh, No: It's a Girl! Do Daughters Cause Divorce?" *Slate,* October 2, 2003, http://slate.msn.com//id/2089142/.

11. Some research has taken an intergenerational approach in examining gender and bequests. Data on 1920 testators showed that among those who treated their children differently, 53 percent discriminated against their sons and 21 percent against their daughters. By 1944, the figures had flipped such that among those who discriminated, 29 percent did so against sons and 50 percent against daughters (Remi Clignet, *Deaths, Deeds and Descendants: Inheritance in Modern America* [New York: Walter de Gruyter, 1992], p. 180). These results are based on small samples and by now are quite dated. More recent analysis by myself and Miriam Ryvicker using the Panel Study of Income Dynamics shows that there is no difference between female and male heads of households in the likelihood of receiving inheritance (though we did not examine the difference between brothers and sisters explicitly). See Dalton Conley and Miriam Ryvicker, "The Price of Female Headship: Gender, Inheritance and Wealth Accumulation in the United States," working paper, Center for Advanced Social Science Research, New York University, 2003.

12. See, for example, Naomi Wolf, *The Beauty Myth* (New York: Doubleday, 1991); Susan Bordo, *Unbearable Weight: Feminism, Western Culture, and the Body* (Berkeley and Los Angeles: University of California Press, 1993); Joan Jacobs Brumberg, *The Body Project: An Intimate History of American Girls* (New York: Vintage, 1997).

13. See Charles A. Register and David R. Williams, "Wage Effects of Obesity Among Young Workers," *Social Science Quarterly* 71 (1990): 130–41; Eng

Seng Loh, "The Economic Effects of Physical Appearance," *Social Science Quarterly* 74 (1993): 420–38; Daniel S. Hamermesh and Jeff E. Biddle, "Beauty and the Labor Market," *American Economic Review* 84 (1993): 1174–94; Steven L. Gortmaker, Aviva Must, James M. Perrin, Arthur M. Sobol, and William H. Dietz, "Social and Economic Consequences of Overweight in Adolescence and Young Adulthood," *New England Journal of Medicine* 329 (1993): 1008–12.

14. Though the stringent weight restrictions that regulated the appearance and behaviors of stewardesses in the past (inducing many to diet excessively, vomit, and even give blood in order to lose weight immediately before their weekly weigh-ins) were made illegal in the early 1990s, weight and height must still be deemed "proportional," and charts are used to determine acceptable ranges.

15. See page 327 of Susan Averett and Sanders Korenman, "The Economic Reality of the Beauty Myth," *Journal of Human Resources* 31 (1996): 304–30. These authors found that "the great majority (as much as 96 percent) of the economic deficit associated with obesity among women in our sample, results from differences in the marriage market (especially lower probabilities of marriage), not the labor market." It should also be noted here that Averett and Korenman also present evidence that the social and economic differentials captured in the data did not cause women's weight gain.

16. Ibid.

17. Deborah A. Dawson, "Ethnic Differences in Female Overweight: Data from the 1985 National Health Interview Survey," *American Journal of Public Health* 78 (1988): 1326–29.

18. John Cawley, "The Impact of Obesity on Wages," *Journal of Human Resources*, forthcoming; an earlier version was John Cawley, "Body Weight and Women's Labor Market Outcomes," working paper 7841, National Bureau of Economic Research, 2000. See also John Cawley, "Obesity and Labor Market Outcomes," working paper, Department of Policy Analysis and Management, Cornell University, 2002.

19. Claud Anderson and Rue L. Cromwell, "'Black Is Beautiful' and the Color Preferences of Afro-American Youth," *Journal of Negro Education* 46 (1977): 76–88; Ronald E. Hall, "Bias Among African Americans Regarding Skin Color: Implications for Social Work Practice," *Research on Social Work Practice* 2 (1992): 479–86; Kathy Russell, Midge Wilson, and Ronald Hall, *The Color Complex: The Politics of Skin Color Among African Americans* (New York: Anchor, 1992); Tracy L. Robinson and Janie V. Ward, "African American Adolescents and Skin Color," *Journal of Black Psychology* 21 (1995): 256–74; Mark

E. Hill, "Color Differences in the Socioeconomic Status of African American Men: Results of a Longitudinal Study," *Social Forces* 78 (2000): 1437–60.

20. Howard E. Freeman, David Armor, J. Michael Ross, and Thomas F. Pettigrew, "Color Gradation and Attitudes Among Middle-Income Negroes," *American Sociological Review* 31 (1966): 365–74; Verna Keith and Cedric Herring, "Skin Tone and Stratification in the Black Community," *American Journal of Sociology* 97 (1991): 760–78; Louie E. Ross, "Mate Selection Preferences Among African American College Students," *Journal of Black Studies* 27 [1997]: 554–69.

21. E. Franklin Frazier, *The Black Bourgeoisie* (New York: Free Press, 1957).

22. According to the 1860 census, 58 percent of the free black population but only 12 percent of the slave population were mulattoes. (Elizabeth I. Mullins and Paul Sites, "The Origins of Contemporary Eminent Black Americans: A Three-Generation Analysis of Social Origin," *American Sociological Review* 49 [1984]: 672–85.)

23. In their intriguing analysis of contemporary eminent African-Americans, sociologists Elizabeth Mullins and Paul Sites, in "Origins of Eminent Black Americans," provide support for Frazier's ideas of social inheritance. Their data show that a predominant number of modern-day eminent blacks are descendants of families that were characterized by antebellum freedom, urban residence, higher education, and occupational attainment—and lighter skin.

24. Keith and Herring, "Skin Tone"; and Hill, "Color Differences."

25. Hill, "Color Differences." Keith and Herring, in "Skin Tone," also point to discrimination as a significant cause of stratification by skin color, and note that this has an especially strong impact on black women.

26. Either way, skin color is—for the most part—exogenous to socioeconomic status. That is, it is a condition of birth—and when differences exist between siblings, it can be thought of as more or less randomly assigned. Thus, in contrast to the cycle of socioeconomic status and obesity, we can be more certain that skin color is playing a causal role in determining the life chances of black siblings.

27. Arguably, another measure of lower status among African-Americans is having a "black-sounding" name. In a fascinating study seeking to measure the extent of racial discrimination in the labor market, Marianne Bertrand and Sendhil Mullainathan (see their "Are Emily and Brendan More Employable Than Lakisha and Jamal? A Field Experiment on Labor Market Discrimination," paper presented at Princeton University's Labor Economics Seminar,

Industrial Relations Section, November 13, 2002) sent résumés with "black-sounding" names—e.g., Aisha, Lakisha, Hakim, and Tyrone—and résumés with "white-sounding" names—e.g., Allison, Meredith, Brendan, and Todd—in response to help-wanted ads in Boston and Chicago newspapers. They found that résumés with "white" names elicited about 50 percent more callbacks than those with "black" names. Further, they found that applicants with "black" names benefit less from improving their credentials, since "black" names with higher quality résumés did not receive significantly more callbacks.

28. The African-American community is hardly the only community to suffer the effects of color bias. For instance, Murguia and colleagues have documented similar differentials by skin color among Mexican-Americans. (See Carlos H. Arce, Edward Murguia, and W. Parker Frisbie, "Phenotype and Life Chances Among Chicanos," *Hispanic Journal of Behavioral Sciences* 9 [1987]: 19–32; Edward Murguia and Edward E. Telles, "Phenotype and Schooling Among Mexican Americans," *Sociology of Education* 69 [1996]: 276–89; Edward E. Telles and Edward Murguia, "Phenotypic Discrimination and Income Differences Among Mexican Americans," *Social Science Quarterly* 71 [1990]: 682–96.)

29. Freeman, Armor, Ross, and Pettigrew, "Color Gradation"; Ross, "Mate Selection."

30. As difficult as it is to negotiate the complexities of skin-color differences within a given racial community, however, *interracial* dating and mating can be even more complicated. In fact, negotiating romantic relationships across racial lines proved problematic for a number of the people we interviewed, and particularly so for women. In general, it was much more common for black men to have had white girlfriends when they were growing up (or as adults) than it was for black women to have had white boyfriends. Sociologists Jerry A. Jacobs and Teresa G. Labov (see their "Gender Differentials in Intermarriage Among Sixteen Race and Ethnic Groups." *Sociological Forum* 17 [2002]: 621–46) have found that this pattern is also true for black-white marriage: while just over 6 percent of college-educated African-American males in the 1990 census married non-Hispanic whites, only slightly more than 2 percent of their female counterparts did the same. (For blacks with less than a college education, the percentages were even less: almost 4 percent of males married white women, while a little over 1 percent of females married white men.) Perhaps unsurprisingly, when such differentials manifest themselves within families, it could be cause for hard feelings among the siblings and—particularly among

women, create feelings of sadness and self-doubt. The literature supports the trends we noticed among the people we interviewed. For instance, Matthijs Kalmijn (see his "Trends in Black/White Intermarriage," *Social Forces* 72 [1993]: 119–46) notes that the rates of intermarriage between blacks and whites have increased significantly since the legal ban on intermarriage was lifted, and that this trend is especially pronounced among black males.

31. S. Montgomery, M. Bartley, D. Cook, and M. Wadsworth, "Health and Social Precursors of Unemployment in Young Men," *Journal of Epidemiology and Community Health* 50 (1996): 415–22; R. Wilkinson, *Unhealthy Societies: The Afflictions of Inequality* (New York: Routledge, 1996), pp. 197–207; R. Wilkinson, ed., *Class and Health: Research and Longitudinal Data* (London: Tavistock, 1986).

32. See Jay Belsky and David Eggebeen, "Early and Extensive Maternal Employment and Young Children's Socioemotional Development: Children of the National Longitudinal Survey of Youth," *Journal of Marriage and the Family* 53 (1991): 1083–1110.

33. Jay Belsky and M. Rovine, "Nonmaternal Care in the First Year of Life and Infant-Parent Attachment Security," *Child Development* 59 (1988): 157–76; Ronald Haskins, "Public School Aggression Among Children with Varying Day-Care Experience," *Child Development* 56 (1985): 689–703; Deborah Vandell and Mary Corasaniti, "Child Care and the Family: Complex Contributors to Child Development," in *Child Care and Maternal Employment: A Social Ecology Approach,* K. McCartney, ed. (San Francisco: Jossey-Bass, 1990); Jay Belsky, "The 'Effects' of Infant Day Care Reconsidered," *Early Childhood Research Quarterly* 3 (1988): 235–272.

34. Indeed, a number of studies have pointed to the benefits of having a mother who is employed outside of the home at least part-time. Interestingly (and somewhat counterintuitively), these benefits even extend to the amount of television watching that is allowed in the home. Sociologists Suzanne Bianchi and John Robinson (see their "What Did You Do Today? Children's Use of Time, Family Composition, and the Acquisition of Social Capital," *Journal of Marriage and the Family* 59 [1997]: 332–344) found that children of mothers who are employed part-time watch significantly less television than do children of mothers who are full-time homemakers, thus increasing the amount of time they can devote to more useful cognitive developmental pursuits and the acquisition of social capital.

35. The figure for both groups combined was a 9 percent difference. See

Dalton Conley, "Gender Stratification Within Families," working paper, Center for Advanced Social Science Research, New York University, 2003. An examination of the debate regarding educational attainment makes it clear that the story is much more complicated than it may initially seem. Boys are almost twice as likely as girls to be held back a grade, while they are marginally less likely to attend private school. Indeed, the debate in the literature over the degree of educational attainment within families evidences the murkiness of gender bias. For instance, some scholars have argued that women's educational attainment has been systematically affected by the gender of her siblings throughout the last century, while men's has not. They claim that women raised only with brothers have received significantly more education than women raised with any sisters (Kristin F. Butcher and Anne Case, "The Effect of Sibling Sex Competition on Women's Education and Earnings," *Quarterly Journal of Economics* 109 [1994]: 531–63; William L. Parish and Robert J. Willis, "Daughters, Education and Family Budgets: Taiwan Experiences," *Journal of Human Resources* 28 [1993]: 863–98). In other words, the more sisters there are in a given family, the fewer educational chances they have, while brothers' educational attainment does not depend on how many other brothers there are in the family. Other scholars, however, have refuted this claim, arguing that sibling sex composition has little effect on educational achievement and that, instead, the addition of each child in a given family simply leads to a modest reduction in educational attainment for all. (Robert M. Hauser and Hsiang-Hui Daphne Kuo, "Does the Gender Composition of Sibships Affect Women's Educational Attainment?" *Journal of Human Resources* 33 [1998]: 644–57; Robert Kaestner, "Are Brothers Really Better? Sibling Sex Composition and Educational Achievement Revisited," *Journal of Human Resources* 32 [1997]: 250–84.) Kaestner did find that sibling sex composition had an effect on the educational attainment of black teens between the ages of fifteen and eighteen. However, this effect was directly opposite that which Butcher and Case, in "Effect of Sibling Sex Competition," had predicted: in Kaestner's data, black teens who grew up with sisters had higher educational attainment than those who grew up with brothers. Such scholars often point out that while it was once the norm for males to have a higher level of educational attainment than females, today men and women have essentially caught up with each other in terms of educational achievement. Thus, they argue that differentials in educational attainment should not necessarily be traced to gender bias within families.

One new addition to this debate is a theory known as the "revised sex minority hypothesis." This hypothesis suggests that regardless of an individual's gender, it is more disadvantageous for him/her to have additional siblings of the opposite sex than of the same sex. The reasons are manifold. First, same-sex siblings may stimulate a more competitive, achievement-oriented environment than do opposite-sex siblings. More importantly, the children who are in the sex minority may find their gender-specific needs unmet and/or devalued, and may also suffer from socialization within the family that conflicts with sex-role expectations within the educational system. So far the data appear to back up this hypothesis; elsewhere in my research, I have found that men are most disadvantaged in terms of educational attainment by the presence of sisters, while women's educational attainment is hurt more by brothers (Dalton Conley, "Sibship Sex Composition: Effects on Educational Attainment," *Social Science Research* 29 [2000]: 441–57.) If further research bears out these findings, what this means is that there is no gender effect per se on educational attainment. Instead, gender effects manifest themselves only in relation to the sex of the individual when we are talking about educational attainment. Thus, while other elements of gender bias still have a clear effect on overall life outcomes, educational attainment seems to be one area within the complexities of family dynamics where the effects of gender bias are much less weighted against females. However, my own test for gender-specific returns to scale (from chapter 3)—using the much larger sample from the U.S. Census—seems to indicate that the sex composition of offspring does not affect their educational outcomes in any systematic way.

36. For these figures, see Conley, "Gender Stratification." Labor force inequality can be traced to occupational segregation rather than to within-job wage discrimination per se. Sociologists Trond Petersen and Laurie Morgan have found that, for observed wage differences among both blue-collar/clerical and professional/administrative occupations, within-job wage discrimination was much less important than was occupation-establishment segregation, which was significant and extensive. (Trond Petersen and Laurie A. Morgan, "Separate and Unequal: Occupation-Establishment Sex Segregation and the Gender Wage Gap," *American Journal of Sociology* 101 [1995]: 329–65.) Like so many other sociological issues, of course, it can be quite difficult to ascertain why this differential exists, but it is clear that family constraints, including that of childrearing, play a role. In fact, there is currently a debate about whether more attention should be paid to labor force discrimination or to the constraints of childrearing. That is, some scholars have argued that some women may "opt"

for less demanding career paths due to the time and flexibility such a choice allows them in managing the burdens of raising children. Others argue similarly that it is the exits from the labor force that women disproportionately take to care for small children that ultimately result in their less prestigious careers—particularly since the burden of child care often comes simultaneously with critical periods in career development. (See Audrey Vandenheuvel, "Women's Roles After First Birth: Variable or Stable?" *Gender and Society* 11 [1997]: 357–68, for a thoughtful review of the complex patterns of maternal labor-force participation after first birth.)

37. Viktor Gecas, "The Social Psychology of Self-Efficacy," *Annual Review of Sociology* 15 (1989): 291–316; Elizabeth G. Menaghan and Toby L. Parcel, "Determining Children's Home Environments: The Impact of Maternal Characteristics and Current Occupational and Family Conditions," *Journal of Marriage and the Family* 53 (1991): 417–31; Kristin A. Moore and Nancy O. Snyder, "Cognitive Attainment Among First-Born Children of Adolescent Mothers," *American Sociological Review* 56 (1991): 612–24.

38. Frank F. Furstenberg Jr., "As the Pendulum Swings: Teenage Childbearing and Social Concerns," *Family Relations* 40 (1991): 127–38; F. Furstenberg and K. M. Harris, "When and Why Fathers Matter: Impacts of Father Involvement on the Children of Adolescent Mothers," in *Young Unwed Fathers: Changing Roles and Emerging Policies,* ed. R. Lerman and T. Ooms (Philadelphia: Temple University, 1993), pp. 117–38.

39. Arline T. Geronimus, "On Teenage Childbearing and Neonatal Mortality in the United States," *Population and Development Review* 13 (1987): 245–79; Arline T. Geronimus and Sanders Korenman, "The Socioeconomic Consequences of Teen Childbearing Reconsidered," *Quarterly Journal of Economics* 107 (1992): 1187–1214; see also Shelly Lundberg and R. Plotnick, "Earnings Losses Caused by Teenage Premarital and Marital Childbearing," paper presented at the Annual Meeting of the American Economics Association, Washington, DC, 1990; Randall J. Olsen and George Farkas, "Endogenous Covariates in Duration Models and the Effect of Adolescent Childbirth on Schooling," *Journal of Human Resources* 24 (1989): 39–53; David C. Ribar, "Teenage Fertility and High School Completion," *Review of Economics and Statistics* 76 (1994): 413–24; Dawn M. Upchurch and James McCarthy, "The Timing of a First Birth and High School Completion," *American Journal of Sociology* 55 (1990): 224–34, for additional evidence that prior research has unwittingly exaggerated the socioeconomic costs of teen childbearing.

40. This approach accounts for both measured and unmeasured aspects of

family background (though, of course, it cannot control for differences that might exist between the sisters, which could also be important). See Geronimus and Korenman, "Socioeconomic Consequences of Teen Childbearing Reconsidered."

41. Interestingly, they and others do not compare brothers and sisters who have a child during their teenage years.

42. See Geronimus and Korenman, "Socioeconomic Consequences of Teen Childbearing Reconsidered."

SEVEN   *Random Acts of Kindness (and Cruelty)*

1. Where the Coxsackie virus was first isolated by scientists in 1948. For a great account of life in a New York State prison from the point of view of a guard, see Ted Conover, *New Jack: Guarding Sing Sing* (New York: Vintage Books, 2001).

2. See, e.g., Judy Dunn and Robert Plomin, *Separate Lives: Why Siblings Are So Different* (New York: Basic Books, 1990).

3. Page 227 of Christopher Jencks, Marshall Smith, Henry Acland, Mary Jo Bane, David Cohen, Herbert Gintis, Barbara Heyns, and Stephan Michelson, *Inequality: A Reassessment of the Effect of Family and Schooling in America* (New York: Harper and Row, 1972).

4. Still, while most parents do not have to face such tough choices, this kind of dynamic may play out in less dramatic situations as well. (Of course, I doubt that it was seen as a conscious choice by her parents at the time; they were merely reacting to rapidly unfolding circumstances.)

5. Though we can never know what would have happened to Missy had it not been for her traumatic incident, she herself compares her own story with that of the daughter of a family friend: a few years ago, well after she and her parents had come to terms with her own attack, this girl was raped, and Missy's mother asked her to speak with the family. The circumstances were different—the girl was raped by someone she knew, and it was less violent than the gang rape Missy had experienced—but the results were the same. The girl had totally shut down and retreated into a shell of shock.

Missy counseled both the girl and her mother. "I told them about what I had gone through and that she couldn't let that happen to her. 'Don't let this scar over. You've got to open it up and you've got to pour antibiotics in it. You have to take care of it, or else it will fester in there.'" Both the mother and daughter took Missy's advice and got the girl into counseling immediately. The mother worked through her own feelings in therapy as well, and she made an extra effort to make her daughter understand that she knew it was not her fault. Last year, Missy received a letter of thanks from the family—they had pressed charges, gone to court, and stuck it out through a trial. The resulting conviction was "better than all the therapy in the world" for the girl, who is now in college and thriving. The story makes one wonder what would have happened to Missy had she enjoyed the same kind of support that she, in turn, provided.

6. A quarter lasts only ten weeks in contrast to semesters, which are generally fourteen or fifteen weeks.

7. Let us start at birth. Kids who are born at a low birth weight because they are born premature (before the thirty-seventh week of gestation) or have growth retardation are less likely to thrive on a number of indicators as compared with the normal birth weight siblings. For example, when we follow kids who were born at a weight of less than five pounds eight ounces and compare them with their siblings who were born at a higher weight, we find that the ones born on the lighter side are much less likely to graduate high school in a timely fashion (that is, by the time they turn nineteen years old). Here birth weight is acting as a stand-in for all sorts of pregnancy-related conditions (such as maternal drinking and smoking) that varied between one child and the next, for the social and economic conditions around the time of birth (again, to the extent that they vary between birth intervals), and for other perinatal health conditions that may be associated with low birth weight (such as prematurity, congenital defects, and so on). When I compared identical twins, I found that the lighter twin is 13 percent more likely to die by the end of the first year of life—which cannot imply good things for being lighter and surviving, either. (See Dalton Conley, Kate Strully, and Neil Bennett, *The Starting Gate: Birth Weight and Life Chances Across Generations* [Berkeley and Los Angeles: University of California Press, 2003].) Other studies demonstrate adult risks of low birth weight on a variety of outcomes but do not use sibling comparisons to rule out other potential causes (such as poverty, maternal behavior, and so on). For example, see H. Sorenesen, S. Sabroe, J. Olsen, K. Rothman, M. Gillman, and P. Fischer, "Birth Weight and Cognitive Function in Young Adult Life: Historical Cohort Study," *British Medical Journal* 315 (1997): 401–3; R. Strauss, "Adult Functional Outcome of Those Born Small for Gestational Age: Twenty-Six-Year Follow-up of the 1970 British Birth Cohort," *Journal of the American Medical Association* 283 (2000): 625–31; J. Rich-Edwards, "Birth Weight and

Risk of Cardiovascular Disease in a Cohort of Women Followed Up Since 1976," *British Medical Journal* 35 (1997): 396–400; M. Hack, D. Flannery, M. Schluchter, L. Cartar, E. Borawski, and N. Klein, "Outcomes in Young Adulthood for Very Low Birth Weight Infants," *New England Journal of Medicine* 346 (2002): 149–57. For a general review of the literature on the sequelae of low birth weight, see F. Bennett, "The LBW, Premature Infant," in *Helping Low Birth Weight, Premature Babies: The Infant Health and Development Program*, ed. R. Gross, D. Spiler, and C. Haynes (Stanford, CA: Stanford University Press, 1997), pp. 3–16.

In the case of identical twins, differences in birth weight are merely the luck of which twin drew the better spot in the womb—closer to the placenta's nourishment. So in the case of twins, the difference in weight is *not* reflecting any other underlying genetic, behavioral, or social condition, but rather is truly random. Thus, it would appear that weight (i.e., fetal growth) itself matters for long-term success. This finding is confirmed by economists Jere Behrman and Mark Rosenzweig—who also compare identical twins—who find that each additional pound of fetal growth is worth another 7 percent of lifetime earnings. (And you always wanted to know how much a pound of flesh was worth. . . .) Jere Behrman and Mark Rosenzweig, "The Returns to Increasing Body Weight," working paper no. 01-052, Penn Institute for Economic Research, University of Pennsylvania, 2001, PDF document available at http://www.econ.upenn.edu/Centers/pier/Archive/01-052.pdf (July 6, 2003).

As we move farther out from birth, it becomes more difficult to sort out cause and effect with respect to health. For example, childhood height (as a general indicator of health) predicts adult income better even than adult height does, but parental income predicts childhood height. (S. Montgomery, M. Bartley, D. Cook, and M. Wadsworth, "Health and Social Precursors of Unemployment in Young Men," *Journal of Epidemiology and Community Health* 50 [1996]: 415–22. Also see R. Wilkinson, *Unhealthy Societies: The Afflictions of Inequality* [New York: Routledge, 1996], pp. 197–207.) So is it really childhood height that predicts adult income, or is it parental income that predicts kids' adult incomes, and height is just a convenient substitute indicator of parental income? Or does child health even affect parental income? Using sibling differences can help clarify these dynamics, since we know that the kids—family fluctuations in income aside—share more or less the same economic circumstances growing up.

Take the case of childhood obesity—an epidemic of alarming proportions in contemporary America. (See, e.g., Eric Schlosser, *Fast Food Nation: The Dark*

Side of the American Meal [New York: Houghton Mifflin, 2001]; also see Greg Critser, *Fat Land: How Americans Became the Fattest People in the World* [New York: Houghton Mifflin, 2003].) Kids whose mothers work are more likely to be overweight than kids whose mothers stay home. However, the two trends of rising childhood obesity rates and rising maternal employment rates have gone hand in hand in recent decades. While it is not likely that the fatness of children is causing mothers to work (although there would certainly be higher food bills for bigger eaters), it could be that the mothers who work the most are disadvantaged in some way that also leads their children to become overweight (like, for example, having less education). By comparing siblings, however, economists Patricia Anderson, Kristin Butcher, and Phillip Levine found that the more mothers worked during the childhoods of siblings, the more weight those kids put on—independent of the mother's or family's general characteristics. (Patricia M. Anderson, Kristin F. Butcher, and Phillip B. Levine, "Maternal Employment and Overweight Children," working paper no. W8770, National Bureau of Economic Research, 2002.)

However, sibling comparisons are not foolproof solutions, since the health of children may also reflect other underlying sibling profiles. For example, kids who experience accidents may be inherently more risk seeking. And it may be that this risk-seeking behavior would have affected their attainment regardless of a particular accident or injury. (Of course, one cannot argue with the fact that certain, very traumatic injuries are the immediate cause of downward mobility regardless of the underlying or distal causes.) Take the case of teen smoking and drinking. When economists Phillip Levine, Tara Gustafson, and Ann Velenchik compared smokers with their nonsmoking siblings, they found that the smoking cost individuals about 4 to 8 percent of their wages. (Phillip B. Levine, Tara A. Gustafson, and Ann D. Velenchik, "More Bad News for Smokers? The Effects of Cigarette Smoking on Labor Market Outcomes," *Industrial and Labor Relations Review* 493 [1997]: 509.)

Of course, it could be that siblings who smoke are "bad" workers in ways that are causally unrelated to their smoking behavior (but which tend to be associated with it). For example, if smokers tend to be nihilistic, then it may be their nihilistic attitude at work that is costing smokers earnings and not the use of cigarettes per se. Or, it could be the case that failure in the rat race stresses people out and causes them to smoke. (Though these same authors use other methods that seem to confirm the numbers they present. For example, they follow individuals over time, tracking their smoking behavior and their wages. This, too, could be problematic since changes in smoking behavior could be associated with other life transitions [like marriage, for example], which could be the "real" underlying causal factor. [Or smoking could be cause and not effect, here, too.] That said, when viewed in combination, the consistency of the results using a variety of methods suggests that their estimates of the economic costs of smoking are probably near the mark. [There are also reasons to expect that the figure they arrive at is an underestimation. Namely, cigarettes are not free. So, higher incomes mean that smokers can afford more cigarettes.])

The same dynamics hold true for alcohol consumption and socioeconomic success. When economists Donald Kenkel and David Ribar compared men who are "sober" with their siblings who are dependent on alcohol, they found that those that drank excessively were 17 percent less likely to get married. (Donald S. Kenkel and David C. Ribar, "Alcohol Consumption and Young Adults' Socioeconomic Status," *Brookings Papers on Economic Activity, Microeconomics* [1994]: 119–61.) These alcohol-dependent men also earned less than their dry siblings. Results are similar for women, too. Although, individual-fixed effects over time show a small, positive effect of alcohol use on wages, this indicates the possibility of both individual-level heterogeneity not addressed by sibling comparisons and the importance of the income effect. Namely, when men earn more money, they can afford more booze.

However, these sibling comparisons may be putting the cart before the horse: alcoholic men may be getting drunk to ease the pain of socioeconomic failure. In order to address this possibility, Kenkel and Ribar also compared levels of drinking that are affected by outside circumstances, like the price of alcohol in a state. They found that drinkers still do worse than nondrinkers. Thus, this "natural experiment" suggests that there is indeed a negative effect of drinking on socioeconomic status, net of the effect of success on drinking behavior.

Drug, alcohol and cigarette consumption, and obesity—though clearly suggestive of poor health—are particularly complicated issues to examine with respect to the link between health status and sibling differences in economic success since they are largely behavioral in nature (though they are also affected by genetic disposition as well). Even when we examine health in early childhood, the causal links are not entirely clear since child health affects parental earnings, social conditions, and behavior. For example, healthier children are more likely to be followed by another sibling in a short interval. (Mark R. Rosenzweig and Kenneth I. Wolpin, "Heterogeneity, Intrafamily Distribution and Child Health," *Journal of Human Resources* 23 [1988]: 437–61.) These same researchers find that children who are healthier at birth are also more likely to be breastfed. (Thus, heroic claims that breastfeeding leads to wunderkinds may be overstated since thriving children are more likely to be breastfed in the first place.) Finally, a study by economists Hope Corman and Robert Kaestner shows that mothers who have an unhealthy child are less likely to be married. The result is that not only do kids who experience illness or injury face their own personal obstacles, they also are "more likely to suffer the consequences of poverty and the poor schooling outcomes that result from being raised in a female-headed household." (Page 389 of Hope Corman and Robert Kaestner, "The Effects of Child Health on Marital Status and Family Structure," *Demography* 29 [1992]: 389–408. Also see, e.g., Rosalyn B. Darling, "The Economic and Psychosocial Costs of Disability: Family-Society Relationships," *Marriage and Family Review* 11 [1987]: 7–24; and Michael T. Yura, "Family Subsystem Functions and Disabled Children: Some Conceptual Issues," *Marriage and Family Review* 11 [1987]: 135–51.) So child health is just one part of a delicate equilibrium of family social and economic conditions. The health of one sibling affects the health status of another sibling, the social status of parents affects the health of offspring, and the health of one child affects the socioeconomic status of that kid him/herself, his/her parents, and his/her siblings. One thing is for certain, however: being healthy is better for overall life chances of success than being sick.

8. She had killed a girl when her car careened into the teenager's bicycle, throwing her off a bridge to her death. She was convicted, but thanks to the attorney, received only probation and treatment for alcoholism.

9. This phrase is a reference to the 1970s television game show *To Tell the Truth,* where three contestants pretended to be the same person. Celebrities first questioned the contestants, then voted for the one they believed to be the real person. After voting, the question was asked, "Will the real [fill in name] please stand up?"

10. The classic article on the topic is by Mark Granovetter, "The Strength of Weak Ties," *American Journal of Sociology* 78 (1973): 1360–80. A number of elaborations on the same basic theme have been pursued. One of the best is the concept of structural holes (i.e., gaps) in social networks leading to success. For this work, see Ronald Burt, *Structural Holes: The Social Structure of Competition* (Cambridge, MA: Harvard University Press, 1992).

11. Malcolm Gladwell, *The Tipping Point: How Little Things Can Make a Big Difference* (Boston: Little Brown, 2000).

12. See pages 38–41 of Gladwell, *The Tipping Point.*

13. Ultimately, however, there is no completely foolproof way to measure

someone's social network. The strategy of using last names—called the Reverse Small World experiment (RSW)—is just one equally mediocre method among many, no matter how the names are generated. (For the details of this part of the study, see the appendix.)

14. For example, network theorist Duncan Watts claims that if you asked everyone if they knew Michael Jordan, most U.S. residents would say yes. "But if you said, 'Who would you trust to look after your kids?' That's not scale-free. As you start to ratchet up the requirements for what it means to know someone, connections diminish." See Emily Eakin, "Connect, They Say, Only Connect," *New York Times,* January 25, 2003, B7. Also see Duncan Watts, *Six Degrees: The Science of a Connected Age* (New York: Norton, 2003).

15. Charles Harrington and Susan Boardman studied one hundred highly successful individuals split by whether or not they came from an economically disadvantaged family of origin. Their intent was to study "what works" rather than what doesn't. They found that "Pathmakers" (as they called these successful adults who beat the odds) were often outsiders within their own families: "[Pathmakers] were more likely to feel hate upon returning to their home of origins as adults. As a result, they reported leaving home to get away from bad environments more often, and they were less likely to maintain contact with their families of origin." Charles Harrington and Susan Boardman, *Paths to Success: Beating the Odds in American Society* (Cambridge, MA: Harvard University Press, 1997), p. 167.

16. For a discussion of this process, see, e.g., Adam Green, "Sexual Orientation and Social Structure: A Comparative Study of Urban Heterosexual and Homosexual Careers," Ph.D. dissertation, Department of Sociology, New York University, 2002.

17. M. V. Lee Badgett, "The Wage Effects of Sexual Orientation Discrimination," *Industrial and Labor Relations Review* 48 (1995): 726–39.

18. David Brooks, *Bobos in Paradise: The New Upper Class* (New York: Simon and Schuster, 2000).

19. Christopher Jencks et al., *Inequality,* p. 227.

20. Alan B. Krueger and Pei Zhu, "Another Look at the New York City Voucher Experiment," working paper, Education Research Section, Princeton University, Princeton, NJ, 2003.

21. See, e.g., Jane Gross, "At Last, Colleges Answer, and New Questions Arise (Getting In: The Last of Three Articles)," *New York Times,* May 7, 2002, A1.

22. Stacy Berg Dale and Alan B. Kreuger, "Estimating the Payoff to Attending an Elite College," working paper no. W7322, National Bureau of Economic Research, 1999.

23. However, they did find that the amount of tuition of a school did matter positively for wages. They also found that college "quality" did matter for those individuals from more disadvantaged backgrounds—another example of how abilities, opportunities, and family socioeconomic circumstances interact to produce particular outcomes.

24. See, e.g., Kathryn M. Neckerman and Joleen Kirschenman, "'We'd Love to Hire Them, But . . .': The Meaning of Race for Employers," in *The Urban Underclass,* ed. Christopher Jencks and Paul E. Peterson (Washington, DC: Brookings Institution Press, 1991), pp. 203–34.

25. She used just a misdemeanor offense in her study. Devah Pager, "The Mark of a Criminal Record," working paper, Department of Sociology, University of Wisconsin at Madison, 2002.

EIGHT   *From Tribes to Markets*

1. There as part of an American Legion Boys Nation delegation.

2. The following biographical information on President Kennedy is largely paraphrased from Lisa Menéndez Weidman and Ellen Shea, "A Biography of John F. Kennedy: The 35th President of the United States," John Fitzgerald Kennedy Library and Museum, University of Massachusetts at Boston, October 26, 2002, http://www.cs.umb.edu/jfklibrary/jfk_biography.html (July 6, 2003).

3. He famously joked to the press: "I have just received the following telegram from my generous Daddy. It says, 'Dear Jack: Don't buy a single vote more than is necessary. I'll be damned if I'm going to pay for a landslide.'"

4. Though Bobby, too, had never been a terribly great student, he appeared competent at the job, as he had been in his previous post as chief counsel of the Senate Labor Rackets Committee Hearings.

5. Or the early morning hours of July 19, depending on whose testimony is to be believed.

6. Though he would make a failed attempt at the Democratic nomination in 1980, Kennedy's presidential prospects were irreparably damaged.

7. In fact, the term "premodern" itself is ill-advised since it implies a march

toward a better and more advanced end (i.e., Western civilization), and therefore judges other societies and prescribes a single path in history; but the term sure beats "primitive," which went out of fashion about thirty years ago.

8. That is to say that even if there are forty status grades of dart-blowers, and an enterprising anthropologist could map a high degree of sibling differences in this system of prestige, for our purposes, we are waving our hands at those differences because, number one, we cannot see them, and number two, from our perspective, all dart-blowers have the same status whether they agree or not.

9. Of course, often the causal arrow goes in the other direction, in that technological changes stimulate a reorganization of labor.

10. "Assets," from the French, *assez*—literally, enough.

11. See, e.g., George Konrad and Ivan Szelenyi, *Intellectuals on the Road to Class Power* (New York: Harcourt Brace, 1979).

12. See Paul Krugman, "For Richer," *New York Times Magazine,* October 20, 2002.

13. About two to three times the rate of comparable European nations. See "Relative Poverty Rate for the Total Population," *Luxembourg Income Study,* May 27, 2003, http://www.lisproject.org/keyfigures/povertytable.htm (July 8, 2003).

14. National Center for Children in Poverty, "Low Income Children in the United States: A Brief Demographic Profile," New York: Columbia University School of Public Health, 2002. To top it off, many Americans do not have access to basic services like health care. About 40 million Americans do not have health insurance. See Committee on the Consequences of Uninsurance, Board on Health Care Services, Institute of Medicine, *Coverage Matters: Insurance and Health Care* (Washington, DC: National Academies Press, 2001).

15. See "Income Inequality Measures," *Luxembourg Income Study,* May 27, 2003, http://www.lisproject.org/keyfigures/ineqtable.htm (July 8, 2003).

16. Ibid. On another measure, called the Gini coefficient, where a higher score means more inequality, the United States scores about .37, almost perfectly equidistant between Mexico's .49 on the high end, and Sweden's .22 and Germany's .26 on the low side.

17. There are a lot of explanations for the unique position among advanced democracies in which the United States finds itself. First, there is the issue of timing. It seems as though the European countries that made the transition to free-market capitalism more recently did so when political institutions were

better able to protect the weak through collective bargaining, welfare state transfers, and universal public services. Another explanation is institutional. That is, the fragmented U.S. political system—which divides power between the federal government and the states, and between three branches of government—makes it difficult to develop a comprehensive safety net in the same way that European countries with strong central governments and a parliamentary system of elections can. (In the United States, it is a lot easier to stop redistribution efforts than to get them rolling.) Another explanation claims that the key aspect of "American exceptionalism" is that we have no history of feudalism (with the caveat of the South before the Civil War). This seems ironic at first glance: feudalism, a form of political, economic oppression in which serfs toiled on the land of their lords, was far more unequal than the image of early America with its citizen-farmers and bountiful land (again with the notable exception of Southern slavery). Given this history of inequality, it would seem to make sense that the European countries with this sort of social history would have *more,* not less, disparity rippling up through the present. But feudalism also developed a culture of state paternalism—the serfs received protection from their lord in return for working his land. Some argue that this arrangement metamorphosized into the modern welfare state, in which citizens pay higher taxes, but can confidently expect their basic economic needs to be taken care of by the government, from cradle to grave. Without such a feudal history, the American cultural tradition of "individualism" mitigates against such paternalism.

Finally, there is the looming shadow of race in America. Some scholars argue that while European powers had racialized "others" in the form of colonized peoples, those "others" were typically far away, with no prospect of the franchise. In other words, European exploitation of nonwhite people usually took place outside the country itself. Thus, providing a strong safety net became a way by which European nations defined themselves in opposition to the "others" whom they were colonizing and denying full political membership. This situation stands in contrast to the United States, where a sizable colonized population was imported. Though black Americans were denied voting rights for most of the history of the American republic, they had begun to secure them by the time the era of government redistribution had arrived. The result was that in order to prevent blacks from participating fully in the American social contract, authority was devolved from the federal government to local authorities, which could then exclude blacks overtly or covertly. The result was a much weaker safety net and one which—for a long time—excluded minorities disproportionately. For example, in order to get social security through the congressional committees that were controlled by racist Southern Democrats, President Roosevelt had to agree to exclude agricultural and domestic workers from the old-age insurance system. This carve-out was done purposely to exclude African-Americans, who were disproportionately employed in these two sectors. It was not until the following decade, when President Truman addressed this gap in the safety net, that blacks were really participants in the social insurance system. Of course, it was that first—white only—generation that really reaped the windfall of social security, receiving payouts from day one, without having paid a cent into the nascent system.

But none of these explanations can account for all cases. Ireland is probably the most recent and most rapidly developing country of the northern European block, yet it displays greater inequalities than, say, the Netherlands, Denmark, or even its sister, the United Kingdom. Canada does not have a feudal past and has a fractured, regional power structure (including semiautonomous states like Quebec), yet it enjoys a much more comprehensive safety net than does America, its southern neighbor. Australia and New Zealand also lack feudal histories and have conquered racial minorities within their national borders yet still have much more progressive social policies than the United States does. Thus, the most probable answer is that timing, institutional structure, cultural history, and race *all* have something to do with the unique position of the United States. In other words, all are necessary conditions, but none are sufficient alone.

18. Gary Solon, "Cross-Country Differences in Intergenerational Earnings Mobility," *Journal of Economic Perspectives* 16 (2002): 59–66.

19. Exchange mobility is sometimes known as "social fluidity."

20. Of course, exchange mobility does not require (and usually does not entail) a one-to-one trade; in other words, an unskilled laborer's son may move up to a skilled labor position, replacing the craftsman whose son has become a manager. Meanwhile the manager's son may experience downward mobility to the level of unskilled laborer, keeping the symmetry of the system intact.

21. Of course, the position of the presidency is, by definition, resistant to structural mobility since there is only one president.

22. An effect of zero would reflect totally random assignment to adult class position—something not theoretically feasible in a capitalist society that is supposed to rely on meritocracy. In this theoretical meritocracy, where only

inherited ability mattered and inherited social position did not count for anything, the parent-child (and sibling) correlation in position would be equal to the genetic heritability for a particular trait. The rest would be random (individual specific) error.

23. See, e.g., Table PF3.1.A of page 1 of http://aspe.os.dhhs.gov/hsp/98trends/Sec1c.pdf; this figure is a slight dip from 1960, when it was 21 percent—of course, at that time, individuals married and entered the labor force at younger ages, so the excess may reflect life course transitions to adult roles.

24. Larry Long, "Changing Residence: Comparative Perspectives on Its Relationship to Age, Sex, and Marital Status," *Population Studies* 46 (1992): 141–58. For the declining rate of mobility, see Claude Fischer, "Ever More Rooted Americans," *City and Community* 1 (2002): 175–193.

25. Andrew J. Oswald, "The Housing Market and Europe's Unemployment: A Non-Technical Working Paper," working paper, Department of Economics, University of Warwick, 1999.

26. B. N. Adams, *Kinship in an Urban Setting* (Chicago: Markham, 1968).

27. See page 11 of Victor G. Cicirelli, "Sibling Relationships in Cross-Cultural Perspective," *Journal of Marriage and the Family* 56 (1994): 7–20.

28. Julie Meyer, "Age: 2000: Census 2000 Brief," issue number C2KBR/01-12 (Washington, DC: U.S. Census Bureau, 2001).

29. U.S. Census Bureau, Table NP-T3-E, "Projections of the Total Resident Population by 5-Year Age Groups, and Sex with Special Age Categories: Middle Series, 2016 to 2020," Internet release date: January 13, 2000, http://www.census.gov/population/projections/nation/summary/np-t3-e.pdf (July 6, 2003).

APPENDIX   *About the Pecking Order*

1. Martha Hill, *The Panel Study of Income Dynamics: A User's Guide* (Newbury Park, CA: Sage Publications, 1992).

2. Dalton Conley, "Sibling Correlations in Socio-Economic Status: Results on Education, Occupation, Income and Wealth," working paper, Center for Advanced Social Science Research, New York University, 2003.

3. Robert M. Hauser and Robert D. Mare, *Study of American Families, 1994* (Madison, WI: Data and Program Library Service, 1997), October 16, 2002, http://dpls.dacc.wisc.edu/SAF/index.html (July 8, 2003).

4. Online documentation can be viewed at GSSDIRS, *General Social Survey,* http://www.icpsr.umich.edu:8080/GSS/homepage.htm (July 8, 2003).

5. James A. Davis and Tom W. Smith, *The NORC General Social Survey: A User's Guide* (Newbury Park, CA: Sage Publications, 1992).

6. From SAF online documentation: *Study of American Families,* http://dpls.dacc.wisc.edu/SAF/safdes.htm. The SAF data can be downloaded at http://dpls.dacc.wisc.edu/SAF (July 8, 2003). These must be combined with the sibling data from the GSS, available publicly as well at http://ww.icpsr.umich.edu:8080/GSS/homepage.htm (July 8, 2003).

7. David R. Featherman and Robert M. Hauser, *Opportunity and Change* (New York: Academic Press, 1978), pp. 242–43; also see Judith Blake, "Number of Siblings and Educational Mobility," *American Sociological Review* 50 (1981): 84–94; Judith Blake, *Family Size and Achievement* (Berkeley and Los Angeles: University of California Press, 1989); D. M. Heer, "Effect of Sibling Number on Child Outcome," *Annual Review of Sociology* 11 (1985): 27–47; B. Powell and L. C. Steelman, "The Educational Benefits of Being Spaced Out: Sibship Density and Educational Progress," *American Sociological Review* 58 (1993): 367–81. (Recent work has expanded the range of sibship measures to include spacing and sex composition. See Powell and Steelman, "The Liability of Having Brothers: Paying for College and the Sex Composition of the Family," *Sociology of Education* 62 [1989]: 134–47; Powell and Steelman, "Beyond Sibship Size: Sibling Density and Educational Outcomes," *Social Forces* 69 [1990]: 181–206; Powell and Steelman, "Educational Benefits".)

8. See Gary Becker, *Human Capital* (Chicago: University of Chicago Press, 1964).

9. L. Steelman and J. Mercy, "Unconfounding the Confluence Model: A Test of Sibship Size and Birth Order Effects on Intelligence," *American Sociological Review* 45 (1980): 571–82; also see Douglas B. Downey, "When Bigger Is Not Better: Family Size, Parental Resources, and Children's Educational Performance," *American Sociological Review* 60 (1995): 746–61.

10. R. B. Zajonc and G. B. Markus, "Birth Order and Intellectual Development," *Psychological Review* 82 (1975): 74–88; R. B. Zajonc, "Family Configuration and Intelligence," *Science* 192 (1976): 227–36.

11. See, e.g., H. D. Grotevant, S. Scarr, and R. A. Weinberg, "Intellectual Development in Families with Adopted and Natural Children: A Test of the Zajonc and Markus Model," *Child Development* 40 (1977): 1699–1703.

12. Downey, "When Bigger Is Not Better."

13. Guang Guo and Leah K. VanWey, "Sibship Size and Intellectual Devel-

opment: Is the Relationship Causal?" *American Sociological Review* 64 (1999): 169–87.

14. Mark R. Rosenzweig and Kenneth I. Wolpin, "Heterogeneity, Intrafamily Distribution and Child Health," *Journal of Human Resources* 23 (1988): 437–61.

15. Arthur S. Goldberger, *A Course in Econometrics* (Cambridge, MA: Harvard University Press, 1991), pp. 248–50.

16. Income presents its own problems in a change model since the birth of additional siblings changes the family size and therefore the income-to-needs ratio, even holding constant income changes. It does not appear that Guo and VanWey, "Sibship Size and Intellectual Development," controlled for "income-to-needs" ratio.

17. Gender should be orthogonal to these variables and thus should not be an issue here.

18. See M. Phillips, "Comment: Sibship Size and Academic Achievement: What We Now Know and What We Still Need to Know," *American Sociological Review* 64 (1999): 188–92; D. Downey, B. Powell, L. C. Steelman, and S. Pribesh, "Much Ado About Siblings: Change Models, Sibship Size, and Intellectual Development," *American Sociological Review* 64 (1999): 193–98; and Guo and VanWey, "Sibship Size and Intellectual Development," for their response.

19. Joshua D. Angrist, "Lifetime Earnings and the Vietnam Era Draft Lottery: Evidence from Social Security Administrative Records," *American Economic Review* 80 (1990): 313–36.

20. The exception is the 1970 draft, for which statisticians have found a degree of bias. (S. E. Fienberg, "Randomization and Social Affairs: The 1970 Draft Lottery," *Science* 171 [1971]: 255–61.) Certain months were more likely to have been selected than others. This, apparently, resulted from the method in which the Ping-Pong balls were mixed. The balls were first organized by month into boxes and then dumped, box by box, into a large vat. This could bias estimates since there is class bias in the seasonality of birth (David A. Jaeger and John Bound, "On the Validity of Season of Birth as an Instrument in Wage Equations: A Comment on Angrist and Krueger's 'Does Compulsory School Attendance Affect School and Earnings?'" *Research in Labor Economics* 19 [2000]: 83–108). This problem was corrected in the 1971 draft after much public criticism. (D. E. Rosenbaum, "Draft Officials Redesign Lottery Procedures to Make the System More Random," *New York Times*, June 25, 1970, p. 17.)

21. For excellent reviews and explanations of this approach, see Christopher Winship and Stephen L. Morgan, "The Estimation of Causal Effects from Observational Data," *Annual Review of Sociology* 25 (1999): 659–706; Joshua D. Angrist and Alan B. Krueger, "Instrumental Variables and the Search for Identification: From Supply and Demand to Natural Experiments," *Journal of Economic Perspectives* 15 (2001): 69–85.

22. This is expressed algebraically in equation 1, below:

$$\beta_{iv} = [(\bar{y}|z_i = 1) - (\bar{y}|z_i = 0)] / [(\bar{x}|z_i = 1) - (\bar{x}|z_i = 0)] \qquad (1)$$

where z_i is a dummy variable indicating membership in either the treatment or control group ("1" for those men with draft-eligible birth dates and "0" for those with draft-ineligible birth dates), x is the average probability of going to Vietnam and y is the average wages post-Vietnam. (This approach can be elaborated into a two-stage least squares estimation [2SLS], but the logic is essentially the same.)

23. In the analysis of family size, the effects of parental age, nativity status (whether or not they were immigrants), parental education levels, income (actually the natural logarithm of total household income), and the average age of the children were all factored out. The first stage is run at the family level, while the second stage is run at the individual level with Huber-White standard errors robust to clustering at the family level. Running the second stage at the individual level allowed me to test whether the effects are different by birth position and gender.

24. J. Angrist and W. N. Evans, "Children and Their Parents' Labor Supply: Evidence from Exogenous Variation in Family Size," *American Economic Review* 88 (1998): 450–77.

25. Another instrument for family size can be the birth of twins (an apparently random event); however, the presence of twins may have other effects on the family since it is an unusual occurrence. In other words, it is difficult to know whether any observed effects on attainment are the result of the unexpected "extra" child present in the family or the presence of twins. Another way of putting this is that families with twins may not be generalizable to the population as a whole. This is not an issue with different sex mixes of children.

26. Neil G. Bennett, ed., *Sex Selection of Children* (New York: Academic Press, 1983).

27. M. Rosenzweig and K. Wolpin, "Natural 'Natural Experiments' in Economics," *Journal of Economic Literature* 38 (2000): 827–74.

28. Powell and Steelman, "The Liability of Having Brothers" and "Beyond Sibship Size"; K. F. Butcher and A. Case, "The Effect of Sibling Sex Composition on Women's Education and Earnings," *Quarterly Journal of Economics* 109 (1994): 531–63; Robert Kaestner, "Are Brothers Really Better?: Sibling Sex Composition and Educational Achievement Revisited," *Journal of Human Resources* 32 (1997): 250–84; Robert Hauser and Hsiang-Hui Daphne Kuo, "Does the Gender Composition of Sibship Affect Educational Attainment?" *Journal of Human Resources* 33 (1998): 644–57; Dalton Conley, "Sibship Sex Composition and the Educational Attainment of Men and Women," *Social Science Research* 29 (2000): 441–57.

29. To address the concern that the effect of the sex composition of the first two children may be having an impact on educational outcomes due to sibship sex composition effects (such as returns to scale for gender-specific goods in the household such as clothes, bedrooms, and so on) and not due to its association with subsequent fertility, I performed analysis control for the sex composition of the entire child population in the household. To get at the returns to scale argument, this is measured as the percentage same sex. We compute the percentage of boys and the percentage of girls, and take the maximum of these two as our percentage same-sex variable. This formulation—as well as a sex-specific measure—was not significant for any of the outcomes under study.

30. We could not test for sex composition effects in two-sib families since such a measure would be collinear with our predicted value. It could be that the returns to scale matter non-monotonically; however, this is a far-fetched possibility. (Even if there are declining returns to scale, our safeguard should be effective as long as the returns to scale for same-sex siblings do not dip below zero [i.e., become negative].) Our control for total sibship sex composition could also be flawed if there exist significant interactions between birth order and sex composition, but these appear equally unlikely, given previous evidence and lack of a strong theoretical reason to expect them.

31. National Center for Education Statistics, *Dropout Rates in the United States: 1995*, U.S. Department of Education, Washington, DC, 1997. Document available online at http://nces.ed.gov/pubs/dp95/97473-5.html (July 22, 2003).

32. This difference represents a flip from the 1950s when public schools had lower student-to-teacher ratios than private schools (26.9 to 31.7 for 1955); the crossover year was 1972. See "Table 56: Enrollment in Grades 9 to 12 in Public and Private Schools Compared with Population 14 to 17 Years of

Age: 1889–90 to Fall 2000," in *Digest of Education Statistics* (National Center for Education Statistics, 2001), http://nces.ed.gov/pubs2002/2002130b.pdf (July 25, 2003).

33. Alan B. Krueger and Pei Zhu, "Another Look at the New York City School Voucher Experiment," working paper, Education Research Section, Princeton University, 2003.

34. See *Digest of Education Statistics.*

35. Ibid.

36. Large-scale sex surveys usually suffer from severe selection bias problems with respect to their response rates. Many surveys attract those types of individuals who want to reveal their sexual practices to others. As a result, surveys like that done by sex magazines or even by Kinsey are skewed to the less "normative" side of sexual expression. Others do not answer honestly and thus may skew the results toward the more conservative end of the sexual spectrum. One relatively good survey is that done by E. Laumann, J. H. Gagnon, R. T. Michael, and S. Michaels, *The Social Organization of Sexuality: Sexual Practices in the United States* (Chicago: University of Chicago Press, 1994). Specifically with respect to the issue of adolescent sexuality, the best resource is the National Longitudinal Survey of Adolescent Health, run out of the University of North Carolina. However, neither of these surveys has the data to address the relationship between sexuality and differences in socioeconomic attainment between siblings (though in later waves, the teenage respondents to the North Carolina survey will be old enough to have registered an adult class status).

37. U.S. Bureau of the Census, *Age: 2000, Census 2000 Brief* (U.S. Department of Commerce: Washington, DC, 2001), page 1. Available electronically at http//www.census.gov/prod/2001pubs/c2kbr01-12.pdf (July 22, 2003).

38. Nationally in 2000, 19 percent of Americans lived in the Northeast, 23 percent in the Midwest, 36 percent in the South, and 22 percent in the West. (See U.S. Bureau of the Census, *United States: 2000, Summary Population and Housing Characteristics* (U.S. Department of Commerce: Washington, DC, 2002), p. 16. Available online at http://www.census.gov/prod/cen2000/phc-1-1-ptl.pdf (July 24, 2003). These census data are for the current residences of all Americans (adults and children), not where current adults were raised. So, while it is clear that we have oversampled the Northeast and undersampled the Midwest, the degree of bias may not be as great as it first appears since there has been an out-migration from the Northeast over the last few decades.

39. U.S. Bureau of the Census, *U.S. Summary: 2000 (Census 2000 Profile)* (U.S. Department of Commerce: Washington, DC, 2002), p. 2. Available

online at http://www.census.gov/prod/2002pubs/c2kprof00-us.pdf (July 24, 2003).

40. Ibid., p. 4.

41. I. de Sola Pool and M. Kochen, "Contacts and Influence," *Social Networks* 1 (1978): 5–51.

42. We did not want to add to the "error" in our results with random "jack-pots" in which a person knew many people from the same family who shared one of the names since this usually reflects one "main" friend and his or her relatives, who are secondary. In other words, we were interested in unique, in-dependent connections. It would be rare for a person to have developed rela-tionships with family members separately, not knowing they were of the same family. While it is also possible that respondents might have checked separate names on the list that actually reflect one social unit (or even family), this is much less likely to occur given the wide number of possible names and our limited list of 250 potential contacts.

43. With respect to the multiple contacts issue, the instructions read as follows:

So, for example, if you know one person with the last name Clark, with the first name David, put a "D" on the line to the left of that name. If you know three Clarks, then put each of their first initials, as in "D, K, M." One important point is that the three Clarks that you know must not be related to each other as far as you know; in other words, you know them independently. That is, if you are friends with David Clark, and through David met his eight children, please do not list them all, just "D" for David—your primary contact. But if you happen to know two or more unrelated Clarks, please enter all their initials.

44. Problems with his approach include the fact that—since these names are drawn from the New York City phone book—the types of names that ap-pear there may be atypical when compared to other parts of the country. For example, there appear to be a higher number of Italian-American- and Jewish-American-sounding names than would be found in a random sample of the U.S. population. So results would be biased in favor of people who live in the New York area or who belong to those particular ethnic enclaves.

45. This list can be accessed electronically at http://landview.census.gov/genealogy/names/dist.all.last.

46. This was not exactly a weighted random sample; it is more accurately

described as a weighted sample without replacement. Given that our target sample size was about 250, the expected number of "Smiths" in our list of names would be about two and a half. Of course, we were not going to list Smith multiple times, so it was not truly weighted to the population distribution, since once a name was picked one time, it was removed from the pool of possibilities.   —

ACKNOWLEDGMENTS

The Pecking Order would not have been possible without a wide array of individuals and institutions. The person without whom this project would never have gotten finished (or would have taken me at least twice as long) is Karen Albright. As my research assistant, she conducted many of the case-study interviews; she also helped with the background research and even coauthored chapter 6—all this while trying to publish her own work and get started on her Ph.D. dissertation. Another critical player was Ylana Beller, the administrator of the Center for Advanced Social Science Research (CASSR), who not only managed the administrative side of the project but, once the writing began, played a key role in finding statistics and researching obscure facts, checking my references, making tables, fixing footnotes, and proofreading the manuscript. Ylana was preceded at CASSR by Lisa Bernhard, to whom I am also indebted for helping manage the interview phase of the project. Justin Seder also helped with the interviews, particularly with the oversample of gay siblings. I am also grateful to the people who transcribed the interviews, most notably Lynn Karow and the anonymous workers at Intercom online. Finally, Brian Gifford and Kate Strully acted as research assistants for this project. Brian's role was helping to manage and analyze the census data; Kate did the same for the Study of American Families and the Panel Study of Income Dynamics.

The reason I could afford all this help is that this project was generously supported by the National Science Foundation in the form of a CAREER Award from the Sociology Program of the Social and Behavioral Sciences Division (Grant Number: SES-9983636) and by a Robert Wood Johnson Foundation Investigator Award in Health Policy Research (Grant Number: 038651). I thank Drs. Alvin Tarlov and David Mechanic, the consecutive directors of the Investigator Awards program. I was also supported by my home institution,

New York University, in the form of research funds and a semester-long research leave.

The book has benefited from comments at various seminars, from colleagues who were kind enough to read chunks of it, and most of all, from my agent and editor, Sydelle Kramer and Dan Frank, respectively. If you've read this far, you've got them to thank. I also have to thank Dan's assistant, Rahel Lerner, and Dawn Davis, the acquiring editor at Pantheon, who left the company before she could see her seed bear fruit. I hope that the book fulfills the promise she saw in the proposal. There are a number of other folks at Pantheon and the Knopf group as a whole who have thrown their weight behind this project; I am grateful to each of them.

Finally, for believing in me (and enduring me) during this process, I would like to thank my family of origin and my family of destination. They include, in age order, Sylvia Alexander, my grandmother; Steve Conley, my father; Ellen Conley, my mother; Alexandra Conley, my sister; E Jeremijenko-Conley, my daughter; and Yo Xing Jeremijenko-Conley, my son. Lastly, I would like to express my gratitude to Natalie Jeremijenko—who has been my life partner—for her support as she saw this project grow from start to finish: talking out ideas at two a.m.; reading sections; and, as has been her habit, challenging all my assumptions about family and beyond.

INDEX